THE GOODMAN THEATRE'S FESTIVAL LATINO

THE GOODMAN THEATRE'S FESTIVAL LATINO

SIX PLAYS

Edited by Henry D. Godinez
and Ramón H. Rivera-Servera

NORTHWESTERN UNIVERSITY PRESS
EVANSTON, ILLINOIS

Northwestern University Press
www.nupress.northwestern.edu

This book has been published with the support of the Andrew W. Mellon Foundation.

Printed in the United States of America

10 9 8 7 6 5 4 3 2 1

Library of Congress Cataloging-in-Publication Data

The Goodman Theatre's Festival Latino : six plays / edited by Henry D. Godinez and
    Ramon H. Rivera-Servera.
        pages cm
    ISBN 978-0-8101-2943-6 (pbk.)
    1. American drama—21st century. 2. Latin American drama—21st century. 3. Hispanic
American theater—Illinois—Chicago. I. Godinez, Henry D., editor of compilation.
II. Rivera-Servera, Ramón H., 1973– editor of compilation.
PQ7084.5.G66 2013
808.829868—dc23
                                                                                      2013025305

♾ The paper used in this publication meets the minimum requirements of the
American National Standard for Information Sciences—Permanence of Paper
for Printed Library Materials, ANSI Z39.48-1992.

For
Nancy, Lucy, and Gaby Godinez
Adela Lamadrid Godinez
Joel Valentín-Martinez
and
Carol Angelique Servera

CONTENTS

ACKNOWLEDGMENTS

This book results from a decade of Latino theatrical activity at Chicago's Goodman Theatre. We thank our many friends and colleagues who have labored in support of Latina and Latino theater artists and audiences at the Goodman and in Chicago. Without the dedication of so many artists, production staff, financial supporters, and audiences, the Goodman's Latino Theatre Festival and this publication would have been impossible. We are especially thankful for the work of Latino artists and theater companies in Chicago who have enriched the city's stages and fed talent, vision, and energy to American theater.

We thank Roche Schulfer, Robert Falls, and the entire staff and Board of Trustees of the Goodman Theatre. Their investment and dedication to Latino theater in Chicago is without precedent and has already left a significant mark in the theatrical landscape of this city. Maria Bechily, the Illinois Arts Council, the Chicago Community Trust, the Joyce Foundation, and the Mellon Foundation have been champions of this work and invaluable partners in the advancement of Latino theater and performance. The Lark Play Development Center, Chicago Latino Network, Instituto Cervantes, and the Consul General of Mexico have been generous collaborators.

This publication is part of the Performance Encounters Project, a public programs and publication venture between Northwestern University Press and faculty in the School of Communication's departments of Theatre and Performance Studies. Working with the Northwestern University Press editorial staff, especially with Mike Levine, has been a delight. We also want to thank our colleagues, especially Joshua T. Chambers-Letson, Tracy C. Davis, Marcela Fuentes, E. Patrick Johnson, D. Soyini Madison, Sandra L. Richards, and Harvey Young, for their ongoing support and intellectual engagement.

We are most grateful for the generous financial support provided by the Andrew W. Mellon Foundation's Universities and the Presses initiative. Their invitation to imagine new ways of publishing in our fields allowed us to develop this project as much more than an anthology of plays. The rich content available online as an extension of this volume is a direct answer to their call and a significant advancement in the ways theater is published and documented.

At the School of Communication, Dean Barbara O'Keefe and her staff provided the key resources and support that made our proposal to the Mellon Foundation possible and viable. We thank her for continuously championing our work in theater and performance at the university.

Henry thanks his wife and daughters, Nancy, Lucy, and Gaby Godinez, for their loving patience and support. He also thanks his mother, Adela Lamadrid Godinez, for never-ending love and encouragement. Ramón thanks Joel Valentin-Martinez for his continued sharing of a life in the theater. He thanks his mother, Carol Angelique Servera, for making that life in the theater possible. This book is dedicated to our respective families who have enabled and continue to enable and inspire the work that we do in the theater and the university.

THE MANY LEGS OF LATINA/O THEATER

Ramón H. Rivera-Servera

Festival Latino brings together six plays that represent the aesthetic and thematic diversity of Latino theater* as showcased at the Goodman Theatre's Latino Theatre Festival in Chicago during its first six installments from 2003 to 2013. Together, the plays that constitute Festival Latino invite new ways of thinking about one of the most historically rich and contemporaneously promising theatrical movements in the United States. Our enthusiasm for this work, implied in the celebratory framing of the festival suggested by our title for this volume, is also a provocation to interrogate the definitional parameters that have governed Latino theater studies to date. *Festival Latino* does this by suggesting a definition of Latino theater that rests on the curatorial framing of the project instead of the more common assumptions of identitarian, thematic, political, or aesthetic alignment of the artists' work with a fixed notion of *lo Latino,* or that which is Latino. That is, in this volume we are interested in pursuing the festival as a framed event—the artists and audiences it convenes and the collective experience it creates—as the definitional locus for a theatrical practice that is as invested in cultivating Latina and Latino theater artists and audiences as it is in circulating their artistry to wider audiences.

Our focus on the curated festival event does not mean an avoidance of the thematic, political, and artistic foundations of Latino theater. In fact, the artists gathered in this collection all participate in some measure

---

*Throughout this book we use the term "Latino" instead of "Latina/o" or "Latin@." We are aware that such a decision defaults the noun for Latina and Latino collectives as masculine. We use "Latino" to conform to the historical usage of the term in representing the movement in the American theater that this book documents, and we intend it to be inclusive.

in addressing Latino experience, provide profound critical commentary on pressing matters to Latino communities, and engage the legacy of Latino aesthetics in theater as much as in everyday life. Nonetheless, the broad range of themes, artistic approaches, and experiences showcased in the Goodman's Latino Theatre Festival often question, rather than assert, the easy assumptions of a homogenous community, culture, and artistic tradition. As such, we arrived at this focus on Latino theater as a curatorial practice in our own struggles to retrospectively define what was specifically Latino about the ten years of activity at the Goodman's Latino Theatre Festival.[1] Each time we asked this question of any of the pieces presented at the festival, we arrived at a different answer.

Latino theater, in its diversity, is simply a multifarious creature as full of wonderment as it is of daring intelligence. We are certainly not the first ones to encounter the definitional dilemma that is pinpointing exactly what is Latino theater. When Latino theater scholar Alberto Sandoval-Sánchez asked *tejana* actress Ruby Nelda Pérez to define Latino theater, she responded enthusiastically that Latino theater is "an octopus with many legs."[2] The very situation of the question, posed at the 1993 Festival Latino of New Plays in San Francisco, California, by a Puerto Rican scholar based in New England to an actress born and raised in San Antonio, Texas, offers an appropriate illustration of what was meant by her response. Latino theater can mean different things depending on who, where, and when you ask. It has been generally described as the theater of Latin American–descent communities who have migrated and settled in the United States. It also accounts for a longer history of theatrical activity in the present territorial United States that predates and endured the annexation of vast expanses of land as a result of war and other U.S. interventions and conflicts. Most significant among these, we find a wealth of indigenous, Spanish, and Mexican theater and performance traditions in what is now the Southwestern United States. We may also consider in this definition the theatrical heritage of Puerto Rico.

Latino theater engages the rich performance histories of Latin American countries that have so significantly influenced Latino aesthetics in the United States. This theatrical inheritance is not only manifest in the European theatrical genealogy introduced by colonization and replenished repeatedly by an internationally aware artistic community, but is also evident in indigenous, African, Asian, and Middle Eastern cultural influences that have shaped and textured the cultural history of Latin America. What is so frequently homogenized as "Spanish America" by uninformed observers results from the foundational and continued presence of indigenous communities, the reverberations of violence from Spanish and Portuguese colonization and slave trade, the rise and troubles of modern nationalism, and the many inward and outward migrations that have and continue to texture Latin American experience. To this we add the long history of struggles for social, economic, and cultural equity that has fueled and frustrated so much of the artistic output of the region. For many Latino artists, this diverse heritage offers a rich palette from where to draw inspiration and thematic as well as aesthetic material of relevance to the present.[3]

As much as Latino theater draws on the historical, it is also a theater of the present. In the United States, the many legs of the octopus that are Latino theater encompass a diverse contemporary demography of Latino theater artists and audiences. The communities assumed under the Latino banner represent more than fifty million residents in the United States originating from twenty-five different Latin American nations. This includes a multigenerational Mexican community with residents in the Southwestern United States region before annexation and their descendants as well as migratory waves dispersed across the national map ever since. At close to 60 percent of the Latino population, they constitute the largest Latino ethno-national subgroup and the fastest growing ethnic group at major theatrical centers such as New York City and Chicago.[4] Puerto Ricans, Cubans, and, more recently, Dominicans follow as the largest components of the Latino population. Smaller but sizable communities hail from El Salvador, Colombia, Guatemala, Honduras, Ecuador, and Peru. Close to 10 percent of the Latino population has roots in one or more of the other fifteen Latin American countries. Each of these communities is diverse in its own right with marked differences in ethnic and racial makeup, class experience, and reasons or circumstances for arrival or incorporation into the United States. But as the Latino banner insists, they also have much in common.

In the midst of all this difference, how is Latino commonality constituted? That is, what brings such a heterogeneous group together in the United States? These questions have been central to what is now an academic field dedicated to researching the political, economic, historical, social, and cultural dimensions of Latino experience in the United States.[5] Assertions of a shared experience, including with language, resulting from Spanish colonialism in the Americas; the pan-Americanism that fueled cross-national collaboration across Latin America; and U.S. military, political, and economic interventionism provide some historical points of contact between Latinos from diverse ethno-national backgrounds. As well, the material and representational histories of racism and xenophobia encountered by Latinos within U.S. borders offer significant and enduring shared experiences. These experiences may result in a collective encounter with stereotypical representations of all things Latino in popular media, anti-immigrant legislation limiting access to rights and services, and the resulting economic, educational, and social marginalities that such negative reception may occasion. Latinos have also been lumped together, by governmental, media, and other corporate interests alike, as a homogenous demographic unit or niche market.[6]

But there are also positive forces that promote the formation of inter-Latino solidarities. Some of them include concerted efforts to coalesce in response to the enduring marginality produced by the historical and continuing pressures described before. Other catalysts of inter-Latino association emerge from those very constraints but evolve into the cultural and social intimacies that anthropologists Milagros Ricourt and Ruby Danta understand as *convivencia diaria*, or everyday conviviality.[7] They are concerned with the kinds of familiarities Latina working-class women in a New York City neighborhood developed by the sheer frequency with which they patronized the same business establishments, religious institutions, schools, and work and leisure spaces. That is, out of finding themselves in the same neighborhood, chosen not necessarily because of a Latino identity but because affordability of housing, business infrastructure, or job opportunities, Latinas increase the probability of meeting each other and forging new relations across their differences. As Henry Godinez explains in his essay, the Goodman's Latino Theatre Festival was intended to serve as a similar engine of inter-Latino *convivencia diaria*. As I have argued elsewhere, it is in the shared time space of performance, assumed in the purposeful and dedicated collaboration among artists who find in their shared experiences the raw materials to develop beautiful and deeply touching works, and in the communion with an audience similarly committed to engaging with the artists and with each other, that *convivencia diaria* produces Latino community.[8]

The Goodman Theatre's Latino Theatre Festival and this anthology participate in the hopeful, collectivizing impulse of *lo Latino* by proposing theater as a site where Latino communities might encounter themselves and others as much in their similarities as their differences. In this sense, Latino theater is also about the future ushered in by the inter-Latino social intimacies that take place among audience members, among theater artists, and between audiences and performers. It also invests in the change of mind or the change of heart that encountering the work on the stage might provoke. Because of the promise of these encounters, and the opportunity they afford to recognize the relevance of aesthetic and social histories to present experience, Latino theater continues to be what Chicano theater scholar Jorge Huerta has termed as "a necessary theater."[9]

The works contained herein demonstrate a wide range of approaches to Latino theater. Some pieces introduce new perspectives to the theatrical canon and to Latino life. Luis Alfaro's *Electricidad* offers an adaptation of Euripides's *Electra* into an East Los Angeles Chicano world where gangs mourn the downed patriarch. Javier Malpica's *Our Dad Is in Atlantis* gives us a portrait of Mexican migration from the viewpoint of children left behind in the homes of relatives as their parents sojourn in search of better futures. Others venture beyond common territory by placing Latino characters, aesthetics, and stories outside an exclusively Latino milieu. Mildred Ruiz and Steven Sapp fuse flamenco, jazz, blues, and performance poetry in *Blue Suite* to tell a story of the struggles of a frustrated and uninspired trumpet player to find himself with the help of his muse in Harlem. Adriana Sevahn Nichols's solo performance, *Taking Flight,* explores the fragility of friendship immediately after the 9/11 attacks to the World Trade Center in New York City. Albany Park Theatre Project's *Home/Land* gifts us with a beautiful and evocative ethnographically devised ensemble piece about the experience of immigrants, Latinos and non-Latinos, in the city of Chicago. This collection, much like the festival itself, crosses the expected borders of Latino theater by bringing works like Malpica's migration play and Raquel Carrió's *Charentón,* an experimental play about failed revolutions (inspired by Peter Weiss's *Marat/Sade*), directly from Mexico and Cuba, respectively, and before a U.S. Latino and non-Latino audience. What makes all of these works Latino? What leg of the octopus do we stand on?

It has been the underlying assumption in the field of Latino theater studies that Latino theater is theater produced by Latino theater artists for Latino audiences. This collection of plays pushes the definition of Latino theater further by offering works that result from the curatorial conceptualization and programming practiced by a Latino curator at an established, Equity Union, Midwestern regional theater to showcase Latino, Latin American, and Spanish theater for Latino and non-Latino audiences alike. Attending to the curatorial frame of the festival, which director and curator Henry Godinez discusses in his essay included in this volume, we arrive at a model of Latino theater that includes pieces by Latino theater artists as well as works by Latin American (and Spanish) artists brought into the framework of Latino theater. It also includes works penned in English, others written in Spanish and presented in the original language (at times with supertitles), and still others translated from Spanish into English as part of a commissioning program. Some pieces tackle Latino experience head-on. Others touch on Latino themes obliquely, and some do not do so at all. What makes these pieces Latino theater is their placement before an audience under the frame of the Latino Theatre Festival. This framing asks audiences to understand the works before them as relevant to our experiences as Latinos and to our understanding of Latinos. This multidirectional relationship to what is Latino is perhaps what Godinez describes as the "universal" in his own account of his work at the Goodman.

Godinez's account of the Latino Theatre Festival offers an important corrective in practice to a Latino theater history that has long sustained a narrative progression from community-based theatrical practice to mainstreaming that stigmatizes the efforts of Latino theater artists to establish themselves in the regional theater circuits or Broadway. Generally, this narrative advances some ambivalence toward the political promise of Latino theater once it leaves the marginal geography of the Latino neighborhood or barrio. Godinez's use of the language of universals is provocative here. While it seemingly introduces an apolitical vision for the theater, it actually reenergizes the potential of Latino theater by placing it, through the framework of the festival, as a critical meeting point and point of view for the theatrical mainstream. At the Goodman's Latino

Theatre Festival, kitchen sink dramatic works produced for mainstream audiences share the space with community performance projects, and the play written by an academically oriented and politically inclined playwright is taken up and performed in a stage reading by an experimental storefront theater ensemble. The legs of the octopus become strategically and productively entangled in a collaborative venture where artists and audiences alike cross their borders of comfort, habits of practice, identitarian assumptions, and even political positions.

The "universals" invoked by Godinez emerge here as a challenge to long-held borders between Latino community performance and American theater. He insists on the idea that Latino theater has been and must continue to be American theater. The Goodman's Latino Theatre Festival offers us a diverse selection of Latino theater within the heightened framework of an internationally visible regional theater platform. The result parallels what playwright, translator, and theater critic Caridad Svich has described as a move "out of the fringe and into the virtual center of contemporary American performance."[10] Godinez, like Svich, is invested in finding alternatives to the always assumed marginality of Latino theater by inviting us to look beyond what theater scholar David Román has described as the "romance with the indigenous." Like Román, *Festival Latino* invites us to become "interested in the different kinds of politics of pleasure that each specific practice brings forth."[11] This does not mean that we do not need to continue to be mindful of the politico-economic differences between commercial, established not-for-profit, and community theaters. What it suggests is that we should explore what's possible in the jumping of scales and in the border crossings between one line of activity and the other. At each of these locations, Latino theater has something important to offer.

The six plays contained in this collection stage for us critically important questions about what Latino theater is and what it might become in the years to come as it grows new legs and expands its reach within the American theater scene. That we must begin to ponder upon the possibilities of an increased Latino presence in the national theater scene is not just a matter of activist advocacy for a growing Latino middle class invested in participating in the public culture of their respective communities but also a matter of survival for a theater mainstream whose idealized primary demographic continues to shrink precipitously. Considering

the projections announced in the 2010 U.S. Census, in just a generation most of the theatrical centers of the United States will count with a
majority Latino population. If theater as a cultural institution wishes to
remain relevant, it will need to engage Latino theater artists and audiences to the point that, perhaps, the very idea of a Latino theater festival
might in the end seem redundant.

Festival Latino should serve as an invitation and a sampler for the
reader interested in exploring the many legs of Latino theater. The collection is by far not a survey of all lines of activity in a field too vast and
diverse to simply contain in a single volume. But we believe it will offer
a provocative range from which to approach what Latino theater might
bring to the table of American theater.

NOTES

The title of this essay is inspired by Alberto Sandoval-Sánchez's groundbreaking study
of Latino theater, *José Can You See? Latinos On and Off Broadway* (Madison: University of
Wisconsin Press, 1999).

1. I have for some time been focusing attention on the work of curators at theater and
   museum venues as critical contributors to the performance event. I argue that curatorial
   labor needs to be more rigorously accounted for in approaches to the arts. For an example
   of this argument in museum contexts, see Ramón H. Rivera-Servera, "Exhibiting Voice/
   Narrating Migration: Performance-Based Curatorial Practice in ¡Azúcar! The Life and
   Music of Celia Cruz" in *Text and Performance Quarterly* 29, no. 9 (2009): 131–48.

2. Sandoval-Sánchez, 103.

3. For one of the richest discussions about the relationship between Latino and Latin
   American communities and theatrical traditions, see Diana Taylor's "Opening Remarks"
   in Diana Taylor and Juan Villegas, eds., *Negotiating Performance: Gender, Sexuality, and
   Theatricality in Latin/o America* (Durham, N.C.: Duke University Press, 1994), 1–16.

4. U.S. Census, 2010.

5. See Juan Flores and Renato Rosaldo, eds., *A Companion to Latina/o Studies* (Malden,
   Mass.: Blackwell Publishing, 2007).

6. On the governmental classification of Latinos through the census, see Suzanne Oboler's
   Ethnic Labels/Latino Lives: Identity and Politics of [Re]presentation in the United States
   (Minneapolis: University of Minnesota Press, 1997). On Latinos as a niche market, see
   Arlene Dávila's *Latinos, Inc.: The Marketing and Making of a People* (New York: New York
   University Press, 2001).

7. See Milagros Ricourt and Ruby Danta, *Hispanas de Queens: Latino Panethnicity in a New
   York Neighborhood* (Ithaca, N.Y.: Cornell University Press, 2003).

8. This is an argument I expand in my book on Latino queer dance. See Ramón H. Rivera-
   Servera, *Performing Queer Latinidad: Dance, Sexuality, Politics* (Ann Arbor: University of
   Michigan Press, 2012).

THE MANY LEGS OF LATINA/O THEATER ❧ XIX

9. Jorge Huerta, *Necessary Theater: Six Plays About the Chicano Experience* (Houston: Arte Público Press, 1989).

10. Caridad Svich, "Out of the Fringe: In Defense of Beauty," in Caridad Svich and María Teresa Marrero, eds., *Out of the Fringe: Contemporary Latina/Latino Theatre and Performance* (New York: Theatre Communications Group, 2000), ix.

11. David Román, *Performance in America: Contemporary U.S. Culture and the Performing Arts* (Durham, N.C.: Duke University Press, 2005), 36.

FESTIVAL LATINO: THE WHY AND WHEREFORE
Henry D. Godinez

It was 1999 and the first time that a Latino playwright had ever been produced on the Goodman main-stage. The play was Luis Valdez's *Zoot Suit,* perhaps the most iconic play in the contemporary Latino theater canon. The response from the Latino community in Chicago was overwhelming, and never before had Latinos flocked to the Goodman in such significant numbers. It was coincidentally the last regular season production in the Goodman Theatre's original home adjacent to the Art Institute of Chicago, before the move to its new state-of-the-art facility on Dearborn Street. However, the first few seasons in the new Goodman Theatre location did not see the inclusion of Latino programming. At the time, as the member of the artistic collective committed to championing Latino work, I was preoccupied with the direction, transfer, and redesign of the Goodman's annual production of *A Christmas Carol.* We were also in the wake of 9/11, and like so many arts organizations around the country, the Goodman sensed a prevailing atmosphere that was less than conducive to risk taking. I nonetheless approached Goodman Executive Director Roche Schulfer and expressed my concern that the audiences that had so enthusiastically come to see *Zoot Suit* wouldn't know where to find us now that we had moved. I was haunted by an anecdote Luis Valdez shared with me on the opening night of *Zoot Suit:* "Now don't let this be like when I was a kid and they'd only let us Chicano kids swim in the public pool the day before they drained it." I responded to Luis with an uneasy laugh and assured him that wasn't going to be the case at Goodman.

A glance at the last twenty seasons of Goodman Theatre programming will reveal a remarkably consistent commitment to writers, directors, and actors of color. It was no surprise then that Roche Schulfer and Artistic Director Robert Falls took my concern seriously, and we began to strategize ways of reconnecting with our Latino audiences. I told Roche about a recent visit to the International Hispanic Theatre Festival in Miami and the amazing international productions I'd seen there. Roche was excited by the idea of a festival as a way to reenergize our relationship with the Latino community in Chicago while at the same time offering a broad spectrum of new work to Goodman subscription audiences.

In the summer of 2004, in association with the International Hispanic Theatre Festival of Miami, we presented the Goodman's first Latino Theatre Festival. Opening in July, and with that season's last main-stage production, Luis Alfaro's *Electricidad*, as its centerpiece, the first Latino Theatre Festival featured two international companies: Compañia Marta Carrasco from Barcelona with their landmark production, *Mira'm, se dicen tantas cosas*, and Mexico's Teatro de Ciertos Habitantes's *El automóvil gris*, directed by Claudio Valdés Kuri. Still, from the beginning we wanted the festival to be more than just an international festival. We felt the festival was an opportunity to showcase the flourishing community of Latino theater artists in Chicago, companies like Teatro Vista, Aguijón Theater Company, and Teatro Luna, each creating Latino work from their own unique perspective and with their own particular agenda. The idea of presenting local companies was not only to expose their work to the large Goodman audience base, but also to afford them the opportunity of interacting with great theater artists from Latin America, Spain, and throughout the United States who were also participating in the festival. The dream was to make it as much a platform for artistic exchange and enrichment for the artistic community in Chicago as it was an opportunity for our audiences to see a variety of exceptional work that represented the diversity of Latino cultural heritage. With the international companies, we wanted Chicago audiences to see a style of theater fundamentally different than anything being done in America, even in a city with Chicago's rich theatrical tradition. Simultaneously, by including Latino theater artists from around the United States, the intention was to create dialogue and to foster relationships in support of a burgeoning national Latino theater movement. And so it was that, beginning with the Goodman's first Latino Theatre Festival in 2004, the standard formula became a combination of the most exciting international, national, and local work we could possibly bring together.

Internationally, my curatorial objective was to bring to Chicago work from Latin America and Spain that challenged our theatrical aesthetic, mostly our inherited addiction to and reliance on realism. At the same time we looked for work that in some way touched upon our common heritage as people of Latin American descent. That common ground was primarily, though not exclusively, a shared mother tongue. Even if the festivals' artists and audiences through the years represented a broad spectrum of fluency, the Spanish language was a bond that all Latinos could trace back to native homelands.

Generally speaking, I felt that much of Latino theater in the United States grappled with issues of identity, which is of course understandable for any community living within a larger dominant culture. The presence of international theater companies afforded us an opportunity to see work from our cultural extended family that was mostly free of the need to articulate, defend, or represent Latino identity, and which instead addressed broader universal themes or simply were more artistically adventurous. The international work that I responded most strongly to tended to be more abstract in nature. In my travels to festivals throughout Latin America and Spain I saw plenty of work that was based in realism, but I found that the more interesting work had very strong physical, ritualistic, and stylized theatrical qualities. Because we wanted the festival to appeal to traditional Goodman subscribers as well as to new Latino audiences, Spanish speaking and non–Spanish speaking alike, the more physically stylized, visually oriented work that I was drawn to seemed like a perfect bridge.

Beyond the obvious audience-bridging benefits of non–text-oriented work, what excited me most about the more physical theater from Latin America and Spain was a profound theatricality that I felt lacking in much of our Chicago-realism-based theater. It felt reminiscent of the poetic qualities of Latino playwrights like José Rivera, Luis Alfaro, Karen Zacarías, Octavio Solis, Nilo Cruz, María Irene Fornés, and others who for me were the lifeblood of the contemporary Latino theater movement in the United States. Only these international companies brought a bold corporal lyricism to their work. One of the most influential and wildly popular of these international companies, with three festival appearances over the years, was Compañia Marta Carrasco of Barcelona, whose work, sadly, is so nontext in nature that it is impossible to represent them in this anthology, at least in print. The digital addendum to this book will undoubtedly capture some of the virtuosity of Marta's extraordinary work. However, the texts that do appear in this anthology represent virtually every key element of the Goodman Latino Theatre Festival formula: theater for youth, new work, and Chicago ensemble–based companies, as well as national and international artists. This is also more than a collection of plays: it represents a broad spectrum of theater creation, from solo work to devised ethnographic work to Spanish-language adaptation.

Very early on we realized that programming theater for youth was vital to the development of new Latino audiences, so we presented companies like Pia Fraus from Brazil and partnered with Chicago Children's Theatre to produce *Esperanza Rising*. In 2008, 2010, and 2013, we presented Albany Park Theatre Project (APTP), a remarkable multiethnic youth theater company that creates and performs original work of astonishing artistic quality. Their nationally acclaimed production of *Home/Land*, published in this anthology and scheduled for the 2013 Latino Theatre Festival, represents the highest level of devised, community-based, socially conscious theater for and by youth. The ensemble of teenage performers from one of Chicago's most culturally diverse neighborhoods conducted the interviews that led to the development of the script published in this book. Like the presence of other Chicago companies throughout the years, APTP's participation in the festival exposed Goodman audiences to the work of an extraordinary and vibrant small Chicago theater company, while at the same time expanding their reach to vast new audiences.

The festival's commitment to new Latino work was a crucial element from the very beginning, starting in 2003 with Ana Castillo's new adaptation of her haunting poem "Like the People of Guatemala, I Want to Be Free of These Memories" titled *Psst . . . I Have Something to Tell You, Mi Amor.* The commitment to new work continued in subsequent festivals with staged readings and productions of plays by Tanya Saracho, Carlos Murillo, and Migdalia Cruz. This commitment to new work culminated in 2010 with the festival fostering a collaboration between the Lark Play Development Center in New York City and five Chicago companies who presented staged readings of five new Mexican plays in translation, all developed through the Lark's U.S./Mexico Playwright Exchange. One of the most powerful of those plays, Javier Malpica's beautiful and devastating *Our Dad Is in Atlantis,* translated from the Spanish by Jorge Ignacio Cortiñas, is a humanized view of immigration issues from a perspective rarely seen in this country—that of Mexican youth. The Lark's unprecedented success in connecting Mexican writers with American playwrights/translators exposed both U.S. audiences and theater companies to the most exciting young writers in Mexico today. The experience nurtured direct relationships between the five Chicago companies and the Lark, creating increased potential for the dissemination of these new Mexican plays in translation beyond New York City, and giving small Chicago companies a vital pipeline to new work.

As we looked to showcase in the festival Latino theater artists from across the United States, we were immediately drawn to groundbreaking pioneers like Herbert Siguenza, Ric Salinas, and Richard Montoya, who together as Culture Clash appeared in two different festivals. However, for some years, the size of the festival and the economic realities of bringing in multiple international companies favored the inclusion of the solo performance, including actress and playwright Adriana Sevahn Nichols's hilarious yet moving solo piece *Taking Flight,* which was a huge hit in the 2008 Latino Theatre Festival, playing to four sold-out houses. By turns funny and profoundly moving, *Taking Flight* celebrates the volatile, loving relationship between two women in the wake of surviving the terrorist attacks of 9/11. Luis Alfaro, who appeared in two festivals with his *Book of Titus and Other Latino Bible Stories,* was also a festival favorite as a solo performer, though his play *Electricidad,* a poetic Latino gangland-inspired adaptation of Sophocles's *Electra,* was the centerpiece of the inaugural Latino Theatre Festival in 2004. It should be noted that the version of *Electricidad* included in this anthology is Luis's most recent version of the text, which is considerably different from the early version (the second production) that was produced at Goodman in 2004.

At times the criteria for inclusion of a particular piece in the Latino Theatre Festival magically lined up on multiple levels, especially with a company like Universes, whose hip theatrical storytelling blends spoken word and music with performance in a way that defies categorization. Certainly for us, the intention was to present a new, unique multicultural form of theatrical expression that we felt would speak to young urban audiences. In a city like Chicago with such a rich history of ensemble work, Universes was an eye-opening inspiration to the many young ensemble companies that flocked to see them. Multitalented writers/performers Mildred Ruiz and Steven Sapp's production of *Blue Sweat* in the 2006 Latino Theatre Festival wove a dreamlike tapestry of words, music, and movement to reveal the complex relationship between a down-on-his-luck horn player and his muse. *Blue Sweat*, published here as *Blue Suite*, highlighted the intersection of hip-hop and theater in a way rarely seen in Chicago before, especially on the stage of one of the city's flagship cultural institutions.

Throughout the evolution of the Goodman Latino Theatre Festival, we strove to engage the city in every way we could through a variety of partnerships with arts organizations, community groups, foundations, corporations, and the city of Chicago itself. Always with the intention of being mutually beneficial, the result was often rewarding, with everything from the Nature Center bringing animals to the Goodman for a Brazilian company's young audience show about the Amazon, to a concert reading with the Grant Park Symphony Orchestra, to a parade of huge insects in Millennium Park, which entertained thousands of people for free, to a young playwrights competition.

It may seem unimaginable—any major regional theater in the United States committing to an event the size and scope of the Goodman's Latino Theatre Festival—yet it is a huge logistic undertaking that only an institution the size of Goodman could possibly successfully accomplish. Certainly one might lament the fact there are no Latino theaters in this country that alone could host a large festival of this kind, though the International Hispanic Theatre Festival in Miami has done so every year for decades through Teatro Avante. The primary difference is that the Goodman pays substantial fees to artists and companies, in addition to paying for transportation and housing. It demands substantial funding above and beyond the regular season's general operating budget, with production and administrative demands that impact every department and practically every staff member. With a large mainstream subscription base and an already lauded commitment to diversity, the Goodman was not necessarily compelled to produce the festival, yet with diversity as a core value and with a sense of responsibility to uphold Chicago's profile as a world-class city, the leadership of the Goodman recognized the festival's importance. The leadership and board of the Goodman believe in its value to the city, the field, and the Goodman Theatre itself.

New audiences were engaged and created, and old ones enriched. The notion that Latino theater is only created and presented in the community for the community has been defiantly challenged. The field of Latin American and Spanish theater around the world can now recognize Latino theater in the United States, a very unique and singular cultural hybrid, as a valued member of the family. Latino theater artists from across the country saw the festival as a place where ideas could be exchanged and relationships nurtured. In their own particular way, each of the plays in this anthology contributed to all of that. Many Latino and non-Latino theater artists alike were enriched with an infusion of creativity and the possibilities these plays offered for new forms of expression. At the center of it all was a sense of unity, of community, of the past, the present, and the future.

THE GOODMAN THEATRE'S FESTIVAL LATINO

ELECTRICIDAD
A CHICANO TAKE ON
THE TRAGEDY OF ELECTRA

Luis Alfaro

PRODUCTION HISTORY

Electricidad premiered at Borderlands Theater in Tucson, Arizona, on September 17, 2003. It was directed by Barclay Goldsmith, with set design by John Longhofer, costume design by Mary Ann Trombino, lighting design by John Dahlstrand, sound design by T. Greg Squires, and choreography by Eva Zorilla Tessler.

Minerva Garcia . . . . Electricidad
Alma Martinez . . . . Clemencia
Rosanne Couston, Rene Skinner,
Albert Soto, Eva Zorilla Tessler,
and Carlota Wilson . . . . Las Vecinas
             (chorus: La Carmen, La Connie, and La Cuca)
Norma Medina . . . . Abuela
Justin Huen . . . . Orestes
Mike Rabago . . . . Nino
Alida Gunn . . . . Cristina

The play was subsequently presented by the Goodman Latino Theatre Festival (June 19–July 25, 2004). It was directed by Henry Godinez, with set design by Ricardo Hernandez, costume design by Christopher Acebo, lighting design by Christopher Akerlind, sound design by Ray Nardelli and Joshua Horvath, choreography by Wilfredo Rivera, original music by Gustavo Leone, dramaturgy by Rick Desrochers, and stage management by Alden Vasquez and Rolando Linares.

Cecilia Suarez . . . . Electricidad
Sandra Marquez . . . . Clemencia
Laura E. Crotte, Sandra Delgado, Tanya
Saracho, and Marisabel Suarez . . . . Las Vecinas
             (La Carmen, La Connie, and La Cuca)
Ivonne Coll . . . . Abuela
Charin Alvarez . . . . Ifigenia
Maximino Arciniega Jr. . . . . Orestes
Edward Torres . . . . Nino

After awhile it comes down to a question
　　of life choices not a choice between you / or her
　　　　this sea town / or that bruising city
　　but about putting one foot in front of the other
　　　　and ending up somewhere
　　　　　　that looks like home.
　　　　　　—Cherríe Moraga, *The Last Generation* (1999)

TIEMPO: Right now, baby.

LUGAR: City of Los, the East Side, by the river. That house at the end of the street over by the freeway.

SONIDO: The city, a live wire, electricity running from a transformer.

CHARACTERS

Agamemnón "El Auggie," (R.I.P.) *El rey, El hombre,* formerly known as Father, a *veterano* from way back, head of the East Side Locos
Electricidad, twenty-three, the oldest daughter, an old-school *chola,* in grief, cannot break the cycle
Clemencia, forty, the mother, total *veterana,* goes way back, has issues
Las Vecinas (*La Carmen, La Connie,* and *La Cuca*), a chorus of *mujeres* from the hood, have seen it all, the *voz* of the city
Abuela, fifty, the grandmother, a *veteran,* old-school *chola, muy* sexy this *vieja*
Ifigenia, twenty, the other daughter, formerly *muy peligrosa,* possibly born-again, looks good in black
Orestes, seventeen, the brother, a Peewee, heir to the *trono,* exiled to Las Vegas
Nino, fifty-two, the godfather, *el atendido,* the most *veterano,* exiled to Las Vegas

STAGING

La Casa de Atridas. We see a yard in front of a casa at the end of the block. Not one of the kept-up ones, *pero una yarda* with dirt, shrubs, stones, and some stuff that didn't fit in the house. *En la yarda* is an *altar* made of stones. Nestled between the stones are objects that live on *altars:* votive candles, burning incense, fragrant flowers, a Bart Simpson piggy bank from the border, old and faded pictures. At the center of the *altar* lies the decomposing body of AGAMEMNÓN "EL AUGGIE" Atridas, the father. *El former rey de la* neighborhood. Eyes plucked. Tongue missing. He is wrapped in a shroud. Sitting in the yard and draped over EL AUGGIE is ELECTRICIDAD, *la* youngest *hija.* She has been sitting in the yard for five days. Waiting. For what? *Quien sabe.* A layer of earth bakes on her. A canvas for the recent Santa Ana's. But you know what? Her makeup is holding on pretty good . . . She wears Levis, a black tank top, and *chancla* flip-flops. Her hair is matted and dirty. She has not spoken for days, but her wailing, which has been heard throughout *el barrio* for days, becomes an echo when it hits the valley at Mariachi Plaza. This homegirl is a young *chola* with old-school ways. Always has, always been. Even at

night when little *cholos* dream of Krispy Kremes and fresh graffiti, ELEC-
TRICIDAD sits with her father. We can clearly see inside *la casa*. The walls
are missing and a wood frame is revealed. We see some furniture inside.
Seventies stuff. Some *cosas* from layaway. Moving nervously through the
house, *como una* bird in a cage, is CLEMENCIA, *la mama*. She is smoking—*pero* always. It helps with the *nervios,* you know. The cigarette is
long. A Virginia Slim. She is dressed in *chola* evening wear. *Y* with some
heel, of course. Sometimes she puts on a hat. When she wants to look
good. *Tu sabes.*

SCENE 1

As I Sit Here

[*An east* los *rooster crows. Daybreak. The sound of work begins. The sweep, sweep, sweep of brooms.* ELECTRICIDAD *sleeps at her altar. The faint sound of* chisme *approaches as the audience sees a trio of* VECINAS *sweep down the street. A* Griego *chorus in housedresses and aprons. Very* mitoteras *these* mujeres. *Their* chisme *is accompanied by the rhythmic sweeping of their brooms.*]

LA CARMEN: *Apoco.*

LA CONNIE: *No me digas.*

LA CUCA: *Ai . . .*

[*Beat.*]

LA CARMEN: Did you see?

LA CONNIE: No, *que?*

LA CUCA: She's still there.

LA CARMEN: There at her *altar.*

LA CONNIE: *Ai,* don't stare *vecina!*

LA CUCA: I can't help it.

LA CARMEN: It's so sad.

LA CONNIE: Such a tragedy.

LA CUCA: A story like this.

LA CARMEN: Makes you wonder.

LA CONNIE: Where you can live these days.

LA CUCA: *Esta asi* all over.

LA CARMEN: Every part of the city.

LA CONNIE: No one can *escapar.*

LA CUCA: Must be fate.

LA CARMEN: Must be luck.

LA CONNIE: Must be the city.

LA CUCA: Especially over here.

LA CARMEN: Split by the freeway.

LA CONNIE: Border the river.

LA CUCA: In the shadow of skyscrapers.

LA CARMEN: But still.

LA CONNIE: It's not right.

LA CUCA: We should say something.

LA CARMEN: I ask you . . .

LA CONNIE: How many neighbors . . .

LA CUCA: Keep a body in their front yard?

LA CARMEN: As if he was a car.

LA CONNIE: Without wheels.

LA CUCA: On cinder blocks.

LA CARMEN: She's all confused.

LA CONNIE: But a body, *mujer?*

LA CUCA: It can't be good for barrio pride.

LA CARMEN: She can't help it.

LA CONNIE: Let her grieve.

LA CUCA: Let her weep.

[*Beat.*]

LA CARMEN: *Apoco.*

LA CONNIE: *No me digas.*

LA CUCA: *Ai . . .*

[*Beat.*]

LA CARMEN: How long can it go on?

LA CONNIE: As long as it takes to forgive.

LA CUCA: *Ai,* but what if she's a grudge-holder?

LA CARMEN: We'll never get any sleep.

LA CONNIE: We'll never get this barrio clean.

LA CUCA: We'll never get back to *una vida normal.*

LA CARMEN: And all of this for what?

LA CONNIE: She wants revenge.

LA CUCA: Who doesn't these days?

LA CARMEN: But, ah *que* sad.

LA CONNIE: What a *tristesa.*

LA CUCA: To lose someone.

LA CARMEN: A father.

LA CONNIE: *El rey.*

LA CUCA: Yes, the king.

LA CARMEN: Even if he was a *cholo.*

LA CONNIE: A warrior.

LA CUCA: A parolee.

LA CARMEN: Protected his family.

LA CONNIE: Protected his territory.

LA CUCA: And all of us.

LA CARMEN: But from what?

LA CONNIE: The elements, *mujer.*

LA CUCA: The city.

LA CARMEN: The other gangs.

LA CONNIE: The thieves.

LA CUCA: *La policia.*

LA CARMEN: And the politicians.

LA CONNIE: Thank *dios* for *cholo* protection.

LA CUCA: And LoJack!

LA CARMEN: But still.

LA CONNIE: It's not right.

LA CUCA: And why do we let them?

LA CARMEN: It wasn't always this way.

LA CONNIE: It was different.

LA CUCA: Another way of life.

LA CARMEN: Do we remember *vecinas?*

LA CONNIE: Remember our story?

LA CUCA: How can you forget a history?

LA CARMEN: Then let us tell it.

LA CONNIE: To our *comunidad.*

LA CUCA: So, that they will know.

[*Beat.*]

LA CARMEN: In the beginning.

LA CONNIE: Before Mayor Bradley.

LA CUCA: And Gloria Molina.

LA CARMEN: Before the great wars of the seventies and eighties.

LA CONNIE: Before the Chicano moratorium.

LA CUCA: And the death of Ruben Salazar.

LA CARMEN: There was the *cholo.*

LA CONNIE: And the *cholo* was no myth.

LA CUCA: He wasn't even a god.

LA CARMEN: No, he was made by man.

LA CONNIE: The product of *racismo.*

LA CUCA: And neglectful *mamas.*

LA CARMEN: The *cholo* was just a homeboy.

LA CONNIE: With his zoot suit.

LA CUCA: And his switchblade.

LA CARMEN: Pushed out by *la cultura.*

LA CONNIE: Chased out of the neighborhood.

LA CUCA: Kicked out of the Chicano tribe.

LA CARMEN: Like a *coyote* he hid in the shadows.

LA CONNIE: In the coolness of midnights.

LA CUCA: His silhouette seen in the doorway of a cantina.

LA CARMEN: But they were "us."

LA CONNIE: Our *otro yo.*

LA CUCA: The dark side of us.

LA CARMEN: Then they came back into the barrio.

LA CONNIE: Causing *desmadre.*

LA CUCA: Claiming their territories.

LA CARMEN: We can't live with them.

LA CONNIE: But we tolerate them.

LA CUCA: And use them.

LA CARMEN: To protect us.

LA CONNIE: And watch our neighborhoods.

LA CUCA: We don't dial the 911 no more.

LA CARMEN: No place for *la policia* in these barrios now.

LA CONNIE: We handle our own now.

LA CUCA: Or we call Father Greg.

[*Beat.*]

LA CARMEN: *Apoco.*

LA CONNIE: *No me digas.*

LA CUCA: *Ai . . .*

[*Beat.*]

LA CARMEN: What is to be done, *vecinas?*

LA CONNIE: *Yo no se.*

LA CUCA: What is to be done?

LA CARMEN: She killed him.

LA CONNIE: Who?

LA CUCA: The mother.

LA CARMEN: *La* Clemencia.

LA CONNIE: What kind of name is that?

LA CUCA: Texas, I bet.

LA CARMEN: She did it with bare hands.

LA CONNIE: But she's a *mujer.*

LA CUCA: How is that possible?

LA CARMEN: She waited after a fiesta.

LA CONNIE: With too many tequilas.

LA CUCA: And Budweiser chasers.

LA CARMEN: He staggered home.

LA CONNIE: Slept and snored.

LA CUCA: She didn't even break a nail.

LA CARMEN: But he beat her.

LA CONNIE: And ignored her.

LA CUCA: And that makes it right?

LA CARMEN: No, of course not.

LA CONNIE: She wanted *algo*.

LA CUCA: Something no woman in this barrio can get.

LA CARMEN: Power.

LA CONNIE: Her own business.

LA CUCA: Her own territory.

LA CARMEN: Wants to own the block.

LA CONNIE: Wants to own the casa.

LA CUCA: Wants to own the *carro*.

LA CARMEN: Be a queen.

LA CONNIE: Be an entrepreneur.

LA CUCA: *Como la* Oprah.

LA CARMEN: She can't see.

LA CONNIE: The price you pay.

LA CUCA: For your ambition.

LA CARMEN: And all *para que*?

LA CONNIE: A piece of the *accion*.

LA CUCA: Her own bank account.

LA CARMEN: He should have known.

LA CONNIE: Isn't it obvious?

LA CUCA: She was trouble from the start.

LA CARMEN: Never marry a woman.

LA CONNIE: From someplace way up high.

LA CUCA: Like the hills of Pico Rivera.

[*Beat.*]

LA CARMEN: *Apoco.*

LA CONNIE: *No me digas.*

LA CUCA: *Ai . . .*

[*Beat.*]

LA CARMEN: Look at the daughter.

LA CONNIE: Our little Electricidad.

LA CUCA: We practically raised her for that mother.

LA CARMEN: She won't talk to us.

LA CONNIE: She's in silence.

LA CUCA: Like *el papa.*

LA CARMEN: Agamemnón.

LA CONNIE: *El* Auggie.

LA CUCA: Another weird name.

LA CARMEN: And who told you all of this?

LA CONNIE: Same person who told you.

LA CUCA: Don't look at me!

LA CARMEN: Oh, you know those *chismosas.*

LA CONNIE: Gossiping.

LA CUCA: *Not like us . . .*

LA CARMEN: And the sister.

LA CONNIE: What happened to the sister?

LA CUCA: Ifigenia.

LA CARMEN: *La Ifi.*

LA CONNIE: Ran off.

LA CUCA: No?

LA CARMEN: How can a *chola* run off?

LA CONNIE: That's like a coyote in the city.

LA CUCA: Spiritual death for sure.

LA CARMEN: And she used to be the meanest of them all.

LA CONNIE: Didn't like the boys too much.

LA CUCA: Cut them up for no *razon.*

LA CARMEN: Danced with girls.

LA CONNIE: You mean she was . . .

LA CUCA: Yes . . . a Catholic-school girl.

[*Beat.*]

LA CARMEN: *Apoco.*

LA CONNIE: *No me digas.*

LA CUCA: *Ai . . .*

[*Beat.*]

LA CARMEN: And the son . . .

LA CONNIE: *El* Orestes, the son.

LA CUCA: Who should've taken his father's place.

LA CARMEN: She killed him.

LA CONNIE: *Tambien?*

LA CUCA: How?

LA CARMEN: *En* Las Vegas.

LA CONNIE: Murdered.

LA CUCA: Like *el* Tupac.

LA CARMEN: She ordered a hit.

LA CONNIE: Like she orders a pizza.

LA CUCA: This is like a whole issue of *Alarma*.

LA CARMEN: Poor Orestes.

LA CONNIE: What is it with this family and their names?

LA CUCA: Must have been raised by *alleluias*.

LA CARMEN: Will Electricidad ever recover?

LA CONNIE: She too is also *muerta*.

LA CUCA: A living dead.

LA CARMEN: And the *mama*?

LA CONNIE: Smoking her *cigaros*.

LA CUCA: Laughing on her *telefono*.

LA CARMEN: Watching *The Price Is Right*.

LA CONNIE: Planning her takeover.

LA CUCA: Plotting against the children for the house.

LA CARMEN: She wants power.

LA CONNIE: She wants money.

LA CUCA: She wants to be single again.

LA CARMEN: But she'll get hers.

LA CONNIE: Don't they know.

LA CUCA: That everything is a circle.

LA CARMEN: What goes around comes around.

LA CONNIE: Everybody pays for their MTA ride.

LA CUCA: The ying and the yang, *comadre*.

LA CARMEN: That woman.

LA CONNIE: That wife.

LA CUCA: That mother.

LA CARMEN: *Mala!*

LA CONNIE: *Floja!*

LA CUCA: *Cabrona!*

LA CARMEN: Doesn't clean her *casa*.

LA CONNIE: Doesn't clean her *yarda*.

LA CUCA: Doesn't clean *la calle*.

LA CARMEN: Thank you, Jesus.

LA CONNIE: That we

LA CUCA: Are not.

ALL: Like them!

[*Beat.*]

LA CARMEN: *Apoco.*

LA CONNIE: *No me digas.*

LA CUCA: *Ai* . . .

[*The pack of* VECINAS *start to sweep their way down the street. You can hear the* chisme *and the sound of their brooms slowly fade away.*]

SCENE 2

Keeper of Dreams

[*Morning. The sound of two freeways meeting each other.* ELECTRICIDAD *stands in the front* yarda. *She looks up at the sky, as if it might be following her.*]

ELECTRICIDAD: *Papa!*
Why do I keep looking up to see heaven,
but I only get as far as the sky?

Why is it the only light that shines on me is the happy face of the helicopter?

I wonder if you could be born-again and really come back?

I am waiting for a cloud to pass by and spit in my mouth.
But the Santa Anas keep pushing them away.
To Vegas, I guess . . .

But I can wait.

When I finally get God to spit down on me, I am going to say that it is a blessing and I am going to use my spit to *gritar* my sorrow, and my rage, and my anger, and all the other *injusticias*.

I don't care how I sound.
I don't care what they think.

I will free you, *Papa.*
From your death.
I will do that.
I don't know how yet, but I will do it.

[ELECTRICIDAD *turns to look at the house.*]

SCENE 3

Confessin' a Feeling

[*In the distance the audience hears a* vieja *coughing. A hack that only an older* vieja *raised on menthols-in-the-box can make. Finally, she spits out a loogie.*

Ai, *thank God.* ELECTRICIDAD *hears it and looks up. We see a woman,* LA ABUELA, *too young to be old, too old to be young. Still trying to make it happen with the Mamie Van Doren. Pointy bra from Woolworths. Maybe a shortened version of a beehive. Can't quite let go of her period, can she? She is accompanied by* IFIGENIA, LA IFI, la hermana. IFIGENIA *is dressed like a sister in a religious order—simple skirt, shoes, and blouse with a cross. Only problem is, her gang tattoos betray her as they sneak out from her neck.*]

IFIGENIA: How long she been sitting out there?

ABUELA: Five days.
Foo-chie!

IFIGENIA: *Hijole,* she's a stubborn *chola.*

ABUELA: Always been.
She sits there forever looking up at the sky, like she's waiting for a UFO or something. And then she has these conversations with herself out loud.

IFIGENIA: Has she talked to *Mama?*

ABUELA: Don't talk to me about *tu Mama!*
She got the Sanitation Department to come out and scoop poor Electricidad up. But *la loca* Electricidad attacked the poor *gabacho* trashman. Pinned him like a pit bull. Threatened to drive-by him. *Y se fue* running, *el pobre.*

IFIGENIA: What's that next to her?

ABUELA: The body, *mujer!*

IFIGENIA: *El Cuerpo!*
Of my dad?

ABUELA: My son.

IFIGENIA: My god . . .

ABUELA: *La loca* has his body there in the front *yarda,* on display, like some Rose Parade float.

IFIGENIA: Somebody's gonna steal it.

ABUELA: No *chansa*. When she brought the body here, she stayed with it. She hasn't left, not even for a *momento*. She even pee-pees in the *yarda*. She's acting like she's at Yosemite or something.
I tell you, she's a *cacahuate*.

IFIGENIA: And how does she survive?

ABUELA: Like all *cholas* do—on the grandmother . . . I leave her *comida* every day. You know, tortillas and stuff. Some Top Ramen. I even bake *pinche* cupcakes for the *loca*.

IFIGENIA: Why do you do that? You don't even like us.

ABUELA: That's true. But let's face it, I do her a *favor* and maybe later she does me a favor. You know the *vida*. You watch your grandmother's back, and your granny watches yours.

IFIGENIA: I got your back, Abuela.

ABUELA: It's so hard. A poor *vieja* like me . . . In my twilight and back to feeding another mouth. A senior citizen *como yo*, making her *los* Rice Krispies, *con el* food coloring, *y todo*. On my *pobre* widow's pension . . .

IFIGENIA: Don't worry, *vieja,*
I'll make sure *Mama* gives you some *dinero*.

ABUELA: *Ai gracias . . .*

And now, even worse, *la loca* stopped talking to *las vecinas*.
She's got them all *aguitadas*. They think she is going to attack them.
When she sleeps, they leave flowers and incense for her. *Pues,* more for the smell of the body . . .

They hired me to *hablar* with her.

IFIGENIA: You charge them?

ABUELA: Well, I'm like a translation *servicio*.

IFIGENIA: My poor sister.

[ABUELA *looks at* IFIGENIA, *kind of surprised.*]

ABUELA: When did you become so nice, hard *chola*?

IFIGENIA: When I realized that someone died on a cross for me.

ABUELA: Oh really, who was that?

IFIGENIA: Don't be disrespectful, old lady.

ABUELA: Why you come back here, hard *chola?*
You been gone so long we thought you gave up the *vida.*

IFIGENIA: Came back to make amends. I'm kinda like on a pilgrimage.
To save the *familia.*

ABUELA: Good luck, *chola.* You got an *hermano* and a *papa* both dead.
You don't got that many people to pilgrim with.

IFIGENIA: What does she do all day?

ABUELA: She sleeps.
She's on the *coyote* cycle.
At night, she talks to herself, or to him, like a *loca.* Laughing and crying. Reliving herself and her *vida. Como una* rerun.
She's planning something, I know it.

IFIGENIA: And how do you know?

ABUELA: I stay up and watch her.

IFIGENIA: *Oye mujer,* you should let her grieve in solitude.

ABUELA: But I'm a retiree! This is what we do. Besides, what kind of *loca* grieves in their own front *yarda* for everyone to see?

IFIGENIA: She just doesn't want to forget . . .
How did she get the body?

ABUELA: She stole it from Forest Lawn the night of the *velorio.*

IFIGENIA: *Y vieja,* how do you know?

ABUELA: *Mujer,* I drove the hearse!

IFIGENIA: Shit, Abuela . . .

ABUELA: She told me she would kick my *nalgas* if I didn't.
So, I broke into the funeral car while she went into the little Chapel of the *Inocentes* and took the body.

Like a flan, he slid off the stretcher and into the hearse. And then she made me drive him *aqui.*
And I don't even have a license!

You know what? She's got like a rabies, I think.
You need to *hablar* with her. She's your sister, *tu sabes?*

IFIGENIA: My *hermana* . . . we never acted like we were sisters.

ABUELA: But, I'm warning you, *cuidado.* She strikes when you least expect it.

IFIGENIA: She wouldn't come at me.

ABUELA: You know her, she'll blame you if you don't take a side.

IFIGENIA: *Esta loca!*

ABUELA: *Pues,* that's what I said, *pero* who listens to the *viejas* anymore?

IFIGENIA: Jesus does . . .

ABUELA: *Ai,* don't start with that *alleluia* stuff, man. If there was a god, I wouldn't be making Government Cheese Quesadillas.

IFIGENIA: OK, scram, old lady.
I want to *hablar con mi* sister.

ABUELA: *Ai,* you girls got no manners, man.

IFIGENIA: We learned it from you, *cabrona.*

ABUELA: No, that comes from your *mama,* the outsider.

IFIGENIA: Oh, now she's an outsider?

ABUELA: Well, look at her. She's not from here. Whittier Boulevard runs a long way, baby.
I told my *hijo,* "Don't take a girl with something, 'cause soon they want everything. Take a girl with nothing and give her something, and it feels like a lot."

IFIGENIA: You really are the *Chola* Most High.

ABUELA: I don't know nothing, but what I know about nothing is a lot.
And I know I hate that *puta*.
No Vegas buffet can satisfy a *mujer* that hungry for power.
And she doesn't even know how to dress!

IFIGENIA: *No seas mala.*

ABUELA: I tell you, the only Mexican I got any respect for these days is
the *Virgin de Guadalupe.*

IFIGENIA: *Vete vieja.*

[ABUELA *begins to walk away.*]

Hey.

HEY!

[ABUELA *stops, surprised at the threat* IFIGENIA *musters, with as much conviction and honesty as she can come up with . . .*]

Que God bless you.

ABUELA: *Ai, gracias . . .*

[ABUELA *keeps walking and mutters under her breath.*]

Religiosa cabrona . . .

[ABUELA *exits.* IFIGENIA *looks at the front yard.*]

SCENE 4

Daddy's Home

[Momentos *later.* ELECTRICIDAD *in the front yard with* Papa.]

ELECTRICIDAD: Oh, you should have seen it, *Papa.*

They had you lying there in that mortuary. On display.
Like a dummy in a store window.

I couldn't have it, *Papa.*
Laying there all night by yourself.

Why do they do that?
Why do they leave someone alone on their first night of dying?
It isn't right, *Papa.*

You are not dead to me.
You are the *rey* of this neighborhood.
Everybody waits for you to give your orders.

No one stopped me from bringing you here.
Thought that I had gone crazy.

They don't know what I am capable of when it comes to my love and
loyalty to you, *mi rey.*

You are the old ways, *Papa.*
You are the history and the reason we know how to live.

I want to live the old *cholo* ways, *Papa.*
Simple and to the point.
You mess with me, I mess with you back.
You want to party, party in your own backyard.
You shoot, I shoot back.
It's simple.
Why can't we live the old ways?

She says I act like a man.
Good.
I'm not a girl.
I'm a *chola*!

DE LOS EAST SIDE LOCOS!

SCENE 5

Always and Forever

[*A forever night in Vegas. The sound of a needle buzzing loudly. It grows
dimmer, and more realistic, as the lights reveal* ORESTES *and* NINO. *They are
both shirtless and glistening with sweat.* ORESTES *sits facing out, looking at
nothing, while* NINO, *with the tattoo gun, sits on a stool, pricking* ORESTES's

chest. A trickle of blood runs from his breast down to his stomach. Suddenly, NINO *hits a nerve.* ORESTES *winces and pushes* NINO*'s hand away. They glare at each other.*]

NINO: You want me to stop?

[ORESTES *looks at* NINO *for a moment, nods "continue," and looks away.*]

Good cholo.

Good.

[NINO *continues to work on* ORESTES*'s chest while the lights fade and the sound of the buzzing grows.*]

SCENE 6

It's Just a Family Affair

[*Still this* mañana. ELECTRICIDAD *in the* yarda.]

ELECTRICIDAD: I scare her.
I know I do.
That's why she took my . . .

Oh, *Papa* . . .
My Orestes. My brother.
My sensitive *hermano,* with the poet's *corazon.*
She's killed him too.

You should hear her, *Papa.*
Me espera.
She wants me to come back inside.
And pretend.

Yo no!
I will not go back inside *con ella.*

As long as I have this memory of you,
I will make *mi casa, la tierra.*
Yes *Papa,* my house is now this front yard . . .

[Ai, *Clemencia, you are so loud on your phone.* ELECTRICIDAD *can hear her.*]

> She laughs at us, mocks us.
> Drives off *en el* Monte Carlo with her *cigaros*
> and her cancer cough that she thinks is so sexy.

> She doesn't sound like *la* J-Lo.
> *Esa cabrona* sounds like *el* John Wayne!

[ELECTRICIDAD *laughs a bitter laugh to herself.*]

> She tries so hard, but everyone knows she's not from the barrio. She never learned our ways.

[ELECTRICIDAD *screams toward the house.*]

> SHE'S ALL *MUY-MUY,* AIN'T SHE, *PAPA?*

[CLEMENCIA *looks out the window.*]

CLEMENCIA: *Callate la boca.*

ELECTRICIDAD: You shut up.

CLEMENCIA: Talking to yourself like some *loca.*

ELECTRICIDAD: Yeah, *y que?*

CLEMENCIA: *Todos los* neighbors think you've gone crazy.

ELECTRICIDAD: Maybe I have.

CLEMENCIA: *Bah, muy dramatica.*
> Save that little Berkeley protest out there for when I sell the house.

ELECTRICIDAD: This is my father's house.

CLEMENCIA: I got Century 21 on speed dial!

> But they won't sell it until you take him back to his bed at the cemetery.

ELECTRICIDAD: *Dejame, pendeja.*

CLEMENCIA: You look as filthy as *tu papa,* lying there in the dirt.
> I am going to call the loco house to come and take you away.

ELECTRICIDAD: They won't know who to take, you old witch.

CLEMENCIA: Don't call me "old"!

[CLEMENCIA *takes a long toke on her* cigaro.]

> *Ai* come on, *no seas asi.*
> Come inside.
> I'll call Yang Chow and order your favorite *chino* food,
> and we can look at old pictures of your father.

[ELECTRICIDAD *throws a stone.*]

> *Ai, malcriada!*
> While you are throwing those stones, clean the yard, you *puerca.*
> And take that *cuerpo* back before Forest Lawn comes and hands me a
> takeaway bill.

[CLEMENCIA *walks away from the window.*]

ELECTRICIDAD: Did you hear her, *Papa?*

CLEMENCIA [*from somewhere inside the house*]: Stop talking to yourself,
I said!

[ELECTRICIDAD *spits toward the house.*]

ELECTRICIDAD: See? She doesn't mourn you.
La noche of your funeral, she put on the K-Earth 101 and served tama-
les and wine coolers.
I didn't even know she could cook!

[*Beat. She looks at him and realizes.*]

> *Ai, Papa,* I'm sorry.
> All this talking makes you tired.
> You are a man of so few words . . .

> But I must tell the stories you told me.
> About who we are and where we came from.
> Or I will forget.

> We were *Aztecas,* huh *Papa?*
> And the *mujer* god of human sacrifices, *Coatlicue,* made the first *cholo.*

And she gave the first *cholo* the switchblade, so that he could leave the barrio and defend himself.
And then she gave the *cholo* the baggy pants, so that he could store the *comida* he shoplifted from the 7-Eleven.
And then she gave him Art Laboe and the oldies and taught him how to dance.

[*"Earth Angel" by the Penguins begins to play in her head. She dances slow* cholo-*style in the* yarda.]

And then she gave the *cholos* house parties and Schlitz, to make them happy.
And she gave them the low-rider and car club, so that they could show off to one another.
And finally she gave them the Boulevard, so that they could cruise and see how beautiful they were . . .

[*She stops dancing.*]

But then, one of her four hundred daughters, *Coyolxauqui*, stood up to her and was like, "Why you get all the power, *vieja*? Why you get to decide everything for us?"

And that's when *Coatlicue* cut her up in four, *carniceria* style, and made the four corners *cholo* world.

First corner, North Side *Locos*, control Aldephia cable.
Second corner, South Side *Locos*, control Vernon slaughterhouses.
Third corner, West Side *Locos*, got all the bail bonds.
And fourth corner, us, the East Side *Locos*, control neighborhood pride and "pharmacy" traffic.

And then she cut her daughter's head off and did a fly ball into the sky, and her head became the moon.

And that's the one I'm trying to see every night, *Papa*.
But she won't show me her expressions.
She's a stone-cold *chola*, that daughter.

And since the beginning of *cholo* time, this is how it was and always will be.

But someone wants to change that.

Oh, you know who I'm talking about.

She says it's progress. She thought that if she killed you, all the ways of the *cholo* would end. But she was wrong, because all she did was offend The Old Council of *Cholos*. Who never forget.

That's why I must say your name, *Papa*.
Or it will lose its power.
I must yell your name out loud or I will forget it, *Papa*.

[*She yells out to the barrio. As if she is calling him back from the dead.*]

AGAMEMNÓN ATRIDAS . . .

VETERANO . . .

DE LOS EAST SIDE LOCOS . . .

CLEMENCIA [*from inside the house*]: *Callate, cabrona!*

ELECTRICIDAD: Every day I will scream your name.
And they will get tired of hearing it and of hearing me,

[*She yells to the house.*]

PERO A MI NO ME IMPORTA!

[*She leans into his body, as if to tell him a secret.*]

Papa, I am going to avenge your death.
Y la muerte of our sweetest, and gentlest, Orestes.

I will turn Ifigenia, my so-called sister, against her.
I will turn the *vecinas* against her, *tambien*.

Oh *Papa*, it is only in the thought of her suffering that I get my *energia*.

Thinking of her lifeless body thrown at the doorway of *El Gato Negro* bar.

[*She laughs at the joy of seeing such an image.*]

The drunks stepping on her as they reach for their *cervezas*.

Yes, I have a *razon* to live!

[*She yells.*]

AGAMEMNÓN ATRIDAS . . .

VETERANO . . .

DE LOS EAST SIDE LOCOS . . .

CLEMENCIA: *Ai*, shut up . . .

ELECTRICIDAD: Oh yes, I would do anything to trade your death with my breath.
Sell my soul to the *diablo*, if only there was one.

[*She thinks about it.*]

There is . . .

[*It's a confirmation and a game plan.*]

Y ella,
Clemencia Atridas,
will have to pay . . .

[ELECTRICIDAD *starts to laugh.* CLEMENCIA *looks out the window and nods her head in disgust. The sound of the current of electricity rises and sweeps away the laughter, as the lights at the altar fade.*]

SCENE 7

I'm Your Puppet

[*Vegas darkness. The sound of breathing and punching. On one side of the stage appear* ORESTES *and* NINO. ORESTES *is plowing away into a punching bag furiously.* NINO *sits on a stool drinking a Corona.* ORESTES *is driven and unstoppable, while* NINO *takes a long slow gulp, gulp, gulp of his* cervecita.]

NINO: Good *cholo*.

Good.

[*The lights fade as* ORESTES *punches away and* NINO *downs his beer.*]

SCENE 8

Earth Angel

[*Midmorning and all the little* mocosos *are in class dozing.* IFIGENIA *enters.* ELECTRICIDAD *sees her and takes her place for battle. She stands with one foot on each side of her father's body.* IFIGENIA *sizes her up and comes closer as if to see the* cuerpo *of her* papa. ELECTRICIDAD *spits in her direction and gets ready for a Braveheart rush. They are staring each other down.* IFIGENIA *comes closer.*]

IFIGENIA: Hey.
They cut out your tongue too?

ELECTRICIDAD: Don't touch him!

IFIGENIA: He was my *papa* too.

ELECTRICIDAD: Is that why you deserted him?

IFIGENIA: What did you say, *pendeja*?

ELECTRICIDAD: You heard.

IFIGENIA: Listen, I didn't even know he was dead.

One of the sisters said, "The king of your barrio *esta muerto!*"
So, I came to see if it was true and pay my *respeto.*

And pray for you, big sister.

ELECTRICIDAD: Pray for me?
Pray that I don't kick your ass, deserter.

IFIGENIA: When I got off the Greyhound, I could hear the cherry bombs screaming a dead man's salute.
I could see the low-riders putt, putt, putt on the Boulevard.
The old-school *cholas* passed by me and give me the "whats up" . . .

[IFIGENIA *nods her head in acknowledgment.*]

And the so-sorrys.

[IFIGENIA *bows her head like you know you're supposed to.*]

They were saying *adios* and giving me condolence.
Knew it must be a *cholo* good-bye.
The sisters didn't lie.
Mi papa is dead.

[*They look at each other, sizing each other up.* IFIGENIA *takes the risk, kneels, and bows to her* papa, el rey. ELECTRICIDAD *knows she is back.*]

ELECTRICIDAD: Where were you?

IFIGENIA: You mean you noticed me gone?

ELECTRICIDAD: Yeah . . .

IFIGENIA: Serving time.

ELECTRICIDAD: Liar.

IFIGENIA: Why you say that?

ELECTRICIDAD: Every time you're gone, you're in jail.
This time nobody could find you.
I gave your *chifle.*

[*She does* IFIGENIA'S chifle.]

But only Helen Keller answered back.
I thought you were a victim, so I looked for you at the bottom of the river, on the railroad tracks, under the freeways.

Then I thought maybe you had walked away from your loyalty.

IFIGENIA: I was doing a different kind of time.
Mostly paying back my past.

ELECTRICIDAD: Man, you're always doing time.

IFIGENIA: Well, I'm a *chola.*

But this time I wasn't doing it in jail.

ELECTRICIDAD: What are you talking about?

IFIGENIA: You better not laugh, or I'll kick your ass.

ELECTRICIDAD: *Dimelo.*

IFIGENIA: I joined a convent . . .

ELECTRICIDAD: Fucking liar.

IFIGENIA: Fuck you, I did.
Why do you think I look like this?

ELECTRICIDAD: And the convent took you in?

IFIGENIA: *Y porque no?*

I'm sorry about *Papa.*
I know you were his favorite.

ELECTRICIDAD: You have to take a side.

IFIGENIA: For what?

ELECTRICIDAD: To avenge your father's death.
From the monster inside *la casa.*

IFIGENIA: I see you've learned a lot of forgiveness out here by yourself.

ELECTRICIDAD: I'm not by myself.

IFIGENIA: *Ya veo.*

ELECTRICIDAD: I'm just doing *lo que* he tells me to do.

IFIGENIA: *Y que es eso?*

ELECTRICIDAD: Planning.
Our father's revenge.

IFIGENIA: Don't forget what he was.
Yes, *rey* of our barrio, but also a mean-ass *cholo.*

ELECTRICIDAD: How do you think he got to be *cholo,* down on his knees
asking Jesus to make him leader?

IFIGENIA: *Hermana,* he gave us these tattoos.
But these tattoos are also scars.

ELECTRICIDAD: *Yo puedo ver que* she poisons your mind.

IFIGENIA: "Forgiveness is a virtue."

ELECTRICIDAD: What are you talking about, *macha*?

IFIGENIA: I just learned that one.
I don't know what the hell it means.

[*Beat.*]

ELECTRICIDAD: You like your convent?

IFIGENIA: It's just like jail, but with better food.
And silence . . .

Listen, *hermana*, your loyalty to *Papa* has always been deep and kind of creepy. You demand so much of *cholo*-hood and its ways. I kind of get your religious loyalty now. But it's time to call a truce and let the House of Atridas mourn and move on.

ELECTRICIDAD: I would rather die on a cross than forgive her.

IFIGENIA: Man, *tu eres* what they call an obstacle to holiness.

ELECTRICIDAD: You really an *alleluia* now?

IFIGENIA: Don't know yet . . .

ELECTRICIDAD: It's like *cholo*-hood, either you are or you aren't.

IFIGENIA: It's different. It takes time.
It's like standing in line at Food-4-Less, you just have to go with it . . .

Is it all true about Orestes?

ELECTRICIDAD: That his own mother killed him?

IFIGENIA: Not even she would do that.

ELECTRICIDAD: She eats her young.

IFIGENIA: Didn't even get a chance to grow into a young *cholo*.
We should bury him with *Papa*.
At Evergreen.

ELECTRICIDAD: They shot him in Las Vegas.
They threw his body into a volcano.

IFIGENIA: A volcano?

In Las Vegas?
Oh yeah . . .

ELECTRICIDAD: I know how she works.
Once she got rid of *Papa*, she knew The Council of Old *Cholos* would
follow the old ways and make Orestes *el* new *Rey del Barrio*.
It's his birth-*derecho*.

But she sees the men and how they hold on to their power.
Oh, she can taste it.
It's like she walked into a Target for the first time—she wants it all.

And now . . .

[ELECTRICIDAD *starts to cry.*]

She killed him.
Lo mato.

[IFIGENIA *goes to comfort her.*]

IFIGENIA: My sister . . .

ELECTRICIDAD: Get away from me!
She took my joy, my Orestes.
And she took my love, *mi papa.*
But when she took, she also gave.

IFIGENIA: Gave you what, *loca*?

ELECTRICIDAD: Gave me this pain.

IFIGENIA: Don't let her.

ELECTRICIDAD: I am going to use it against her, and give honor back to
La Casa de Atridas.

[IFIGENIA *tries to move toward her again.*]

IFIGENIA: Come on, man . . .

[ELECTRICIDAD *slaps her hard against the face.*]

ELECTRICIDAD: Don't, *puta*!
You left me here alone.

I didn't have any backup.
She knows it and she's already taken more than she deserves.
You broke the *cholo* code.
You walked away.

IFIGENIA: Forgive me . . .

[*An awkward silence and look passes between them—too much so that they turn to face* Papa. IFIGENIA *starts to cry.*]

ELECTRICIDAD: Don't.

IFIGENIA: Shut up.

ELECTRICIDAD: What do you got to cry about?

IFIGENIA: He was a *cabron.*
Look at what he left us.
Our own jails.

ELECTRICIDAD: *Yo no.*

IFIGENIA: Oh yeah, you. *Mama.* Me.
All trapped.
Even in his *muerte,* he still won't let us go.

[*In* IFIGENIA's *grief, she tries to go to him.*]

Papa? Por favor, let us go.

ELECTRICIDAD: Leave him alone!

[IFIGENIA *reaches out to touch him.*]

No, I said!

[IFIGENIA *leans in, and* ELECTRICIDAD *jumps on her. They fall to the ground and do an old after-school fight. They both have each other by the hair. Neither wants to let go. Finally* IFIGENIA, *maybe feeling overpowered, pulls away. Oh man, this might be the first time she lost a fight to her* hermana.]

IFIGENIA: You crazy bitch!

ELECTRICIDAD: No one touches him!

IFIGENIA: You're lucky I know about that "turn-the-other-cheek" shit.

ELECTRICIDAD: I am making plans, Ifi.
I am going to take her last breath without raising a finger.
Just watch me.
I am not going to walk away from this body until her stillborn heart rests in my hands.
Until I hear the final little song that a last breath makes.
Until I look up and the gods smile at my loyalty.

Help me destroy her, my hard *chola* sister, who always lent a fist in loyalty to the *Casa de Atridas*.

IFIGENIA: I am out of my jail.
But I see that you have just entered yours.
Your solitude has made you *loca, hermana*.

Your grief ain't *sopa, babosa*.
Don't let it boil.

ELECTRICIDAD: My grief is the match that fuels the fire of my revenge.

IFIGENIA: That's poetic . . . but stupid.

The sisters gave me a gift, idiot.
It's called "forgiveness."
You should try it.
Otherwise, you are going to destroy yourself . . .

ELECTRICIDAD: Not me, her.

IFIGENIA: The sisters at Immaculate Conception say . . .

ELECTRICIDAD: You mean the dykes?

[IFIGENIA *looks at her, gets up, and dusts off.*]

IFIGENIA: *Llamame* when you are ready to talk some sense.

ELECTRICIDAD: At your funeral, deserter.

IFIGENIA: Get over yourself, you stupid bitch—Jesus loves you!

[*The lights begin to fade, as the audience hears the sweeping of the brooms.*]

SCENE 9

Reasons

[Ai, *you could almost feel the morning* frio *leaving your* cuerpo. *The faint sound of* chisme *makes its way through the neighborhood again. The chatter grows louder as the audience sees* LAS VECINAS *sweep their way down the street.*]

LA CARMEN: *Apoco!*

LA CONNIE: *No me digas!*

LA CUCA: *Ai . . .*

[*Beat.*]

LA CARMEN: Did you hear *La Electricidad?*

LA CONNIE: She's going to do something.

LA CUCA: To *la mama.*

LA CARMEN: But what?

LA CONNIE: I couldn't hear good enough.

LA CUCA: She got all soft and dramatic.

LA CARMEN: They always scream at each other down the street.

LA CONNIE: And right when they got something good to say.

LA CUCA: We can't hear them!

LA CARMEN: It can't be good.

LA CONNIE: Not for us.

LA CUCA: Not for this barrio.

LA CARMEN: The daughter planning.

LA CONNIE: The mother scheming.

LA CUCA: *Ai,* even the sister praying is scary.

LA CARMEN: *Vecinas,* it isn't safe.

LA CONNIE: Not like it was.

LA CUCA: It never was.

LA CARMEN: No, it used to be.

LA CONNIE: I never locked the door.

LA CUCA: *Porque eres mensa.*

LA CARMEN: We're trapped.

LA CONNIE: We don't say anything.

LA CUCA: *Dame un* break.

LA CARMEN: We just live with it.

LA CONNIE: *Lo aceptamos.*

LA CUCA: Like a way *de vivir.*

LA CARMEN: I knew a time.

LA CONNIE: A time *mas calmado.*

LA CUCA: More simple.

LA CARMEN: Call me old-fashioned.

LA CONNIE: Call me old school.

LA CUCA: Call me old ways.

LA CARMEN: *La casa.*

LA CONNIE: *El* Porch.

LA CUCA: *El barrio.*

LA CARMEN: Cleaning.

LA CONNIE: Cooking.

LA CUCA: Sweeping.

LA CARMEN: *La familia.*

LA CONNIE: The *vecinos.*

LA CUCA: *Los* kids.

LA CARMEN: It wasn't always like this.

LA CONNIE: It was different.

LA CUCA: It was?

[*Beat.*]

LA CARMEN: *Apoco!*

LA CONNIE: *No me digas!*

LA CUCA: *Ai . . .*

[*Beat.*]

LA CARMEN: Why don't we start a *Barrio* Watch?

LA CONNIE: Whose children are these?

LA CUCA: Where are the mothers?

LA CARMEN: Are all the fathers dead?

LA CONNIE: *Cuando* is it enough?

LA CUCA: Who will stand up and be *contada?*

LA CARMEN: Who wants to be the *primero* to complain?

LA CONNIE: Whose barrio is this?

LA CUCA: Who paid for their house?

LA CARMEN: When did we give away our neighborhood?

LA CONNIE: When is too much enough?

LA CUCA: Why don't we own anything?

LA CARMEN: Why are we all asking questions?

LA CONNIE: Because *vecinas . . .*

LA CUCA: We're afraid to give the answers.

[*Beat.*]

LA CARMEN: *Apoco.*

LA CONNIE: *No me digas.*

LA CUCA: *Ai . . .*

[*Beat.*]

LA CARMEN: Look at this city.

LA CONNIE: City of the *futuro.*

LA CUCA: *Ciudad* with the most of everything.

LA CARMEN: *Chinos, Japones, Coreanos.*

LA CONNIE: *Salvadorenos, Cubanos, Armenios.*

LA CUCA: *Rusos, Suecos, Polacos.*

LA CARMEN: This city with no center.

LA CONNIE: No heart.

LA CUCA: All border towns.

LA CARMEN: *Ai dios mio, vecinas!*

LA CONNIE: It just hit me!

LA CUCA: This the wild, wild, *oeste . . .*

[*Beat.*]

LA CARMEN: *Apoco.*

LA CONNIE: *No me digas.*

LA CUCA: *Ai . . .*

[*Beat.*]

LA CARMEN: Lock your doors.

LA CONNIE: Say good-bye to the *noche.*

LA CUCA: *La luna* no more.

LA CARMEN: The moon drips blood.

LA CONNIE: For them.

LA CUCA: *Los* cholos.

LA CARMEN: *Con sus* ways.

LA CONNIE: *Con sus* gangs.

LA CUCA: *Con su* violence.

LA CARMEN: So different.

LA CONNIE: But yet . . .

LA CUCA: They look just like us . . .

[*Beat.*]

LA CARMEN: *Apoco!*

LA CONNIE: *No me digas!*

LA CUCA: *Ai* . . .

[*The pack of* VECINAS *start to sweep their way down the street. You can hear the* chisme *and the sound of their brooms slowly fade away.*]

SCENE 10

You're Still a Young Man

[*Vegas night. The sound of a punch and a grunt. On one side of the stage appear* NINO *and* ORESTES. *They are both shirtless. They stand facing each other as* ORESTES *tightens up and gives* NINO *a nod, indicating the silent "OK."* NINO *punches him in the stomach.*]

NINO: Eighteen . . .

[ORESTES *tightens up and gives him the nod again.* NINO *punches his* pansa.]

    Nineteen . . .

[ORESTES *is winded but tightens up and gives* NINO *another nod.* NINO *punches him again.*]

Twenty.

[*Oh man, that hurt . . .*]

How you feeling?

[ORESTES *tries to catch his breath.* NINO *hugs him.*]

Good *cholo.*
Good . . .

[NINO *lets go of him.*]

Didn't mean to do so many, young homeboy, but I was bored.
Just trying to kill some time.

[ORESTES *is doubled over.*]

The sooner you get the skills of the warrior, the faster we leave Vegas
and go back home.

[ORESTES *comes up.*]

ORESTES: When, Nino?

NINO: Soon, young homeboy.
Your *papa* will be calling us back any *dia.*
And you have to be *listo.*

ORESTES: Yes, *mi maestro.*

NINO: He's going to be so *cholo* happy when he sees that his attendant
turned the little lion king into the *poderoso* heir to *La Casa de Atridas.*

You know what, *mijo?*
I like it when I got purpose . . .

ORESTES: I know he must be thinking about us right now.
Six months is enough, right, old *viejo?*
Cholos can't live in exile, it's against our nature.
That's why they call us "homeboys," right?

NINO: Exile?
Que's eso?

ORESTES: Exile.
Es como, kicked out.
Banished.

NINO: *Ah,* I thought you said X-Filed at first.
You kinda freaked me out.

ORESTES: Remember, Nino, when we first got here?
How lonely we were?
Every night at the Cheetah's Strip Club?

NINO: Oh. You stopped going?

ORESTES: I wish we were in our *tierra.*
I can't sleep here with all these lights.
I miss our one-bulb barrio too much.

NINO: Your *papa* sent you away to protect you.

ORESTES: Remember that light in our bathroom, Nino?
The one that had that string that you pulled on to give it life?
Man, how I would sit on that toilet and stare at that bulb for hours.
So small, but so full of light.
I used to think it held my dreams . . .

How I would cry at night when *Mama* pulled the string and killed it.

NINO: Yeah, man, Vegas ain't our lady.
Cholos are all about darkness and midnights.

ORESTES: I miss *mi hermana.*
My Electricidad, my *Trici.*
I wish she could see this.
A million lightbulbs.
A million dreams.

My *corazon* is empty without my sister.
That's why I'm painting her on my heart, old man.
So that I don't forget her.

NINO: To each his own . . .

ORESTES: I have to go back.
If only to bring my sister here and show her what her very name has inspired.

NINO: Then you have to be *listo.*

[NINO *comes up from behind and easily grabs* ORESTES *by the neck and takes him down.*]

Oh, man, we're going to be here forever . . .

[NINO *helps* ORESTES *up.*]

Toughen up, *puto.*
I'm running out of nickels!

[*They walk away as the sky does a big* vuelta *from* noche *to* dia *in a casino minute.*]

SCENE 11

We Are Family

[*The yard.* Medio dia. *That quiet time between morning and* All My Children. CLEMENCIA *enters* la yarda, *a bit* nerviosa *and* fumando, *of course.* ELECTRICIDAD *sits up, ready to strike.*]

CLEMENCIA: Don't worry. I won't touch him.
Lo toque enough when he was alive.

ELECTRICIDAD: It won't do you no good to come beg his forgiveness.

CLEMENCIA: Oh, you're funny.

We need to talk.

ELECTRICIDAD: I have *nada* to say to you, murderer.

CLEMENCIA: I am not charging you *renta* in this *yarda.*
The least you can do is talk *conmigo,* "tenant."

Listen, I'm sorry I called the sanitation on you.
But I'm a homeowner now. "Property values," *mija.*

ELECTRICIDAD: I know what you did.

CLEMENCIA: Oh really? Raise you so that you could turn on me like this?

You're just like him.

ELECTRICIDAD: *Que bueno.*

CLEMENCIA: Stubborn. Unforgiving.
If I did anything wrong, it was that I let him give you too much of his *filosofia.*
I let him try to shape you to his hardness.
I let him show you the destructive ways.

ELECTRICIDAD: He taught us the *cholo* way.

CLEMENCIA: Yeah, but how?

Everyone forgets what a bully he was.
He made us think that we couldn't grow and change and make something better than what we are.
He beat me and made me scared of the world.
Scared of crossing over these bridges.

It was the only way he could control us.

Like the petty thief that he was, he took our dreams.

ELECTRICIDAD: And you murdered them.

[ELECTRICIDAD *looks at her with an absolute lack of fear.*]

You took your hands to him when he was at his weakest.
Then you told everybody that someone broke in.
You blamed it on one of the *locos* from the four directions.

Nobody broke in. Only you.

Into this house. Twenty-three years ago.

Te estoy viendo, cabrona.
You're like an X-ray. His *sangre*-stains are all over you.

CLEMENCIA: You got some way of looking at the world, my daughter.

Don't forget that I was the one that convinced the Repo man to give
us another chance on the Monte Carlo.

ELECTRICIDAD: You let the pit bulls attack him!

CLEMENCIA: Yeah, well, he gave us another chance, didn't he?

I made sure the mortgage never died.
I made sure you kids always had your *cholo* wear.

I even scared the *vecinas* into buying all that Avon, so we wouldn't
starve when your *papa* got lost in some City Terrace thighs.

Oh, don't look at me that way.

You think it's easy being a woman in this *hombre* world?
Those *hombres* are ruthless *conmigo*. And they will be with you too.
They want one thing from us. And they always take it.

But when we want a cut. A place in their world. Our fair share.
Well . . . *Vas a ver.*

ELECTRICIDAD: You're the queen of excuses, Clemencia.
I can't wait to see what you'll say when the hands wrap around your
neck. I'll be here waiting.

CLEMENCIA: You think you can sit there forever?
You think he isn't going to leave you at some point?
They always leave you, these men.

And then what? Who will watch your back then?

Everyone smells the *oportunidad* that an empty throne brings.
Without backup, little *nina,* you're like a wounded *coyote* out there.

[Ai, *hold on* cigaro.]

Let me protect you.

ELECTRICIDAD: Desperate.

[Un *puff* importante.]

CLEMENCIA: You know how I met your sweet *papa*?
On the boulevard.

I was thirteen.
He smelled good, like VO5, and I flirted.
What's wrong with that, huh?
I was an innocent.

But he took my girlhood from me.
In the back of a car.
And he brought me here.

My father looked at me and called me a tramp.
My mother hid in a back room to save herself a black eye.
And he sold me to him.
Because he thought I was dirty.
This is what they do.

Did I get to *escojer*?

No, my stubborn daughter, I didn't get to choose.
And neither will you.

History just keeps repeating itself.
Cholos don't move forward.
They just keep going farther into the past.
Oldies, oldies, oldies.

And I want to change it.

I want to take back every bruise your father gave me and turn it into
a dollar.
I want the memory of every one of his punches to be a kiss that could
make me believe in myself.

I am going to make a business.
In his name, if you want.

I could give you a cut.
Then you could have a piece of him that's worth something.
The piece that makes *dinero*.

[ELECTRICIDAD *glares at her.*]

You and I are cut from the same cloth, Electricidad.
Imagine us working together.

ELECTRICIDAD: Together, ha!

CLEMENCIA: These *hombres* wouldn't know how to deal with the both of us.
They wouldn't be able to ignore us, I'll tell you *eso.*
Think about it.

Then you could honor his *nombre,* if that's what you want to do.
We could even make a statue and put it out here where his stinky body sits.

Come on. Come back inside the casa.

ELECTRICIDAD: Not into that living coffin.

CLEMENCIA: A mother sacrifices.
I never did. I admit that.

Just like you, I like the "running around" too much.
I was never good with the "domestic."
But then again, I never meant to be a mother.

But now we have to start *pensando* about our *futuro.*
You and I are survivors.

ELECTRICIDAD: *No tengo nada* in common with you, monster.

CLEMENCIA: You hate me *porque me ves* inside of you.
We are more alike than you can ever imagine.

ELECTRICIDAD: Lies.

CLEMENCIA: No *seas mensa.*
This could all be yours.
Yes, even the house.

ELECTRICIDAD: Why would I want this house?

CLEMENCIA: Oh, you love this house *mas que yo.*
You can't wait to live out the last of your days in the past.
Looking out this window at a world that would never have us.

Not me.
I am going to forget all this, sell this house and buy a condo.
In Pasa-fucken-dena!

[CLEMENCIA *takes a deep drag of the cigarette.* CLEMENCIA *smiles at* ELECTRICIDAD.]

I would have even given him to you.

[ELECTRICIDAD *is caught off guard.*]

ELECTRICIDAD: *Callate!*

CLEMENCIA: Oh, I know you wanted him.

ELECTRICIDAD: Stop it.

CLEMENCIA: You did, didn't you?
Hard *chola* with no friends to call her own.
Your sister always in jail, and your little brother too soft for his own good.
Little *chola* whose only friend was your hard *papa.*

He took the soft skin from you and made you a warrior.
And you are stupid enough to thank him for it.
But why wouldn't you?
You were in love with him.

ELECTRICIDAD: I hate you . . .

CLEMENCIA: That ain't a new *sentimiento.*
I hate me too sometimes.

Listen to me.
I am offering you things.
Attention.
Partnership.
Motherhood even, if that is *lo que quieres.*

All of the things that no one ever gave me, I am offering to you.

But you must pay me for it.

ELECTRICIDAD: I will pay for your casket.

CLEMENCIA: Pay me for being your *mama*! I never wanted it.
They took being a girl from me and they gave me "mother."
I didn't ask for it.

No, my daughter, I'm not old enough to be old.

It's all yours, Electricidad.
Make a choice.
There's nothing to stand in your way now.
You could change the destiny of *La Casa de Atridas*.

MIRA MENSA, TAKE SOMETHING FROM ME!

ELECTRICIDAD: It's your last breath *que quiero*.

[*Beat.* CLEMENCIA *composes herself.*]

CLEMENCIA: OK.

I am going to start a neighborhood association.
And you are going to be the first item on the agenda, *cabrona*.

Last *chansa*. Are you going to come inside or not?

ELECTRICIDAD: I'll come to your funeral, old lady.

CLEMENCIA: I'm going to go back inside and use up my "anytime minutes."

[*She flicks her cigarette butt on* AUGGIE's *corpse.* ELECTRICIDAD *frantically runs over to him and tries to pick it off him.*]

Don't say that I didn't warn you.

[CLEMENCIA *walks into the house.* ELECTRICIDAD *turns to watch her leave.*]

SCENE 12

Que Viva Las Vegas

[*The nighttime glow of Vegas neon. The distant* sonido *of the ker-ching, ker-ching of a slot machine on a winning play.* ORESTES *and* NINO *are backstage, working at a buffet.* NINO *sits on a white bucket sipping a Malt 40, while* ORESTES *struggles with a tray full of dirty dishes.*]

NINO: Young *cholo*, come sit.

ORESTES: We're on a shift, old man!

NINO: Don't worry about it.
I just paid a *mojado* to do our work.

We got *cholo* matters to attend to.

[ORESTES *comes and sits with* NINO.]

ORESTES: OK, lazy *viejo, dime.*

NINO: A few days ago, someone tried to take you out.

ORESTES: What? Are you messing with me?

NINO: Someone showed up to stop your *corazon.*

[ORESTES *looks like a little* mocoso *all of a sudden.*]

ORESTES: Should I be worried, old man?

NINO: Relax, nervous *cholo.*
I took care of it.
No one will hurt the next king while the old *viejo*'s around.

ORESTES: Was it one of the *Locos* from the Four Directions?

NINO: Don't know.
He came knocking to your doorstep. Said he was from the IRS.
What a *pendejo*! Everybody knows *cholos* don't pay taxes . . .

I put on my Chiclets face.

[NINO *does his* pobre *Chiclets* cara.]

And he lowered his guard.

He came in and looked around. Said he would wait.

I offered him a Malt 40, and I held it out for him to grab.
When he reached for it, his sleeve raised and I could see he had a tattoo from back home.

He looked down and realized his mistake, but it was too late.
The bottle was already on the way to his head.

I tried to get something out of him. I cut off a couple of fingers, hoping he would talk, but he was a "professional."

You have to admire a man's loyalty.
I injected him with bleach, because there's no point in making a man suffer.

ORESTES: I know they're gonna get me. I don't think like you. I don't have the "*cholo* instinct."

NINO: Listen, young *cholo*. Word's coming through the *cholo* satellite that things are not good back home.
In *El Mundo del Cholo* the Four Directions are at war.
The North Side *Locos* are moving into the hills.

The East Side *Locos* don't got no way to grow.
We're trapped between three freeways and a *Pollo Loco*.
La Casa de Atridas is vulnerable.

But never underestimate the great *cholo* leader of the East Side.
He knew to send you away.

Your job, little homeboy, is to *reemplazar a tu papa*, when his time comes to go to the barrio in the sky.
You need to be ready when The Council of Old *Cholos* call on a new leader.

I will be there as your sergeant, *a tu lado*.

ORESTES: Thank you, old *viejo*.
For saving my life.

NINO: We have to step up your training.

ORESTES: Yes, *viejo*.
But what if they're setting us up?

NINO: That's the life.
It's surprise destiny, *mijo*.
That is why we will come back in the middle of a midnight.
Just in *caso*.

ORESTES: You're not setting me up, are you, Nino?

NINO: Good *cholo.*
  Trust no one.
  Not even your Nino.

[NINO *looks away.*]

  But you hurt my feelings, son.

ORESTES: Oh, Nino, I'm sorry . . .

NINO: I'm just testing you.
  Toughen up, *puto.*

  Now we will see what you are made of.

ORESTES: But, what if I'm not ready?

NINO: You have to be.

ORESTES: Why?

NINO: Because it's been like this since the beginning of *cholo* time.

  I didn't make the *pinche* rules.
  I'm just the *pendejo* that follows them.

[*As they turn to leave, the sun comes up over the state line.*]

SCENE 13

Smoke Gets in Your Eyes

[*Afternoon. El sol is out getting a tan, ese. The altar. We see* ABUELA. *She is carrying a plastic bag for the* mandado. *She approaches the altar slowly.* ELECTRICIDAD *sits staring at the sky.*]

ABUELA: *Mija,* you want to *comer* something?

ELECTRICIDAD: No, Abuela. Not today.

ABUELA: *Te estas* killing yourself.
  You're starting to look like *una* lizard out here.

ELECTRICIDAD: *Dejame mujer!*

ABUELA: Is that what *El* Auggie would have wanted for you?

ELECTRICIDAD: What do you care about *mi papa*?

ABUELA: *Ai*, he was my son.

ELECTRICIDAD: Well, then, why didn't I see you shed a *lagrima* at his funeral?

ABUELA: I don't cry no more, it messes with my makeup.

Why don't you go inside now, *mija*?

ELECTRICIDAD: How much did they pay you?

ABUELA: *Que me dices?*

ELECTRICIDAD: How much did they pay you, *cabrona*? To come out here and make me go inside.

[ELECTRICIDAD *stares at her, burning a hole through* ABUELA.]

ABUELA: *Ai*, forty dollars, OK?

ELECTRICIDAD: I knew it.

ABUELA: A *vieja* has to make money somehow.
Besides, *las vecinas* are "concerned."
Can you blame them? They clean and clean, and now they got a body in a *yarda*.

ELECTRICIDAD: *Que se vayan al diablo!*
I hear those old *cabronas* sweeping and "concerning" about us all day.

And you. Drop the act.

ABUELA: What act?

ELECTRICIDAD: If you want to talk, drop the senora bit.

ABUELA: *Que me dices, nina?*

ELECTRICIDAD: Have it your way . . .

[ELECTRICIDAD *runs up to* ABUELA *and spits a loogie in her face. Ooh, she may be up there, but* ABUELA's *going to go all Stallone on her granddaughter. She starts chasing her.*]

ABUELA: *Ai, desgraciada!*
You piece of trash *de la calle!*
I'm not too old to kick some barrio ass, you little peewee.

ELECTRICIDAD: Ah, there you go, that's the Abuela that I know.

[ABUELA *wipes the loogie off her face, and* ELECTRICIDAD *begins to laugh.* ABUELA *sees her laughing, it's been so long.* Ai, *it's not that bad. She's laughing, the* pobre loca.]

ABUELA: *Ai, mija.* You remind me so much of me when I was young.
I used to go up to people all the time and spit in their face. Especially guys I liked.

[ABUELA *looks down the street. She hikes up her* falda *and pulls out a pack of Winston cigarettes tucked into her stockings. She pulls a lighter from deep inside her cleavage and lights up.*]

ELECTRICIDAD: Abuela, you must tell *las vecinas* to keep their distance.
This is my grief and my anger and it might last my lifetime.

ABUELA: Lifetime . . .?
OK.
They already paid me, what do I care.

[CLEMENCIA *sticks her head out the window.*]

CLEMENCIA: You, what are you doing here?

ABUELA: *Visitando con mi* granddaughter.

CLEMENCIA: Look at you, showing your varicose. You're polluting my yard, old lady. Visiting hours are over. Go home, *vieja.*

[ELECTRICIDAD *throws a stone toward the house.*]

Ai, stop it.

Vete vieja.
I feel old just looking at you.

[CLEMENCIA *pulls her head back inside.*]

ABUELA: Your father always settled for so little . . .

[ELECTRICIDAD *stares at* ABUELA *hard. The silence and the stare make* ABUELA *uncomfortable.*]

ELECTRICIDAD: Abuela, *te tengo que* ask you something.

ABUELA: *Ai,* those forty dollars were for my *cigaros* . . .

ELECTRICIDAD: Not that.

ABUELA: *Pues!*

ELECTRICIDAD: Listen, if you tell anyone, and I mean it, *vieja,* I'll go down to your little *casita* and break all your Princess Diana plates.

ABUELA: *Ai, que* mean!

[*Beat.*]

ELECTRICIDAD: I'm going to kill her.

ABUELA: Ha, take it from a *chola* who's been there.
If you think this is going to help you sleep at night, it doesn't.
It makes you a victim of the *noche.*

Little girl, the way of the *chola* is to keep those thoughts inside.

ELECTRICIDAD: But what if I left the way of the *chola*?

ABUELA: If only.
You can't.
What are you going to do, go off to a convent like your sister? No, you have the soul of an old *cholo.*
This is your life. Learn to live with it.
Look at your *papa.* Still hanging out on a front yard. A true homeboy!

ELECTRICIDAD: But if I killed her . . .

ABUELA: Ooh, if it was so easy, we probably all would be doing it.
Even *cholos* have standards.
No one kills the mother.

It has to stop.
All these guns, all these *drogas,* that's not who we are.
Murdering our own, and for what?

ELECTRICIDAD: Don't you ever think about it, Abuela?
   About getting out?

ABUELA: What for?
   I'm already dead.

   See my crosses?

[ABUELA *pulls down her blouse, and on her breast there are three tattoo crosses.*]

   They killed *a mi* husband and my two children.
   I am one of the living dead.
   A *chola* in limbo.

ELECTRICIDAD: Then why do you stay?

ABUELA: The same reason we all do, young *chola*.
   Where do *cholos* go in a world that won't have us?

   This is the *mundo* we know. Good or bad.
   Es lo que es.

ELECTRICIDAD: But, if I could stop this pain . . .

ABUELA: *Ai,* this is getting too *pesado*.
   Let's smoke a joint.

[ABUELA *leans back and pulls a joint out of her cleavage.* ELECTRICIDAD *looks on admiringly.* ABUELA *lights it, takes a toke, and passes it to* ELECTRICIDAD.]

ELECTRICIDAD: How long you been a *chola*, Abuela?

ABUELA: Oh, since I was an infant.
   I used to shoplift from my baby carriage.

[*They laugh.*]

ELECTRICIDAD: *Cabrona.*

ABUELA: I got jumped into my first gang when I was nine.

ELECTRICIDAD: Wow.

ABUELA: Yeah, I been a *chola* so long, they should have a beer named after me.

But the *mundo de la chola* was so *differente* back then.

[Ai, una memoria. *Maybe it's funny, maybe it's deep. Definitely means something to remember it.*]

I used to work in a nightclub.
The *Del Rio.*
Not a lot of good *dinero,* but what an education!

We didn't have *chola* teachers like you have now.
We were *las* originals!

The first Cleopatra eyeliner was laid down by me!

I used to have a big ole beehive. I did!
I used to have to use three cans of Aqua Net to make it stay up there.
I kept everything in my hair.
Knives, joints, food stamps . . .

And the hombres . . .
Ai, the men.
They traced themselves on your tattoos with their tongues.

ELECTRICIDAD: *Puta.*

ABUELA: No *pendeja*—"liberated."

Pero, it's all different now.
The *mundo* of the *chola* is *muerte y* sadness.
What your *mama* did, changes *todo.*

Listen, young *chola,* if you are going to follow the way of the *chola,* you must accept *la muerte* as a fact of our life.
I know I did.
Otherwise, you become the ghost to all of your memories.

[*Una orden.*]

You've got to walk away from him now.

ELECTRICIDAD: *Mi papa?*

ABUELA: Yeah.
   You've got to walk away from this body.
   This *cuerpo* wants you to go with him. Into the lonely after-*vida*.
   But you are still alive, young *chola*.

ELECTRICIDAD: She took his last breath and now she wants his soul, to
   scare the gods into thinking that she is ruthless enough to be a king.
   I am going to wait here until it all disappears.

ABUELA: *Mensa,* you will wait forever.

ELECTRICIDAD: My choice!

ABUELA: You will suffer a fate worse than your *papa.*

ELECTRICIDAD: What could be worse?

ABUELA: He lies here in eternal sleep.
   Free from his worries now.
   Free from all of his responsibilities as *rey del barrio.*

   But you? You're a stubborn *chola.* Nothing satisfies you.

ELECTRICIDAD: You don't know shit, old lady.

ABUELA: You're an open book, young *chola.*
   That's the difference between our generations.
   You don't know how to make the mask.

ELECTRICIDAD: For what?

ABUELA: Your feelings.

   Tu mama sees them.
   So do the *vecinas.*
   You give yourself away, peewee.

ELECTRICIDAD: OK, get lost.
   I have to talk with my father.

[ABUELA *stands and puts on her* rebozo. *She puts out the joint. She flicks the roach onto the* altar. ELECTRICIDAD *looks at* ABUELA con respeto. ABUELA *begins to walk away.*]

ABUELA: Later, gator.

ELECTRICIDAD: After a while, crocodile.

ABUELA: *Y mija, cuidate.*

It's hard to keep your balance on the edge of a knife.

[ABUELA *leaves.*]

SCENE 14

I Only Have Eyes for You

[*Afternoon. The house.* CLEMENCIA *stands at the window. She is dipping cotton balls in nail polish remover and doing her nails.* IFIGENIA *stands next to her, holding a large ceramic of the* Virgen *under her arm. She places it on top of the TV.* CLEMENCIA *looks at it for a moment, then grabs it and puts it on the floor.*]

CLEMENCIA: She's been sitting out there for a week.

IFIGENIA: I know.
It's called reflection and patience, *Mama.*
She's finding out about herself.

CLEMENCIA: Yeah, what did she find out?

Did she tell you she knew something, or is she just doing the crazy whispering-to-her-*papa* act with you too?

IFIGENIA: Try loving her, *Mama.*

CLEMENCIA: Don't start with me, Ifi.
I have tried giving her my love.
I have none left.

IFIGENIA: No, *Mama.*
You have enough love to last a *chola* lifetime.

CLEMENCIA: Good, 'cause that *chola* out there really sucks it out of you.

[*Takes a good look out the window.*]

IFIGENIA: *Mama,* did you hurt Orestes?

CLEMENCIA: No!
   No.
   Tu papa sent him away.
   Things are going down.
   He did it for his safety, for his own good.

IFIGENIA: Where is he?

CLEMENCIA: I don't know, Catholic school, I guess . . .
   Have you seen him? . . .

[IFIGENIA *doesn't believe her.*]

IFIGENIA: I never got a chance to say good-bye.

CLEMENCIA: Were you gone again?

IFIGENIA: A year, *Mama*!

CLEMENCIA: A year. Really?
   I thought you were living in the garage.
   Estabas en la jail, *mija?*

IFIGENIA: An order.

CLEMENCIA: An order?

IFIGENIA: An order.
   In Fresno.

   Like with nuns.

CLEMENCIA: You're a born-again *chola*?
   Oh, that's a good one.

IFIGENIA: I am *buscando.*
   Looking for answers.

CLEMENCIA: Me too.

IFIGENIA: Well then, let me help you, *Mama.*

CLEMENCIA: She blames me for everything.
   Why do they always blame the mother?

Tell me, why do they do that?

IFIGENIA: They teach you a lot at the convent, *Mama.*
About turning the other cheek, and things like that.

CLEMENCIA: That's not what I asked you.

IFIGENIA: And you learn about forgiveness.

CLEMENCIA: Yeah, so?

What have they taught you that I didn't teach you?

[*A long beat.*]

IFIGENIA: "Unconditional love."

CLEMENCIA: What does that mean?

IFIGENIA: It means love, like . . . beyond the barrio.

CLEMENCIA: Look, I'm going to go out there and finally stop this.

IFIGENIA: Be nice, *Mama.*
Just go *calmada* wanting to do good.

CLEMENCIA: Listen, do me a *favor.*

IFIGENIA: What?

CLEMENCIA: If she goes off . . .

IFIGENIA: I'll call the police.

CLEMENCIA: Oh no, no, we never call the police.
They always take away the mother.

IFIGENIA: It says in the Bible . . .

CLEMENCIA: Just get a stick.

IFIGENIA: A stick is not the answer.
Love is.

CLEMENCIA: If she comes after me, you get her.

IFIGENIA: No way, man, I won't fight her!

CLEMENCIA: *Ai,* you Christians are such a pain in the ass.

> OK, OK.
> I'm going to go out there all peaceful and stuff.
> I'm going to show her my "unconditional love."
> But if that *cabrona* doesn't take my "unconditional love,"
> I have to do something, right?
> Jesus did.

IFIGENIA: Maybe we should pray?

[*Beat.* CLEMENCIA *looks at* IFIGENIA *intently.*]

CLEMENCIA: You love me, Ifi, right?

IFIGENIA: . . . OK.

CLEMENCIA: Well, then, if your god says it—you should say it.

[*Oh, boy. This is an act of kindness for* IFIGENIA.]

IFIGENIA: . . . I love you.

CLEMENCIA: I love you . . . Mother.

[Ai, *Jesus give me the patience.*]

IFIGENIA: I love you . . . Mother.

[CLEMENCIA *smiles. It's the little victories.*]

CLEMENCIA: They all blame me for Electricidad.
> That I didn't give her guidance.
> But it wasn't me. It was her *apa.* He gave her this barrio.

IFIGENIA: Refuge.

CLEMENCIA: You love me, Ifi, right?

IFIGENIA: I just said I did!

CLEMENCIA: Say it again, Jesus.

IFIGENIA: Damn, I love you, OK?

CLEMENCIA: I love you . . . Mother.

[*OK, Jesus, I am going to kick her ass.*]

IFIGENIA: Mother . . .
  I love you.

CLEMENCIA: Hm . . . no one ever says that to me.

IFIGENIA: I love you.
  Really.
  Yeah, OK.
  I love you.

[CLEMENCIA *finally takes real notice of* IFIGENIA'*s sincerity. Or struggle with it. She doesn't like what she sees.*]

CLEMENCIA: Go find me a stick!

SCENE 15

Sincerely

[*Dusk, that time when day starts to clock out and night is showing up for his shift.* IFIGENIA *exits the house quietly and slowly crosses the yard. She is carrying her statue of* la Virgen. *She is trying to escape without being noticed.* ELECTRICIDAD *notices her and yells across the* yarda.]

ELECTRICIDAD: Hey, where you going? Heaven?

IFIGENIA: Shut up, stupid!
  I'm running away again.
  I can't do it.
  She's testing my patience.
  It's like being tempted by the devil.

  The sisters want me back.
  I know they do.

ELECTRICIDAD: You going away far?

IFIGENIA: Fresno far.

[*Beat.*]

ELECTRICIDAD: Too bad.

IFIGENIA: Wow, you sad I'm going?

[*So many feelings. What to do with them.*]

ELECTRICIDAD: No . . .

IFIGENIA: It's OK, Electricidad.
You can tell me. Please.
It's just me. *Tu hermana.*

[ELECTRICIDAD *starts to cry. But why?* IFIGENIA *holds out her hand. Close enough to offer, but not be bitten.* ELECTRICIDAD *doesn't know whether she can touch it or not.*]

Don't bite it, bitch.

[ELECTRICIDAD *reaches out and grabs her hand. She brings it to her cheek. Has it been so long since she has held the living? She surprises* IFIGENIA, *and herself, by kissing it. The action is so honest and real, that they become awkward, all of a sudden. They both pull away.*]

ELECTRICIDAD: Have you really found a god?

IFIGENIA: I don't know . . .
I'm doing a lot of waiting for him.

ELECTRICIDAD: Me too.

IFIGENIA: I sit in this thing they call a grotto. It's just kind of like a clean backyard.
And you think about him and ask him if he'll come.

ELECTRICIDAD: Yeah?

IFIGENIA: Yeah. And if he can't come, can he fill you with stuff.
Goodness and shit.
Sounds stupid, huh?

It kinda works.

ELECTRICIDAD: Really?

IFIGENIA: The sisters leave me out there by myself all day.
They buy me cigarettes.

They're afraid of me . . .

They make good cake.

[*Beat.*]

ELECTRICIDAD: Does he ever talk back?

[*Silence.*]

IFIGENIA: That's what it's like at the convent.

ELECTRICIDAD: Do you remember how I was?

IFIGENIA: What do you mean?
Like a little girl or something?

ELECTRICIDAD: No, the way I used to be, before she gave me the darkness.

IFIGENIA: She didn't give you the darkness, Electricidad.
You found that on your own.

You have a *chansa*, my sister.
To make a choice.

I did, and I left.

[*Beat.*]

ELECTRICIDAD: I have a confession.

IFIGENIA: I'm not a priest.

ELECTRICIDAD: That's OK.

I'm going to kill her.

IFIGENIA: OK.
I can't stop you.

ELECTRICIDAD: That's not very godlike, letting us all kill each other.

IFIGENIA: I think God will forgive me if I marry him.

You know what? I want to live with the silent nuns.
The silent nuns who don't talk anywhere as much as you and *Mama*.
The silent nuns who give me cigarettes and leave me alone.
The silent nuns who don't hear all the noise in this barrio.

ELECTRICIDAD: Do you really believe it?

IFIGENIA: I want to. So bad.

ELECTRICIDAD: Maybe . . . you should stay?

IFIGENIA: You don't want me to stay.
You just don't want to be alone.
Big difference.

[ELECTRICIDAD *looks away.*]

Don't hurt her.
You'll be hurting yourself.

[IFIGENIA *picks up her statue. A shout from* CLEMENCIA *can be heard from inside the house.*]

CLEMENCIA: *IFI?* . . .

IFIGENIA: I have to go.
Now.

[IFIGENIA *starts to leave.*]

ELECTRICIDAD: We could have been friends.

[IFIGENIA *stops and wonders if maybe this would be her calling.*]

IFIGENIA: We can be sisters!

CLEMENCIA: *IFI?*

[*So many choices. Trying to imagine them all so quickly. Make one, make one, make one . . .*]

ELECTRICIDAD: *Vete.*
Go, *cabrona.*

[*They look at each other. They give the* cholo *nod to one another.* IFIGENIA *begins to run as if she is running for her life.*]

CLEMENCIA: *Ifi?* . . .

[*A transformer begins to sizzle.*]

SCENE 16

This I Swear

[*The sun is tipping his hat a final adios.* LAS VECINAS *enter* la yarda. *They sweep at twice the pace. They gossip quickly and nervously.*]

LA CARMEN: *Vecina*s, I got a feeling in my bones.

LA CONNIE: Me too, my knees started hurting.

LA CUCA: Oh good, I thought it was my *artritis.*

LA CARMEN: The sun is shutting its eyes.

LA CONNIE: He's closing early.

LA CUCA: Up there he can see what is going down.

LA CARMEN: Something is not right.

LA CONNIE: The *chisme* is traveling fast.

LA CUCA: The *tiendas* roll down their metal doors.

LA CARMEN: The bus took a detour.

LA CONNIE: The *perros* are beginning to howl.

LA CUCA: And they ran out of tamales at *la marqueta*!

LA CARMEN: The *aire* is thick.

LA CONNIE: The *noche* belongs to them.

LA CUCA: Tonight they are going to use it.

LA CARMEN: Lock your doors.

LA CONNIE: Close your *ventanas.*

LA CUCA: Pray a rosary.

LA CARMEN: Light a candle.

LA CONNIE: Ask the *Virgen*.

LA CUCA: Burn the incense.

LA CARMEN: Offer up an orange.

LA CONNIE: Sleep on the floor.

LA CUCA: Don't get near the window.

LA CARMEN: Trapped in our casas.

LA CONNIE: Trapped in our *yardas*.

LA CUCA: Trapped in our barrios.

LA CARMEN: Say good-bye to the *noche*.

LA CONNIE: *La luna* no more.

LA CUCA: *Que* destiny guide her.

LA CARMEN: Oh I know this feeling.

LA CONNIE: I know it too, *vecina*.

LA CUCA: Oh, this feeling . . .

[LAS VECINAS *march off. We hear the sound of three doors slamming and three locks locking.*]

SCENE 17

In the Still of the Nite

[*A Vegas night,* otra vez. *The sound of the needle buzzing. It grows dimmer and more realistic as the lights reveal* ORESTES *and* NINO. *They are, once again, shirtless and glistening with sweat.* ORESTES *sits, facing out, looking out at nothing with the stone-cold* cholo *stare.* NINO *pricks his chest with the tattoo gun. We see the trickle of blood running down* ORESTES's *chest, but this time the audience doesn't see* ORESTES *react to the pain. Suddenly the sound of the gun stops.* NINO *wipes and pulls away to reveal the face of* ELECTRICIDAD *on* ORESTES's *breast.*]

NINO: *Listo.*

[ORESTES *looks down at his chest intently. He looks up at* NINO *and smiles.*]

ORESTES: It's good, old *cholo.*

NINO: Better than the Sears Family Portraits!

ORESTES: Which one should we do next?

NINO: The next tattoo you will have to earn.

ORESTES: But I have.
   With my loneliness.

NINO: That lonely tattoo you already got.
   Right there.

[NINO *points to clean skin on* ORESTES.]

ORESTES: It's clean.
   There's nothing there, Stevie Wonder.

NINO: Those spaces get filled in with experience.

ORESTES: Yeah right.

NINO: Look at this.

[NINO *pulls up his shirt to reveal a canvas of* tatuaje *over his stomach and chest.*]

   Everybody thinks that when you go to the big house, we just sit
   around tattooing to kill time.
   It's just the opposite.
   We work as fast as we can to show everyone our history.

ORESTES: Give me my history, *viejo cabron.*

NINO: I have, little one.

   You have worked every muscle.
   You have sharpened every shank.
   You even know a little Bruce Lee.

   But do you know why you throw the punch, young *cholo?*

ORESTES: For the kingdom.

NINO: That's right.
For the kingdom, *ese*.

ORESTES: It's time to go back my loyal *atendido*.

NINO: Yes, *mi rey*.
When the sun starts to wave good-bye over the pyramid, we will get on *El* Greyhound.

We'll arrive in the darkness of midnight.

To be safe, we will split up.
I'll check out last call and you can say hello to your *familia*.

ORESTES: Finally I get to see *mi papa*.
And my beloved sister.

To our lives, Nino!

NINO: Or to our deaths, *baboso*.

Barrios never stay the same.
You're gone a week, and they take down the mural.

Are you *listo*?

[NINO *throws a surprise punch at* ORESTES, *who stops it in midair.*]

Good *cholo*.

Good . . .

[NINO *hugs* ORESTES.]

SCENE 18

Baby, I'm for Real

[*Darkness sets in as* cena *is being served and the Hollenbeck police eat their* burritos. ELECTRICIDAD *sleeps next to* apa. CLEMENCIA *enters, tiptoeing quietly into the* yarda. *She carries a bottle of her nail polish remover and a lighter! She opens the bottle and begins to pour it all over* EL AUGGIE. *She stands and looks at him.* ELECTRICIDAD *smells the alcohol and wakes up.*]

ELECTRICIDAD: What are you doing here, *loca!*
Que estas haciendo, cabrona!

What are you doing?

[CLEMENCIA *clicks the lighter and turns on a flame.*]

No!
Stop.
Please.

[CLEMENCIA *starts to come near the body. She holds the lighter like a gun.*
ELECTRICIDAD *is paralyzed with fear.*]

If you have a heart . . .

CLEMENCIA: I have a heart.
I have a heart!

That's why I took these hands to him.
For years he took his hands to me, why couldn't I?

It's only right, isn't it?

I took his last breath so that we could finally make something of
ourselves.

I did it for you, Electricidad.

But your problem is that you feel too much.
For him.

[CLEMENCIA *begins to weep.*]

So did I . . .

ELECTRICIDAD: Then stop, please . . .

CLEMENCIA: It's too late for that.

Have you ever seen your *suenos* go up in flames?

I have.
He was my dream.

ELECTRICIDAD: You are going to pay for this.
For eternity.

CLEMENCIA: I already am.

[CLEMENCIA *leans in to light the body.*]

> *Electricidad.*
> Your very name means light.
> I gave it to you.
>
> And now, *mi hija.*
> I am going to turn you off.

[*She lights the fire.* ELECTRICIDAD *begins to scream. A scream of rage and grief through* el barrio. *The electricity crackles as it meshes with the crackling of the fire.* CLEMENCIA *is destroyed. She stands looking at the flame. She tries to light a cigarette, but her hands shake uncontrollably.* ELECTRICIDAD *lies in a corner in a fetal position, weeping. The crackling of the fire can be heard loud, louder, loudest.*]

SCENE 19

War (What Is It Good For)

[*The* noche *washes over the barrio like a good detergent.* LAS VECINAS *enter* la yarda.]

LA CARMEN: *Vecinas,* did you see it?

LA CONNIE: I saw it.

LA CUCA: I even turned off *la novela.*

LA CARMEN: Oh, they have done things.

LA CONNIE: *Cosas* to one another.

LA CUCA: That offend all the gods.

LA CARMEN: She lit up the *noche.*

LA CONNIE: With his body.

LA CUCA: Like burning trash in the back-*yarda.*

LA CARMEN: Set him on fire.

LA CONNIE: Like in *India*!

LA CUCA: We don't do that here.

LA CARMEN: His body . . .

LA CONNIE: slowly roasting . . .

LA CUCA: Like a *Pollo Loco*.

LA CARMEN: Oh, they don't realize.

LA CONNIE: What they have done.

LA CUCA: Called on the dark spirits.

LA CARMEN: The flames.

LA CONNIE: So high.

LA CUCA: Like the riots.

LA CARMEN: But it's one family . . .

LA CONNIE: That destroys . . .

LA CUCA: This barrio.

LA CARMEN: The smoke.

LA CONNIE: So thick and black.

LA CUCA: You could see the devil inhaling.

LA CARMEN: And her screams.

LA CONNIE: Screams of *injusticia*.

LA CUCA: So mournful.

LA CARMEN: So heavy.

LA CONNIE: So sad.

LA CUCA: So lonely.

LA CARMEN: I could weep.

LA CONNIE: I could grieve.

LA CUCA: I could pray.

[*They nod their heads for the lack of* palabras. LAS VECINAS *march off. We hear the squeak of three doors closing on a world.*]

SCENE 20

Woman to Woman

[*Oh, it's dark. The* Eyewitness News *is over, and midnight is peeking his head around the corner.* ABUELA *enters* la yarda. *She got the 411 on the* chisme *line. She sees* ELECTRICIDAD *lying over the ash remains of the* altar. *She is dark and dirty.*]

ABUELA: *Ai, dios! Mija? Mija? Que paso?*

[ABUELA *looks at the house and realizes what has happened.*]

Oh my *dios. Esa cabrona* did it. All the devils in hell are *cantando* her praises.

[ABUELA *turns to face* la casa. CLEMENCIA *paces in the house. She is nervous and frantic. This is worse than when she took out* AUGGIE. ABUELA *comes to the front of the house and screams for* CLEMENCIA.]

DONDE ESTAS, DAUGHTER OF *EL DIABLO?*

[CLEMENCIA *comes out front.*]

CLEMENCIA: Don't even think about coming in, old lady.
There's nothing here for you to pickpocket.

ABUELA: What have you done?

CLEMENCIA: Cleaned up your messes.

I took care of the *hombre* you couldn't control.
You should thank me.
THANK ME!

ABUELA: Never.

CLEMENCIA: This is for you *tambien*.

> For the generations of undisciplined men that have wasted our lives.
> For the years that I had to sit there and watch him bully you *y* every-
> one else.
> For the drinks I poured.
> For the dinners I made.
> For the parties I threw.
> For the money he wasted.
> For the love without love that I had to make.
> For the *ninos* that I had to raise.
> For the sacrifices we make . . .

ABUELA: Not like this.

CLEMENCIA: You too, *vieja*.
> Show me the sacrifices on your heart.
> I know you made them.

ABUELA: Not for this.

CLEMENCIA: Don't act like Mother *Teresa*, you bitch.

> I cleaned up a mess.
> Your mess.
> The mess you made.
> The mess your mother made.

ABUELA: *Sin consciencia.*

CLEMENCIA: Oh, I have a conscience. If not I would have taken care of you too. For letting him become the monster that he was.

ABUELA: Now you think you are a god.

CLEMENCIA: Listen to me, *cabrona*.
> I am going to do something that none of you ever did.
>
> I am going to change this neighborhood.
>
> I am going to bring the four directions together and we are going to make it right.

I am going to run *La Casa de Atridas.*
Oh yes, I am.
And I am going to make it better than he ever did.

And you know why?
Because I am the mother!

[ABUELA *runs away from the house.*]

THE MOTHER!!

[CLEMENCIA *tries to light a cigarette, but it just ain't going to happen. She buries her face in her hands.*]

SCENE 21

You'll Lose a Good Thing

[ABUELA *goes into* la yarda *and tries to help* ELECTRICIDAD *up.*]

ABUELA: We have to go.
Vamonos, hija.

[*But* ELECTRICIDAD *does not get up.*]

Vamonos before she comes back and sets you on fire.

[ELECTRICIDAD *violently resists.*]

Vamonos chola. Por favor.
Let's go.
Make a choice. Towards the living.
Your grief is going to kill you. Find a way!

[ELECTRICIDAD *pushes* ABUELA *away.*]

I am going to help you.
Enough *ya*!
Let us leave the house of *Atridas.*

ELECTRICIDAD: Only her death will set me free.

ABUELA: *Babosa.*

[ABUELA *tries to grab* ELECTRICIDAD *to drag her.* ELECTRICIDAD *turns and gives* ABUELA *a big fat Rocky Balboa across the jaw.* ABUELA *instinctually reaches over and grabs* ELECTRICIDAD *by the hair and slaps her hard across the face in an old-school* chola *kind of way.* ELECTRICIDAD *can't believe it. Who knew the old* vieja *was* yoda tambien.]

ENOUGH!!

You're a baby *chola. No honor.* No respect.

You say you're old school, but you haven't learned our ways.
You don't know what it means to be *chola.*

[ELECTRICIDAD *is stunned. She looks at* ABUELA *for the longest time unable to speak.* ABUELA *begins to walk away. Finally, in her desperation,* ELECTRICIDAD *breaks down.*]

ELECTRICIDAD: Abuela. Don't go.
　　Ayudame.
　　I can't.
　　I can't anymore.

[ABUELA *goes to* ELECTRICIDAD.]

　　Help me.

ABUELA: *Si,* young *chola.*
　　Si.

　　Gracias.
　　The old *veterana* will help you.

[ABUELA *runs to* la esquina. *She screams to the end of the block.*]

　　Vecinas!
　　Vecinas!
　　I know it's late.
　　But *esta* coming out of the darkness!
　　Ayudenme.

[ABUELA *looks up, as if to see the electricity raging through the power lines.*]

SCENE 22

What You Won't Do for Love

[Ai, *it's midnight, why's everybody up?* LAS VECINAS *run into the* yarda *all ready for a little* accion. ABUELA *joins them.*]

ABUELA: OK, *mujeres.*
   We don't have a lot of *tiempo.*
   We're going to do a *limpia,* but more car-wash style.
   She wants to walk away. Right, *mija?*
   You are going to walk away, right?

ELECTRICIDAD: *Si,* Abuela.

ABUELA: Go for it, *vecinas.*

[LAS VECINAS *grab her like a stray dog. They wash her with Handi Wipes and* un spray que tiene algo *that smells like clean toilets at King Taco. As they clean her they are barking orders at one another until* ELECTRICIDAD *speaks to them, and they stop what they are doing.*]

ELECTRICIDAD: Why do you do this for me?

LA CARMEN: To *ayudar.*

LA CONNIE: To remember.

LA CUCA: To preserve.

LA CARMEN: A custom.

LA CONNIE: Our way.

LA CUCA: Our *gente.*

[LAS VECINAS *go at her, pulling her hair back with a rubber band, cleaning her face and hands, etc. All of this is done very quickly, as if they could feel* CLEMENCIA's *breath over their backs. When they finish, they stand back to reveal her, and* ELECTRICIDAD *looks strangely angelic.*]

LA CARMEN: *Mijita.*

LA CONNIE: It's time.

LA CUCA: To let him journey.

[*They all look at the* altar.]

LA CARMEN: Say good-bye.

LA CONNIE: Say good-bye.

LA CUCA: Say good-bye.

[*Beat beat beat, like a* corazon. *She looks at the* altar.]

ELECTRICIDAD: Good-bye . . .

[*Beat.*]

LA CARMEN: Wow, it worked!

LA CONNIE: *Que bueno.*

LA CUCA: *Vamanos vecinas.* I'm tired.

[LAS VECINAS *leave.* ABUELA *goes to* ELECTRICIDAD.]

ABUELA: *Ai,* what a *noche.*
I'm too old for all of this.

What do you want to do?
Do you want me to sneak you into the Senior Projects?

ELECTRICIDAD: No, Abuela.
I'm going to stay under the freeway tonight.

You go.
I want to pick up his ashes.

ABUELA: Well, give a *chifle* in the morning, and I'll make you a waffle.

ELECTRICIDAD: Gracias, Abuela.

ABUELA: Welcome back to the living, young *chola.*

Ai, these Payless *chanclas* are killing me . . .

[ABUELA *leaves.* ELECTRICIDAD *looks up at* Coyolxauqui, *the moon face.*]

SCENE 23

Reunited and It Feels So Good

[*The second hour of morning.* ORESTES *can be seen in the distance. He does a* chifle *down the block that belongs only to his Trici.* ELECTRICIDAD *freezes when she hears it.*]

ORESTES: Electricidad, my sister.
   You look like a statue.
   The most beautiful statue in Caesars.

[ORESTES *whistles again while he runs into the yard.*]

   Electricidad, *mi hermana!*

[ELECTRICIDAD *screams in horror. She runs to a corner and crouches in fear.*]

   Trici, que paso? My sweet sister, it's me.

ELECTRICIDAD: Go away!

ORESTES: What's up, *esa?*
   My little lightbulb, I'm back.
   I have returned in the middle of a midnight like all smart *cholos* do.

ELECTRICIDAD: Go away, young ghost.

ORESTES: A ghost? No, I am an *hombre* now.
   You don't recognize me *porque* I have changed.

ELECTRICIDAD: Please don't haunt me.

ORESTES: *Que esta pasando?* I have dreamt of this moment for months. If you don't welcome me, I will die more than a spiritual death. You're freaking me out, man.

ELECTRICIDAD: Just tell me if you are a ghost.

ORESTES: Only of the past. Here I am, flesh and blood, *mi hermana.*

ELECTRICIDAD: Orestes . . .

[ELECTRICIDAD *goes to him and touches his face. If he's not Casper, could it really be him? She holds him.*]

You look like . . . a man.

ORESTES: Yes, my sister.
I been doing my pull-ups and stuff.

I know my creases and my cuffs.
I know the hand signals and territories.
I even know how to read the map of our tattoos.
Oh man, *Trici*, I did so many pull-ups, I sleep like this.

[*He puts his hands over his chest, pull-up style.*]

Nino even taught me "the look."

[*He gives her a stone-cold scary* cholo *look.*]

Cool, huh?

[*She smiles. He giggles, out of embarrassment.*]

ELECTRICIDAD: Where were you?

ORESTES: In the desert. Wandering in exile.
Sent away by *mi papa*, for the good of our barrio.

ELECTRICIDAD: She didn't kill you?

ORESTES: Who?

ELECTRICIDAD: Clemencia.

ORESTES: What are you talking about?

ELECTRICIDAD: They said she had killed you.
She put a hit out on you.

ORESTES: A hit?
It was *mi mama*?
Oh my God. I can't believe it.

ELECTRICIDAD: So much has changed, Orestes.
Since you've been gone, darkness has set on this side of the river.

ORESTES: But I'm her favorite.

ELECTRICIDAD: *Oh, Orestes . . .*
There's so much you don't know.

ORESTES: Tell me before my heart explodes.

ELECTRICIDAD: She killed *Papa*.

[Esto *is too much* para el joven.]

ORESTES: *Mi papa*'s dead?

ELECTRICIDAD: Clemencia killed him.

ORESTES: She couldn't have.

She knows the rules.

ELECTRICIDAD: There are no more rules, Orestes.
In the time you left, *el mundo* of the *cholo* has changed.

ORESTES: My *papa* . . .

[ORESTES *starts to cry. He holds* ELECTRICIDAD. *Suddenly they seem way smaller and younger than they are.*]

ELECTRICIDAD: She says he was ruining us. But it's *una mentira*.
And just to prove her disrespect for *el mundo* of the *cholo*, she set him on fire, so that he could not visit us in the after-*vida*.

ORESTES: Electricidad, I'm scared.
Who is going to protect us?

ELECTRICIDAD: You are, young *cholo*.

ORESTES: Me? I came back to stand at my father's side.
To be his right-hand *mano*.
I can't lead. The East Side *Locos* will eat me up.

ELECTRICIDAD: Orestes, you don't understand.
I was going to walk away, homeboy. I was going to forgive her.
How could I have doubted myself? Doubted you, the *nuevo* king?

ORESTES: But I'm not.
Not yet.

ELECTRICIDAD: Time moves differently for us now, my brother.

Orestes, for the good of *el barrio*, for the East Side *Locos*, your family—you must say *adios* to the little homie inside of you.

This is a special night.
Like when you first got jumped in.

ORESTES: What do you mean?

ELECTRICIDAD: Before you hear the first drop of *el* newspaper,
before you can smell the *pan dulce* rising,
before *el sol* says *buenos dias*—
you will become a man.

ORESTES: I don't understand. What's going on around here?

ELECTRICIDAD: Tonight you will bring the barrio back together again.

Do you know how?

SCENE 24

Oh What a Nite

[*At the same* momento, *in another part of the barrio,* NINO *stands on* un lado de la calle *and sees* ABUELA *walking home.*]

NINO: *Oye viejita,* I haven't seen a pair of legs that juicy since they stopped serving *carnitas* at *El Tepeyac.*

ABUELA: *Ai,* low class *viejo, cabron.*
Mind your manners, *puto.*

NINO: *Con una boca* like that, you definitely have to be an East Side *Loca.*

ABUELA: Who is there that knows my past?

NINO: The man they used to call *La Lengua* . . .

ABUELA: Nino!
What are you doing here, sexy old *viejo*?

NINO: Just back from X-file.

ABUELA: What is that?

NINO: *Como una* vacation.
But forced.

ABUELA: So, you were doing time?

NINO: Yeah, doing time, so to speak.

ABUELA: *Cuanto tiempo* you've been gone old man?

NINO: Six months.

ABUELA: *Hijole,* a lot has happened in the barrio.

NINO: Did they take away the mural?

ABUELA: No, worse. A lot worse.

> *Ai viejo,* if you get through your twenties, you think you can live in
> the life *por vida,* but I never thought I would be one of the *viejas* ask-
> ing: what happened to the good old days?

> What happened to rock around the clock?

NINO: *Y el Pachuco* Hop.

ABUELA: Beehives.

NINO: Low-riders.

ABUELA: Wine coolers.

NINO: *Mota.*

ABUELA: Oh, the good old days.

> Nothing's good anymore.
> This is not why we became *cholos.*
> They're all killing each other now.
> They don't live by the rules of the *mundo,* now.

NINO: Man, when I hear this, it gives me *pena* to have these tattoos.

ABUELA: They had a barbecue tonight.

NINO: Sounds good.

ABUELA: You can't imagine what she cooked . . .

> Listen, *viejo,* there is a lot to *hablar* about.
> But right now I just want to forget.

NINO: Yeah, me too.
I'm old, I just want to hang out with a *cervecita* and listen to some oldies.

ABUELA: Why don't you come over?
I just got into senior housing.
We could put on an eight-track and catch up . . .

NINO: Show me the way, sexy senior . . .

SCENE 25

Angel Baby

[*Back in* la yarda.]

ELECTRICIDAD: This is bigger than you and me.
This whole barrio is calling on you.
She killed him with her bare hands, Orestes.
And that is how she must die.
An eye for an eye.
And you must do it.

ORESTES: But, she's my *mama*.
And besides.
I've never killed anyone.
I haven't even kicked anyone's ass.

ELECTRICIDAD: She isn't your mother anymore.
She is the murderer of your father.

ORESTES: Why don't we start with the house and just take it away from her?
Kick her ass and throw her out into *la calle*.

ELECTRICIDAD: What are you talking about?
Things have changed, Orestes.

It's what *Papa* would have wanted.

ORESTES: He wouldn't have wanted this.

ELECTRICIDAD: You have to do it.

It's your job.

ORESTES: But what if I don't want it?

ELECTRICIDAD: What are you talking about!
You are the next king.

We can't be doing everything for you.

ORESTES: But, but . . . you, you're the one that's all eager to get rid of her . . .

ELECTRICIDAD: I can't, Orestes.
Don't you understand?

I want nothing more than to take these hands to her neck.
But it isn't our way . . .

I give her to you.
With a smile . . .

ORESTES: But, I . . . can't.

ELECTRICIDAD: Where is your loyalty?

Everyone is circling *La Casa de Atridas.*
They all want a chance to take the throne.
To take our way of life.

Your return.
Is a sign, my brother.
That all will be made right in *el barrio* once again.

ORESTES: But I thought.
I thought maybe, maybe, we could go.
I could show you the city of your name.

ELECTRICIDAD: We can't leave here!
This is your territory.
This is where you will rule.

ORESTES: Maybe we don't need this?
Maybe we could make other rules.

ELECTRICIDAD: Like she did?

ORESTES: We can run out of here.
    If we really wanted, we could.
    Just you and I, *mi hermana*.

ELECTRICIDAD: Orestes, you are breaking my *corazon*.
    What will it take to reclaim your father's legacy?

ORESTES: His legacy.
    Not ours.

ELECTRICIDAD: Stop playing around!

    It is your duty.
    All the East Side *Locos* will respect and accept you.
    When they see that you have returned and that you have made things
    right again.

ORESTES: Who cares about this barrio?

ELECTRICIDAD: This neighborhood has been waiting.
    They expect it.
    You will gain your honor.

    This is your kingdom, Orestes.
    Take it!

ORESTES: I can't . . .

[*She slaps him hard on the face.*]

ELECTRICIDAD: Don't disgrace your father!
    Show them that you can be the leader.

    Kings don't get crowns.
    They take them!

[ORESTES *starts to cry. She holds him while she speaks.*]

    Sssh.
    Calmado, young homeboy.

    Orestes, remember when we were small and they left us?
    Two weeks.

Do you remember that?
And we didn't know where they had gone.

Ifi ran away into *el barrio* all angry and we didn't see her.
And you and I were left alone *en la casa.*

And I told you that it would be OK.
And I did, didn't I?
I made it OK.
We made burritos and we watched TV until they came back.

Who taught you how to hide under the freeway?
Who taught you how to sneak into R-rated movies?

ORESTES: This is different.

ELECTRICIDAD: Remember when *Papa* showed us the animal instinct?

ORESTES: Please . . .
Don't . . .

ELECTRICIDAD: When he brought that *vato* home from the North Side
Locos and he told us that we were going to kill him.
That he was going to give us the animal instinct.

Remember he had him all tied up and he threw him on the floor in front of us?

ORESTES: We were watching cartoons.

ELECTRICIDAD: Oh yeah . . .
I remember.

And *Papa* made us kick him and kick him and kick him, and the *vato* started crying. And *Papa* didn't let us stop until he could tell he wasn't breathing.

ORESTES: I wanted to cry.

ELECTRICIDAD: But you didn't, young warrior.
You didn't.

ORESTES: I looked at you, instead of him.

ELECTRICIDAD: Right, you looked at me . . .

Papa gave us a dollar and told us to go out and play.
No big deal, right?

Look at me.
Look at me now.

Find your courage.
Find your rage.
Find your darkness.

ORESTES: I am so scared.

ELECTRICIDAD: You have been born-again, Orestes.
You were dead once and now you have come back.
Not even your father, the king, got this chance.

ORESTES: But I'm just . . . a homeboy.

ELECTRICIDAD: No, you're not.
You're a *cholo.*

Call on the god of human sacrifices, *Coatlicue,* and moon face, her
daughter to give you enough light in *la casa.*

Do it.
And be the king.

It's OK.

Look at me.

[*They both turn and look toward* la casa. *He slowly sneaks into the house.*]

SCENE 26

Natural High

[*It's three in the morning. The barmaids are slipping their tips under pillows
while the* panaderos *are getting up to roll their* pan dulces. ELECTRICIDAD
turns around and looks up at moon face. She starts laughing.]

ELECTRICIDAD: I call on the darkness inside the Four Directions.

Find the courage.
Find the rage.
Find the darkness.

Find the courage.
Find the rage.
Find the darkness.

Finally, a chance for *la familia* to be together again.
Without her.

Find the courage.
Find the rage.
Find the darkness.

Let the gates of hell open.
Now!

[*A helicopter roars by on a freeway chase.*]

SCENE 27

Dedicated to the One I Love

[*The rooster stands by the time clock, restless to announce* la mañana. ORESTES *can be seen as a shadow in the house.* ELECTRICIDAD *can be seen in* la yarda. CLEMENCIA *can be seen in the house, illuminated by the television and smoking a cigarette. She laughs with the tele.* ORESTES *enters her room.* CLEMENCIA *is surprised.*]

CLEMENCIA: Orestes?

[CLEMENCIA *stands and paces. She doesn't know what to say or how to act. She waits to see what* ORESTES *will do. They stand awkwardly facing each other. As if in a standoff. Finally* ORESTES *moves toward his mother. She stiffens. He grabs* CLEMENCIA *and hugs her.*]

Orestes, *mi hijo*!
You surprised me, homeboy.

You've come back . . .

Where were you?

[*He holds onto her.*]

You are still *mi hijo,* right?
Mi hijo?
My little baby, my little boy?

[*He nods yes. Oh, maybe he can't do this.*]

You love me, Orestes?
Say, I love you, Mother.

[*He doesn't respond.*]

OK, it's OK.

My most sensitive one.
My *razon para vivir.*

[*While in her arms, he starts to cry. She relaxes a bit. Maybe the* cabron *can't do it.*]

Ai, mijo.
You missed *tu mama.*
Pero how good that you came home.
Now, we can be a family . . .
I was never good at making one.
I didn't know how.
Pero, now you and I, *y* Electricidad, if she wants.
We can be a family.

[*He pulls back and looks at her. He has a glazed looked on his face. It scares her. She must not let him know.*]

You know it wasn't me, right?
Tu sabes que tu apa.
He was a bully.

Made him do crazy things.
He wanted to beat the *cholo* into you.
I couldn't let him do that, my sensitive one.

Tu sabes, don't you?
I know you do.

[*He moves toward her and goes for her neck awkwardly.* ELECTRICIDAD *starts to whisper her incantation from the yard.*]

ELECTRICIDAD: Find the courage.
Find the rage.
Find the darkness.

CLEMENCIA: *No!*
Mi hijo!
No . . .

[CLEMENCIA *pushes him away violently.*]

Stop it.
You don't know what you're doing.

[*He loses his grip as she pulls away. He starts crying.* ELECTRICIDAD's *incantation grows louder and more forceful with the scene.*]

It was me, Orestes.
It was me that tried to save you.
From this *vida.*
This *vida* that surely would have killed you.
I saved you.
I did it.
This is not your life.

[*He moves toward her.*]

Que te dijo?
She lies.
She lies, Orestes.
Esta loca.
She's gone mad.

[*He grabs her and won't let go.*]

Don't try it, *cabron.* Don't!

[*She pulls away and grabs a switchblade. He grabs it away from her and reaches for her neck.*]

No sabes.
You don't know what I did for you.
I saved you . . .

[*He is crying. He holds her down, but he cannot do it.*]

Por favor, no.

You don't know.
How hard it is.

I'm just like you.
Nobody showed me shit.
Nobody gave me . . . nothing . . .

All I wanted was to make it better.
To get us out of here.

Forgive me.

I gave you. *Mijo.*
I gave you my . . .

Unconditional . . .

[ELECTRICIDAD *screams from the yard.*]

ELECTRICIDAD: *ORESTES!* DO IT!

[*And with that, he cuts his mother's throat.*]

SCENE 28

Feelings

[*The east* los *rooster crows. Daybreak is peeking its head around the corner. There is a quiet and a calm.* ELECTRICIDAD *lies on her father's ashes.* ABUELA *and* NINO *run into the* yarda.]

ABUELA: *Mija,* why didn't you leave?
   Donde esta Orestes?
   Have you seen Orestes?

[ELECTRICIDAD *looks at* ABUELA *and smiles.*]

Something has happened!

What have you done?
Dime, what have you done?

A la casa, viejo.
Por favor.
Hurry.

[NINO *runs into the house, sees what has happened, and screams for the boy.*]

NINO: Orestes!

[ABUELA *puts her hands to her mouth, stifling her cry. She weeps as she looks at* ELECTRICIDAD. NINO *screams from inside the house.*]

Mi Orestes!
Alguien!
Ayudenme!

ELECTRICIDAD: Orestes?

[ABUELA *goes into the house, sees the* tragedia, *and runs out screaming.*]

ABUELA: *Eres un demonio!*
  Is this what you wanted?

ELECTRICIDAD: Orestes?

[NINO *runs for help and* ABUELA *runs after him.* ORESTES *walks out of the house. He is covered in blood. He is laughing. He has gone mad. So many dreams gone.* ELECTRICIDAD *is terrified. She is afraid to get near him. He goes to her.*]

Orestes?

[ORESTES *falls to his knees over* Papa's ashes. ELECTRICIDAD *kneels to him and cradles him in her arms.*]

Orestes?
Orestes, please . . .

[ELECTRICIDAD *and* ORESTES *hold each other* en la yarda, *while the morning comes into the neighborhood.*]

SCENE 29

Together

[*A* nuevo dia. *The sound of work begins. The sweep, sweep, sweep of brooms.* ELECTRICIDAD *and* ORESTES *are kneeling at the* altar.]

LA CARMEN: *Apoco.*

LA CONNIE: *No me digas.*

LA CUCA: *Ai . . .*

[*Beat.*]

LA CARMEN: Did you see?

LA CONNIE: Oh yes.

LA CUCA: Victory.

LA CARMEN: Electricidad got what she wanted.

LA CONNIE: The gods answered her prayers.

LA CUCA: All is good?

LA CARMEN: Peace at last.

LA CONNIE: Now we can go back to our lives.

LA CUCA: To the way we live.

LA CARMEN: The family.

LA CONNIE: Together again.

LA CUCA: *Que bueno.*

LA CARMEN: Let's close the doors.

LA CONNIE: On this *mito.*

LA CUCA: *En La Casa de Atridas.*

[*Beat.*]

LA CARMEN: What is to be done, *vecinas*?

LA CONNIE: What can be done?

LA CUCA: We never learn.

[*Beat.*]

LA CARMEN: *Apoco.*

LA CONNIE: *No me digas.*

LA CUCA: *Ai . . .*

[*Beat.*]

TAKING FLIGHT

Adriana Sevahn Nichols

For my beloved husband, Jonathan.
Your love and support has been the anchor
that made it possible for me to
take flight . . .

The way of love is not
a subtle argument.

The door there
is devastation.

Birds make great sky circles
of their freedom.

How do they learn it?

They fall, and falling,
they are given wings.

—Rumi

PRODUCTION HISTORY

Taking Flight was developed by Center Theatre Group/Kirk Douglas Theatre for the festival Solomania! 2006. Michael Ritchie was artistic director; Charles Dillingham was managing director. The play was developed with the assistance of Philip Himberg and Mame Hunt at the Sundance Institute; Juliette Carillo and director Tony Plana at the 2004 Hispanic Playwrights Project Festival at South Coast Repertory; Diane Rodriguez's 2004 Women's Writing Retreat, hosted by the Latino Theater Initiative at the Mark Taper; INTAR's 2002 New Works Lab called "9/11: Writers Respond"; and director Giovanna Sardelli's boundless insight and partnership.

Taking Flight was first produced by the Center Theatre Group in Los Angeles on May 14, 2006. The play was written and performed by Adriana Sevahn Nichols.

The performance was directed by Giovanna Sardelli, with sets by Edward E. Haynes Jr., costumes by Candace Cain, lighting by Jose Lopez, percussion by Michito Sanchez, sound design by Adam Phalen, and video by Daniel Foster/EyeAwake Studios. The production stage manager was Scott Harrison.

Goodman Theatre Production, August 15–17, 2008:

Director . . . . Giovanna Sardelli
Performer . . . . Adriana Sevahn Nichols

PLAYWRIGHT'S TECHNICAL NOTES

The overall tone of this play, technically, should be very simple. The entire play is performed by one actor. The only set pieces or props that are essential are a chair, live white flowers, a bowl or vessel to float the flowers in, and a black cardigan sweater. Fake flowers should not be substituted as they are an offering to the goddess Yemaya. Even one live, beautiful white flower will do.

The lighting should be magical, transporting us from location to location, easily, depicting the stark fluorescent sterility of the hospital, to the eerie apocalyptic New York streets, to the warmth of the flashback memories, to the "Vegas/magenta/mambo/magic" world of Esperanza.

The Rumi poem should be displayed somehow during the preshow cue and become prominent as the house lights are going down, before the start of dialogue.

When there is an actress other than Adriana Sevahn Nichols performing the play, please substitute all references to Adriana with the real first name of the actress. It is important that she feel herself inside this story.

[ADRIANA *enters the stage carrying the bud of a live white rose. She regards the audience. She offers a silent prayer as she places the open blossom into a bowl of water. She walks in a circle around the playing area, arms outstretched, preparing the space. When complete, she reaches into the bowl of water and gathers some in her hands. She throws it onto the circle. Lights shift. The circle is alive. She enters it.*]

ADRIANA [*on her cell phone*]: Hey, Rhonda, it's me. Listen, I'm running late. I just got out of the workshop. The Introduction to the Shamanic Journey workshop at the Open Center?! Hold on. [*Addressing the audience directly*] I'm so sorry. I just had to make this call. I'll be right with all of you.

[*Back to* RHONDA] Rhonda, it was amazing. This guy, his name is Machete, El Gran Shaman of Peru. I mean I called him Birdman, because his spirit animals are like the Condor and all of the sacred birds of the Mayans . . . or was it the Incans? Anyway—no, listen, so all of these freaks are there, right? Like total losers. Quasi-spiritually wounded children types. They all circle around him like he's some freakin' rock star, but me wise woman in waiting . . . I hold back. I wait until every last groupie had groped him for a blessing. And Rhonda, when I looked into his eyes, I knew, that he knew, that I KNOW!

What? I thought your fitting was next Thursday? Well, we'll figure it out later—listen, listen! I bought this really amazing gourd rattle—it's to call in the spirits. I can't wait to show you. And sweetie, Birdman and I know each other from before. I'm getting it's somewhere between my lifetime as the priestess of Athena and the beheading in France. Oh! I saw this flyer for this workshop, it's called, "Celebrating the Goddess Within," we have to go! I think it would be great for you to do this workshop before you get married. I don't know . . . we'll dance, we'll sing, we'll eat chocolate. It'll be great!

What??? I thought you were going with purple and mauves?

[*Covering the phone, she whispers to audience*] I'm so sorry she talks so much.

[*Back to* RHONDA] I don't know. I'll have to see it—look, I'm hopping on the train right now. OK. I love you too. Bye.

[*She hangs up.*]

[*To audience*] My best friend Rhonda and I are planning her wedding for next fall and she is driving me crazy talking endlessly about the minutiae of every last detail, every day. The day Brian and I get married, it will be by a mountain stream or on a beach somewhere—you know . . . simple . . . home-cooked . . . a handful of special people. Not Rhonda. So far her guest list is pushing two hundred and that's small to her.

[RHONDA *speaks with a very heavy Long Island "Jewish American Priestess" accent. Her laugh is deliciously annoying and reminiscent of Fran Drescher and a blender crushing ice. Lights shift.*]

RHONDA: Honey, you remember how I told you my dream was to get married in the Italian countryside? Well it's going to come true. Mike and I just found the place.

ADRIANA: Oh. That's great.
[*To audience*] Shit. I have already been feeling stressed out about financing the bridesmaid dress I will never wear again and the expensive gift I'll have to give them. I mean, Rhonda has always been so generous to me and now a ticket to Italy???

RHONDA: Are you ready for this? We just found a little fake Tuscan villa, on a vineyard, right out on the tip of Long Island.

ADRIANA [*whispers to audience*]: Thank God!

RHONDA: And, in the middle of all those grapes, it came to me. I'm gonna have gold, crimson, and burnt orange decorations. A harvest theme. And I'm gonna walk down that aisle in an apricot-colored taffeta Vera Wang with hair extensions down to my waist.

[RHONDA *laughs.*]

ADRIANA: Okaaay . . . It's starting to sound like the Godfather meets the Mists of Avalon.

RHONDA: Oh shut up. I'm not done yet! So, what was my second dream???

ADRIANA [*unenthusiastically*]: To have Bon Jovi play at your wedding—
OH MY GOD!!! You got Bon Jovi to play your wedding?????

RHONDA: No, Einstein, but I got the best Bon Jovi cover band on Long
Island to play for the ceremony, and they gave me a great deal 'cuz I
told them I have hot-lookin' bridesmaids in corsets and they could
stay for the party!

ADRIANA: Great. So I'm gonna have a drunk Bon Jovi wannabe waiting
for my tits to pop out of my dress?

RHONDA: Don't worry. Brian will give him that icy Nordic stare of his
and scare him off.

ADRIANA: What about the klezmer band your parents hired?

RHONDA: I'm putting them outside the bathroom. Now shush . . . sit
down. I worked out the opening, I want you to see it, and then you
can show me your magic gourd.

[*We hear the dramatic opening of a rock-'n'-roll Bach fugue that sounds like
the opening to Bon Jovi's "Let It Rock."* RHONDA *speaks over the music. She
paints each image as the musical interludes accompany her epic plan.*]

OK . . . The iron gates to the vineyard fly open . . . This is where you
guys start filing in down the aisle. Bridesmaids . . . Bridesmaids . . .
Bridesmaids . . . Bridesmaids . . . My little cousin with the flower
petals. Now . . . silence . . . I enter . . . everyone sees my dress. I look
gorgeous. I look at my father. I take my father's arm.

[*Beat.*]

OK, I don't know what do with this part. I was hoping you could
help me. But when Bon Jovi starts singin', that's when I'm gonna start
walking down the aisle towards Mike. You ready?

[RHONDA *gives herself space to walk down the aisle.*]

Oh my God, what are you cryin' for already? She's so dramatic!

Aaaannd . . .

[*As the electric guitar plays a marchlike rhythm,* RHONDA *does a rock-'n'-roll walk down the aisle.*]

What do you think????

[*The phone rings. Music stops as lights shift.*]

ADRIANA: Hello? Mike! Oh my God! I told you she was. Where is she? What? Uh-huh . . . Uh-huh . . . What does that mean? Do you think she's going to make it? She did? No, I'll be there . . . I don't know . . . but you tell her I'll be there . . . I will . . . you too . . .

[ADRIANA *hangs up the phone. She dials frantically.*]

They found Rhonda. Yeah. No, it's not good. She's in ICU. Look, Mike just called. They don't know if she's going to make it and he said that she was asking for me, so . . . I wanted to ask if you'll go to the hospital with—no, I can't ask Brian. He's home, but I can't ask. No, it's OK, I understand. You too—

[*She hangs up.*]

[*Back to the audience*] I call three other people before I finally reach Gabriella, a mutual friend of mine and Rhonda's. She is my last hope, so when she says, "I'll go to the hospital with you even though Rhonda didn't ask for me," I am so relieved. Gabi is a champion synchronized swimmer and she sees everything as a competition, which can be so exhausting, but I appreciate her honesty and I am grateful not to have to go alone.

[*She paces.*]

I have no idea how the hell I'm going to get down there and I don't know what the hell to wear. I mean, what do you wear to maybe say good-bye? Do you get dressed up? After all, Rhonda is the high priestess of the fashion police. No! That's ridiculous. I'm going to wear a gray T-shirt, an old pair of jeans. No makeup. My hair pulled back. That seems respectful. I'll try and get a cab to Fourteenth Street and then pray for a miracle. I take my grandmother's rosary beads with me, just in case.

[*She takes rosary beads from a small altar. She holds them as she prays . . .*]

> *Abuela. Por favor. Cuidame a Rhonda. La queiro ver. Y ayudame a llegar al hospital. Te queiro tanto. Gracias.*

[*Lights shift to a tight special—inside the cab. We hear a quiet outdoor hum of the city.*]

The cabdriver looks at me intently through the rearview mirror. I cry most of the drive. I tell him the little I know about Rhonda's condition. It helps me to keep talking. He shakes his head . . . and he says . . .

CABBIE [*in a heavy Haitian accent*]: You know what scare me now . . . dis enemy . . . is like a ghost . . . you don see . . . you can't see . . . so who do you trust?

ADRIANA: I notice the tiny brand new American flag he has taped to the meter. It's around 9 P.M. when he drops me off. He won't take any money for the fare, not even a tip, he says,

CABBIE: Dat what you tole me, miss, break my heart. But I gon' pray for you and your friend.

[*Lights shift.*]

ADRIANA: I start trying to convince the cops on York Avenue to let me cross the barricade.

[*To* COPS] Excuse me, officer, my friend is in ICU and—

COP NUMBER ONE [*heavy New York accent*]: Only residents with the proper ID, ma'am, next—

ADRIANA: First Avenue . . . Officer, my friend is in ICU and she's—

COP NUMBER TWO [*African American*]: I'm sorry, ma'am, it's just too dangerous, I can't let you by here, next—

ADRIANA: Second Avenue . . . Officer, please—

COP NUMBER THREE [*irate New York accent*]: I'm not tellin' you people again—now back it up!!

ADRIANA [*back to audience*]: I am now a wreck on Third Avenue. I march right up to the Highway Patrol cop with the kind eyes . . . "Please, officer, my friend is in ICU—I gotta get down there—she's asking for me and she may not make it through the night"—He puts his hand on my shoulder and he tears up. I knew I had found my man, or maybe the cabbie had just started praying . . .

[*She crosses through the barricade.*]

My cop with the kind eyes starts flagging down every vehicle allowed past the barricade, but no one will take me. Finally, this tiny blue Honda Civic pulls up with a tired-looking doctor still in his stethoscope, scrubs, and clogs. He agrees to take me. I tell him about Rhonda's condition and ask him if there is any way he thinks she can survive . . . The deep breath he takes before he answers . . . tells me no. When we get within a few blocks of the hospital, cops yell at us to get out of the car. No private vehicles allowed past the checkpoint. But I don't want to get out of the car alone—thankfully my doctor, Dr. Earl Noilan, says he'll walk with me.

[*Lights shift. It is dark. There is a faint sound of a gritty wind and distant siren that penetrates the eerie silence. She moves slowly.*]

We get out of the car. I can't see. The black smoke is so thick I can't see the names of the streets. My lungs feel as if they are being squeezed. I can't get any air. We move slowly . . . feeling what we can't see . . . I begin to feel nauseous . . . from the smell . . . the horrible smell that I taste in my mouth. We are lost in a labyrinth of streets. I can't breathe . . . my chest hurts . . . then I remember . . . I have a doctor next to me . . . so I ask him if it would be OK if I hold his hand . . . and he says of course and reaches his warm hand out to me.

[*Lights shift.*]

We turn the corner and we are blinded by an apocalyptic veil of white light and there in the midst of this eerie cloud is the front entrance to the hospital. It looks like the set of a movie . . . like maybe some TV show had lent the hospital those big lights they use for the night shoots. The entrance is shrouded in an endless wallpaper of missing people flyers . . . fluttering smiles . . . last seen . . . last wearing . . .

Mike is standing out front and Gabi is right there next to him. I hug my doctor good-bye and as I watch his green form reenter the dark ash, I think . . . I should bake him some cookies.

Well, Gabi is wearing her sexy ivory-colored sundress and makeup and of course I immediately feel underdressed.

[*They enter the hospital.*]

It's hard to believe that twelve hours ago this place was a major medical center. Now, the entire hospital is running on a generator, no lights or AC in nonessential areas. The phones are dead. And outside every window is the relentless blizzard of black ash. We stop briefly in the bathroom on the first floor to collect ourselves.

ADRIANA [*while fixing her hair in the mirror, to* GABRIELLA]: Should we say a prayer?

GABRIELLA: Here in the bathroom?

[ADRIANA *nods.*]

[*Tentatively*] OK.

[*They take hands.*]

ADRIANA: Great Spirit . . . Abuela . . . and all those that watch over us. Thank you for getting us here safely. Thank you for taking care of Rhonda today. Please keep her safe from . . . [*Prayer becomes inaudible while* ADRIANA *continues and the sound of a toilet flushing loud and long drowns out her voice.*] and help us to know what . . . [*Flushing toilet again.*] . . . [*After toilet gurgles settle.*] . . . Thank you.

GABRIELLA: That was beautiful.

ADRIANA: Thanks. You ready?

[*To audience*] We take the dark stairs up to room 302.

[*A lone sound of a heart monitor beeping.*]

We enter Rhonda's room . . . quietly.

[ADRIANA *crosses to center, where the chair is placed with the black sweater over the back. This will become the hospital room and bed whenever referred to as such.*]

She looks beautiful. I am so relieved to see that her face has been untouched. It's hard to get close to her because of all of the equipment around her. Her heart monitor starts racing when she sees us. She struggles to speak around the respirator tube in her mouth . . .

RHONDA [*heavily drugged*]: I'm so fucked up . . . I'm so fucked up.

ADRIANA: Gabi and I stand on either side of her bed side, holding both of her hands like two book-ends not knowing what to do. Rhonda can't take her eyes off of Gabi, she looks so luminous in her sundress.

RHONDA [*struggles to speak*]: Oh, Gabi, you . . . Goddess . . .

ADRIANA [*to audience*]: Shit, hello? I dress down out of respect and I am virtually invisible.

RHONDA: Oh . . . Yemaya . . .

[*Lights shift. We hear soft ocean waves.* RHONDA *rises out of the chair and comes forward. She is completely healthy and strong as she embodies this memory. This will be true of all flashbacks.*]

Adriana and I were goin' on this retreat called, "Celebrating the Goddess Within," and part of our homework was ta choose a goddess and start a relationship with her. So I didn't know what goddess ta pick. And I was talkin' ta Adriana about it, so she asks me, "What do I love most in nature?" So I tell ha, I love the sea. I'm from Oyster Bay, Long Island, and I've always loved the ocean. So she starts tellin' me about this goddess that her grandmother used to pray to called, Yemaya. So Adriana takes me up to this place called a botanica.

[*She laughs.*]

We walk in and there is this weird-lookin' creature behind the door— well I mean it wasn't alive or anything, but like this figure, made out of wood with coconuts all around it and pennies and candles—black candles—which made me a little uncomfortable. It was a teeny tiny little place, but there was all this stuff for the money, the health, the good luck—it all felt a little hokey to me, you know, like a lot a voodoo tchotchkes, but then we got to this section where they had all a this stuff of Yemaya, the goddess of the sea [*A soft, sensual drumbeat sounds . . . magic enters the story.*] and she is so beautiful. She has this really long dark hair and it looks like she has a bit of a tan. She's in this beautiful flowing white dress, nice figure, and her arms are open like . . . like she was calling me and when I looked at her I felt such peace, that I knew I had found my Goddess.

[*Drumbeat ends.*]

So I got a Yemaya candle. A royal blue one to bring with me on the retreat. And they put some silver sparkles on it—I could choose between silver and gold—I chose the silver because I did not think the gold matched Yemaya's outfit. Adriana had chosen the goddess, Oya.

[*She laughs.*]

Oyaaaaa! I couldn't resist asking if she was the goddess from Minnesota? So Adriana looks at me real serious like she does sometimes and she goes, "No. Oya is the goddess of the wind and the cemeteries. She's a warrior goddess symbolizing female power, righteous anger, and the storms of change!" You know Adriana can be so dramatic sometimes. So I said well OK honey, that sounds festive. So she got her burgundy-colored candle with everything on it and off we went—laughing and walkin' arm in arm down Amsterdam Ave. Oh!! They were filming *Law & Order* on the corner and we were trying to see Jesse Martin. I think he's so cute. And I was tellin' Adriana, "See, she shoulda been carrying around her headshots!" 'Cuz, I mean you never know, that coulda been a great opportunity for her.

We really had fun that day . . . the day I fell in love with Yemaya, the goddess of the sea.

[*We hear the return of the ocean waves.* RHONDA *recedes back into the chair. She takes two slow deep breaths. Her heart monitor starts beeping again.*]

ADRIANA [*to audience*]: The nurses are busy, checking and filling, checking and emptying and occasionally smiling softly at us. Rhonda is covered from her chest to her feet in a stiff white sheet. Now Gabi had already warned me that she gets faint at the sight of blood and yet I know that we both want to see what the hell happened to our friend. We don't want to wake her, or hurt her, so very gently we begin sliding the sheet up. Rhonda's toes poke out at us still sporting the Black Cherry Pedicure she had gotten with me at the Pinky nail salon on Broadway [*nervous giggles*] . . . We continue pulling the sheet up—

Rhonda fades back into consciousness, she pulls the entire sheet back with a grand flourish, and says that she wants us to see her.

Gabi nearly hits the floor, as she whispers "that she'll be right baaaack."

[*Beat.*]

So there I am, alone with Rhonda. I look down at her mangled body. It looks like she's been turned inside out. She is lying in a pool of blood-soaked bandages. Her legs from the knees down have been ground up like meat and what is left of them is being held together with thick steel rods and screws . . . parts of her have been sewn closed like a rag doll with thick black thread and staples, and from the side, I can see the skin from her upper back is missing, and is a gaping hole. I stare . . . not recognizing her body . . . one that I know so well. Holding the sheet up, she says,

RHONDA: See . . . see what happened?

ADRIANA: Like a little kid that can't wait to show you her boo-boo. And I say . . .

[*To* RHONDA] I see you. I see you.

[*We hear the pulsing of a delicious mambo beat and are jolted by the heat of fabulous magenta lights.* ESPERANZA, *born out of the depth of this pain, explodes into the room. She is a cross between Carmen Miranda and Doctor Phil "in the hood." She takes the audience to a realm of the goddess and Caribbean magic. She may not have the budget of Celine Dion, but when you're the real thing, baby, who needs it!*]

ESPERANZA: Good evening, ladies and gentlemen!
I am Esperanza an I will bring you hope
I will take away your pain and then ju and I will smoke!

Whepa!!

I am the life of the party of life!
Oh jes, I am the real thing, baby.
No crazy Birdman from Peru.

[*She makes fun of him with a birdcall.*]

Pleassse!

I am Esperanza Middleschmerz
A crazy name
I know

Ju ask why?
Bueno ju didn't ask why
Pero theatrically I say why
So we can keep this going
Because ju people are berry berry quiet.

So you ask why?
I tell ju

Because I believe that without hope
there is no heart
an without heart
there is no life
so I am hope
ju know?!

An then Middleschmerz
That's berry berry creative.

[*She addresses a man in the audience.*]

Ay Papi, ju look confuse,
Middleschmerz is the pain that the womans hab
in the middle of the month
An that's why . . .

I am the hope
in the middle
of the pain!

Whepa!!!!

OK Adrianita, listen to me berry carefully . . . dis is what you hab been waiting for your entire codependent life. This is the big Kahuna. Are ju ready Mamita becuz we hab work to do!

[*We hear the pulse of Afro-Cuban drums.* ESPERANZA *smells the air . . . obviously she is in her element . . . the darkness is no match for her.*]

Shhh!! We hab to clean this room because this air is full of death. Sssssut. *Ay un muerto aqui, un espiritu atrasao,* an we habs to get him out. Ahhhaa . . . don thinks ju can hide from me, you hungry ghost. Ju will not take this buriful girl with you!

[*She speaks to* ADRIANA.]

Oye Nena muevate we don't hab time! Look if ju jus going to stand there then get out of my way because I hab a life to save.

[ESPERANZA *goes to the head of* RHONDA'*s bed.*]

Ay Dios mio, mi cielo, dis bed is facing west! I'm going to turn ju to the morning light . . . so much darkness . . . we need light!

Adriana, take this stalk of yerba buena and Florida water and I want ju to beat the darkness out of this floor.

[ESPERANZA *shows her how.*]

Clean. Everything must be clean. Because the devil hides in corners and under the dust of all the peoples that came here to die.

Hand me my cigar and my botella de rum . . .

Ay Maria Santisima y en el gran nobre de Jesus
Ayudame mis Santos a salvar esta pobre muchacha . . .

[ESPERANZA'*s body shakes as she becomes possessed with the Holy Spirit. She circles the bed in a rhythmic Afro-Cuban dance. She alternates between puffing cigar smoke and spraying rum, through her mouth, onto* RHONDA, *after each line.*]

Que se vaya de aqui todo los espiritus atrassado . . . huhhhh
y la echiseria . . . huuuh
y la macumba . . . huhhh!!!!

[*Her dance builds to a fever pitch as she battles with the dark spirits until she is satisfied that* RHONDA *is safe. She stops in a grand and abrupt gesture and addresses the audience . . .*]

Ay People I am getting too old for dis. I need a little refreshments. A little piña colada.

[*She sips water.*]

Bacardi 151, baby! Ayyyy yai yai yaiiii!

[*She holds her forehead.*]

I have, how ju call it, a little brain freeze!

Ok, where was I . . . *Aqui!*

[ESPERANZA *stands behind* RHONDA's *chair, like a guardian, as she prays over her.*]

Yemaya . . . *madre de los mares* . . . lady of the moon . . . protect your daughter . . . Rhonda . . . she needs ju now. Send *los angelitos* of light to surround this child of yours and keep her safe from the dark spirits that try to take her today.

[ESPERANZA *sings praise to Yemaya.*] Yemaya *oro mi nee a ye o* . . . Yemaya!

[ADRIANA *puts her hand in the vessel of water and offers it to the goddess . . . she whispers . . .*]

Hekua Yemaya . . . Hekua . . .

[*Lights shift. Sound of heart monitor beeping.*]

ADRIANA: It's Rhonda's third night in ICU. I wash my hands before making my way to her bedside. Since the slightest infection could kill her, it's a rule that everyone has to wash their hands upon entering her room. There's a little sink with a sign above it that says, "Quiet healing in progress." We are also supposed to wear gloves, but I don't because Rhonda hates how they feel, so I make sure that my hands are immaculate before I touch her. I stare at her as she sleeps. Her body trembles softly. She still has the respirator tube stuffed down her throat, IV poles everywhere, monitors beeping . . .

Her bed is made of sand and it looks like a big blue inflatable boat that you'd pile into on a cool summer lake. It keeps rippling quiet waves underneath her so she won't have any pressure on her wounds and with her thick mane of crimson-colored curls cascading all around her, she looks like a mermaid taking a rest, on a floating island.

[*Lights shift. Flashback. A cacophony of gongs and chants in women's voices.*]

ADRIANA [*chants . . . uninspired*]: Earth my body
Water my blood
Air my breath
And fire my spirit

We are at the "Celebrating the Goddess Within" weekend retreat. It is Saturday afternoon already and I am wondering when the hell we are going to get to the "celebrating" part?? We're all sitting around in this circle grabbing the stupid talking stick, that's the thing with the feathers that's supposed to make you tell the truth, and the women are moaning, "I feel . . . I feel . . ." Oh my God, if I have to listen to another story about somebody's horrible abuse, or neglect, I am going to lose my mind. I can't believe Rhonda and I paid good money for this. Look, I love putting on the really fun goddessy kinda clothes and the jewelry and sitting around eating delicious meals that we all help each other cook . . . and getting the sleepover giggles in the tents . . . like that part is fun . . . but then why the hell don't we just go camping and cut out all the psycho crap???

Anyway . . . we're sitting around the circle and for some reason none of us notice that Rhonda is missing. All of a sudden we hear this laughter coming from outside the door and we're all like, "What the hell is going on?" Rhonda bursts into the room and she howls in laughter . . . huuhhuuaaaaahuuaaaa . . . she is stark naked . . . dripping wet . . . looking gorgeous . . . and she like . . .

RHONDA: Oh my God, you guys. Oh my God. I went into the pond. I just jumped into the pond. It is so gorgeous in there. You have to come. You have to come. Just come on!!

ADRIANA: So we looked at our "group leader" and she's like go! Go! Thank God. Free from that stupid circle. [*Reenacting the entire scene*]

We strip off our clothes and we run down . . . to this freezing cold pond . . . Rhonda leading the way . . . her big titties flapping in the breeze . . . I'm screaming . . .

I'm not doing this, Rhonda. I have Dominican blood in me. I hate cold water. You understand? I take hot baths, hot showers. I swim in warm oceans. No no no no no.

RHONDA: Oh c'mon, Adriana, you're gonna love it. You're gonna love it. C'mon!

ADRIANA: No, Rhonda, I can't it's too cold. It's too cold.

RHONDA: C'mon, Adriana. C'mon. Take my hand. Count of three. Here we go. C'mon. One. Two. Three. AAiiiiihhhhhhhhhhhhhhiiieeeeeeeee!!!!!!

[*They hold hands as they jump into the pond's icy depths.*]

ADRIANA [*gasping and shivering*]: Oh my God.

RHONDA: Isn't it gorgeous?! Isn't it wonderful?! C'mon, fix your hair honey. Fix your hair.

[RHONDA *throws her head back, into water, holding her nose.* ADRIANA *repeats the motion.*]

ADRIANA [*shivering through blue lips*]: Uh huh huh huh . . . huh. Oh it is beautiful. It is beautiful in here. Ooooooooowhooo. Uh huh huh . . . the sun is just like . . . huh huh . . . so beautiful. OK I'm getting out . . . it's just too cold!!!

RHONDA: Oh you're a wuss!

ADRIANA: Rhonda is just swimming around like a fish in there. I can hardly believe it . . . I mean she's scared of so many other things, but to see her swimming in that water, just like a mermaid . . .

[*Sound of beautiful melody as the audience sees* RHONDA *embody this moment of freedom and beauty. The heart monitor fades back in as* ADRIANA's *memory recedes. She returns to* RHONDA's *bedside.*]

The ICU nurse comes in to check Rhonda's vital signs every ten minutes. They've been doing this for the past three days. Her doctors are worried. She has a severe infection. Her temperature has spiked up to 103, so they are keeping a close watch.

[*Beat.*]

I decided not to make the same mistake of dressing down again because Rhonda has no memory of me being there that first night, but she has total recall of Goddess Gabriella in her flowing white dress. So I am wearing an unforgettable magenta sari and a lapis moonstone necklace. Rhonda startles me as she snaps back into consciousness and grabs hold of my sari . . . "Honey . . . hi . . . what is it . . . are you in pain . . . what do you need . . . oh God . . . let me go call the nurse??" She maintains her white-knuckled grip on the folds of my sari as she pulls me close, and mouths . . .

RHONDA [*with great effort*]: Is that new?

[ADRIANA *nods.*]

RHONDA: You look . . . beautiful . . .

ADRIANA: And that was a glorious moment because it meant our Rhonda was still here and Goddess Gabriella had now been replaced by Goddess Adriana!

[*Lights shift.*]

My lack of wardrobe and fashion sense has always been of great concern to Rhonda, she being the unparalleled high fashion priestess of the upper Eastside. It boggles my mind the way she puts things together. The colors, the textures, the accessories, the purse. Jesus, I just grab whatever is clean and I'm good to go. Not Rhonda. She had a . . . has . . . a ritzy Wall Street job. She's an investment banker. ~~She hates it, but her clothes habit makes her a slave to it. But~~ the best part is that whenever she'd clean out her closets, ~~which was often~~, she'd call me to come over and pick up a bag of goodies. This sweater ~~was in the last bag she gave me.~~

[*She takes the sweater off the back of the chair. She puts it on.*]

I hate it. It's just not me. ~~I remember how happy she was because . . .~~

RHONDA: . . . it comes with a matching sleeveless shell and I think this J. Crew ensemble will be just perfect for your auditions.

ADRIANA: I don't wear corporate black sweater sets to auditions. Oh no! I wear a low-cut V-neck with a Miracle Bra that cuts off my circulation for all those slutty *puta* calls I go on.

Well whenever I had an audition, I'd run over to her place, the night before, to run lines. She loved helping me, she even gave me direction, but she hated all the ethnic crap I'd go out for. You know, the . . .

[*Touching herself while gyrating*] "*Ay Papi* you feel so good! *Ay Dios mio. Dios mio!*"

[*Sobbing widow*] or "I was afraid to call the police because I didn't have the papers."

[*Overworked pregnant mother of twelve*] or "Jose Miguel Felipe Ramirez Gonzales, *sientate en esa mesa, y come t'el arroz con pollo. Cono!!!*" [*She slaps the child.*]

Rhonda would say . . .

RHONDA: I don't get it. I just don't get it. You're so talented, why do you go out for all this garbage? You don't even look Latin to me. You should be a lawyer on *Law & Order* or Sarah Jessica Parker's new best friend on *Sex and the City*.

[*Beat.*]

ADRIANA: Well, Rhonda has been wearing a hospital gown for the past month. She is still in ICU. Same room. Same bed. Her doctors have told her family that she probably won't be able to walk again, but they haven't told Rhonda that, they just keep saying they're doing their best to get her home by Thanksgiving.

Since her only accessory now is a plastic ID bracelet which reads September 11th 9:13 A.M. . . . whenever I go to visit, I like to bring beauty and fashion to her. I take great care in coordinating the clothes, the hair, the makeup, the jewelry, the purse. As soon as I enter her room she says,

RHONDA: Come here let me see you . . .

ADRIANA: I walk towards her . . . slowly. Do a little turn followed by a shaky leg extension so she can see my shoes. She loves shoes! They're usually the same old shoes, but she always asks to see them and I always show her. I wait for her blessings . . .

RHONDA: Hair looks good . . . that new?

ADRIANA: She drinks me in with her eagle eye and in these moments we are far from room 302 . . .

[*A hard rock song begins playing.*]

RHONDA: I love you, JON BON JOVI!!!!

ADRIANA: We are back in her living room on East Eighty-Third Street, eating soy cheese doodles, and talking about sex . . .

RHONDA: You! You got a nasty reputation.
Sing it, Adriana!!

[*She hands* ADRIANA *the hairbrush microphone.*]

ADRIANA: We're in a tricky situation.
I don't know what he says here.

RHONDA: C'mon, you know the words . . . Here we go . . .

So tell me is it true?
They say there ain't nobody betta . . .

ADRIANA: 'Cuz now that we're together show me what you can dooooo!!

RHONDA: We're under the gun / Out on the run—
Ooohhh. I got a stitch. Keep dancing. Keep dancing!!!! I'm so exhausted.

[*She sits. Music fades . . .*]

Mike had me up all night. We did it three times!!! He's been takin' these zinc supplements. He's like a rock.

ADRIANA: OK. I'm totally jealous. I can't even remember the last time Brian and I had sex. He's so tired from work. He comes home around midnight, and he's exhausted—can you believe he actually said this to me the other day, "Well, you need to be more visually stimulating." What the hell does that mean!? Am I supposed to slink around all night in patent leather boots and a nurse's outfit waiting for him to get home? I don't think so! How about a little date, dinner, a present . . . it takes time for me to warm up.

RHONDA: Well honey, you gotta speed things up a bit . . . you know . . . help the guy out. I know what your problem is. You gotta get over trying to have the ideal orgasm from the "Look Ma no hands" school already. So God put your love button a little too far north . . . what are you gonna do? You're gonna get a rocket pocket!

ADRIANA: A rocket pocket?

RHONDA: A rocket pocket! It's so small it fits in the palm of your hand. You just hold it there while he's doin' his thing and . . . zzzzz . . . zzzzz . . . zzzzzzz . . . OH MY GOD!!! I got the website right here for you. It's called "Opening Pandora's Box."

[*She laughs.*]

And sweetie, you gotta mow the lawn, you know? Trim those hedges so Brian can find your garden of paradise. He's from a cold country. He's used to hairless women. I think you should surprise him. I'm telling you, he won't be able to keep his hands off you. I got it! Hold onto your labia minora honey 'cuz I'm taking you to get your first Brazilian bikini wax, my treat, you're gonna hate me during, but boy are you gonna love me after . . .

[*She laughs. Lights shift back to ICU.*]

RHONDA [*semi-drugged*]: My doctors scheduled the skin-grafting surgery for next Monday, 'cuz Mike has the day off for Columbus Day. I was wondering if you could come too so he's not here alone.

ADRIANA: Sure sweetie. I'll just have to tell Brian we—

RHONDA: Oh my God . . . Brian?! Honey, I forgot. Oh my God . . . Why haven't you said anything? Is he all right?

ADRIANA: He's OK . . . he's OK. He was fifteen minutes late for work, so he got there right after the second plane hit. He saw a lot of—Are you sure you want to talk about this?

RHONDA: Yeah. I wanna know.

ADRIANA: Well, he was late for work, so he got there around nine fifteen, but the trains had stopped running to World Trade . . . they made them get off at Chambers Street. He saw the flames and this big hole and for some reason he just kept walking towards it, to work. He saw a lot of people jump . . . or fall. Rhonda, he remembers what they were all wearing. Meanwhile I'm standing in the middle of the living room watching all of this on TV and the phone is dead. I couldn't stop shaking. I didn't know if he was alive. I didn't know if you were alive. I wanted to go down there but I didn't know what I'd do or how . . . I mean Giuliani said the city was in lockdown . . . so I just starting praying. I promised that if he walked through that door, I was going to hold onto him and never let go. That I would marry him the next day . . . you know, forget the stupid wedding . . . just keep holding on. But when he walked through that door, he didn't want to be touched. He wouldn't eat or talk. He just sat in front of the TV in his dusty blue suit, watching the towers come down over and over. I spent the rest of the day calling all of the hospitals every fifteen minutes looking for you, until Mike called, nine hours later, and said they had found you.

RHONDA: I wish I could remember, but all I got is . . . pieces. I remember walkin' outta the train station on Courtlandt Street. I was gonna stop at Borders to pick up an anniversary card for Mike. I crossed Church Street and I remember feeling the ground shake . . . I thought it was the subway . . .

ADRIANA [*to audience*]: The man that found Rhonda would fill in the blanks. He tracked her down at the hospital. When I got him alone he told me . . .

[*Lights shift.*]

MAN: There were about two hundred people in the street just screaming and running for cover from the hot metal . . . sheets of glass . . . concrete after the plane hit . . . debris is flying everywhere . . . and I see this beautiful redhead . . . long curly hair . . . runnin' next to me . . . I hear this loud crash and I turn around to make sure the redhead's OK . . . and I see her on the ground, half a block away. I run back . . . she's in pieces . . . her legs below the knees . . . corkscrewed and dangling . . . her whole back is open . . . there's so much blood . . . and she's still tryin' to get up . . . so I just tell her to "Stay still honey, stay still" . . . I take off my jacket and tie it around her to hold her together . . . then I cover her with my body so the stampede of people won't trample what is left of her, while I scream for help!!!!! This guy flags down an ambulance. They get the people outta there who aren't as injured, but she's in too many pieces to lift her onto the stretcher—she's bleeding out—we gotta get her outta there, so we grab a sheet and slide it under her and with great care, we load her onto that ambulance . . . such a beautiful girl . . .

[*Lights shift. We hear an upbeat shopping samba.*]

ADRIANA [*enthusiastic*]: OK. Ready to pack the bag of goodies for Rhonda's visit!
Skeleton and bat decals for the Halloween manicure.
Purple velvet headband with batwings.
Purple feather pom-pom magic wand and pen.
Purple and green silk butterflies to hang over her bed.
Photos of trees and the ocean to create a view.
And a big picture of Yemaya . . .

   I arrive at the hospital with my bag of treasures, dressed to the nines. It is a week before Halloween and perfect sweater weather. I am wearing the matching black J Crew sweater set Rhonda had given me, a fabulous pair of Ann Taylor black pants . . . I splurged on, and my Franco Sarto calf length boots. Marshalls. I even put on full makeup and hairspray. It took me an hour and a half to get ready and I am already feeling a blister on my baby toe, but the look on Rhonda's face when I walk in the room is totally worth it . . .

RHONDA [*on morphine . . . dreamy with energy*]: C'mere let me see you. Oh honey. You look wonderful.

[*She laughs.*]

Stand on that chair. I want to see all of you. Hair looks good. Love the boots. I'm not crazy about the sweater though.

ADRIANA: Sweetie, you gave this to me.

RHONDA: I did? Well now I know why. Can you give me my water? Look at all this . . . Honey thank you. It feels like my birthday and Christmas and Hanukkah and—

ADRIANA: Rhonda's nurse interrupts as she announces the arrival of some visitors. I like to call them "fringe friends" . . . you know . . . the ones that stroll in usually around a holiday with frozen smiles, presents, exciting updates, and leave thirty minutes later feeling oh so good about themselves for having stopped by. I stand by Rhonda's bedside like a sentinel enjoying how awkward and uncomfortable and useless they seem to feel. "Did you wash your hands?" I bark. "And make sure you put on the gloves." I move about the room anticipating Rhonda's every need, flaunting my intimate knowledge of her world. I confer with her nurses as though we are colleagues, and delight when the Fringes inevitably have to run off somewhere . . . Bye . . .

RHONDA: Good-bye. Tell me the truth, Adriana, do I look awful? My hair?

ADRIANA: No. And, madam, today is your lucky day 'cuz I am going to wash and style your hair.

RHONDA: How are you gonna do that?

ADRIANA: Well . . .

[*She looks around . . . improvising.*]

I am going to tie this garbage bag around you like an enormous hood. And I'll use the pee-pee pan to catch the water.

RHONDA: No. That's disgusting. Ow . . . wait . . .

[*She pushes the morphine button.*]

. . . Ow . . .
Owww . . . [*Struggling to breathe*] Owww . . . No . . . I told them . . . I need more fucking morphine.

[RHONDA *screams in pain.*]

Owww . . . No . . . Owwwww!!!!!!!!!

ADRIANA: Alarms start screeching around her. I'm afraid to leave her alone. I run to the door. "Nurse!! Nurse room 302!!" A crowd of nurses rush into her room. They push me outside . . .

[*Lights shift. We hear a strong Afro-Cuban drumbeat . . . the rhythm sounds like a heartbeat.*]

ESPERANZA: *Ay Dios mio!* Look who jus' arrive at Chez Esperanza's Beauty Salon?! It's Rhonda e-bri-body! Go Rhonda. Go Rhonda. *Ay nena,* ju looks like a self-conscious Americano on a Caribbean cruise who hasn't had enough piña coladas to let the *fuego* out. *Dale Mamaita,* today is jour lucky day, because I am taking you on an unforgettable trip. When ju leave here . . . ju going to be a new woman!

ADRIANA: Just give her more morphine! They need her chart, she's had too much, they need her doctor, he's in surgery, they need to call the anesthesiologist, he's not here. More white coats running down the hall and she's still screaming.

ESPERANZA: I am going to wash and style jour hair because we know these crazy nurses don't know how to handle our kind of hair. Right? How's that water temperature?

RHONDA: I feel cold.

ADRIANA: My God. Will someone help her????

RHONDA: Can you see all the hair I've lost?? Tell me the truth, Esperanza.

ESPERANZA: E'cu me. E'cu me. E'cu me! Ju hair is beautiful. An judging from how often you hab to shave that little toto of jours, ju hab nothing to worry about! Ju see Mami, sontimes life take ju all the way back to the beginning to start again. Sontimes ju hab to let go of everything ju counted on . . . jour home . . . jour name . . . and even jour hair . . . an like a baby ju start again . . .

ADRIANA: Why is she so quiet? What's wrong?!

RHONDA: I like it here, Esperanza. Can I stay?

ESPERANZA: *No mi vida.* But I'm going to put my homemade avocado con diet 7 Up special hair conditioner on ju, a secret recipe from my Abuelita, and I jus want ju to keeps breathing . . . that's it, Mamita . . . in . . . and . . . out . . . in . . . and . . . out . . . [*Whispers*] Go Rhonda. Go Rhonda.

[*The heart monitor continues to beep . . . Lights shift back to ICU.*]

ADRIANA: When they finally let me back into her room . . . they say that I can only see her for a few minutes. But that it would do her good. I'm so afraid to leave. And I am afraid to go home.

[*Lights shift.*]

It's Thanksgiving night and Brian is pissed at me because he says I didn't put enough thought into our Thanksgiving dinner. Which is ridiculous since neither one of us likes turkey and we both agreed we weren't going to make a big fuss this year.

[*The phone rings.*]

[*To* BRIAN] I'll get it.

[*She answers the phone.*]

Hello.

RHONDA [*stronger*]: It's me. Did you guys have a nice Thanksgiving?

ADRIANA: No. [*Whispering*] He's in a mood.

RHONDA: Well why don't you come to the hospital for a little while? I sent Mike to his parents' house 'cuz he hasn't spent any time with them and my family already stopped by for "the visit." Drove me crazy the whole time.

ADRIANA: I don't know sweetie. It's late.

RHONDA: Just for a little bit?

ADRIANA: I don't—

RHONDA: Please. Pleeeeaasse??

ADRIANA: OK. Can I bring you anything?

RHONDA: Yeah . . . a mushroom, onion, and olive pizza.

ADRIANA: You got it.

[*She hangs up.*]

Rhonda has started eating solid food and when she is not nauseous, which is still most of the time, she gets these cravings. I delight in satisfying them, but often by the time I get to the hospital with her special request, she's nauseous again. So her nurses are the best-fed nurses on the floor.

[*Lights shift. It is nighttime at the hospital.* RHONDA's *TV is on full blast. An epic soundtrack is playing.*]

RHONDA: Honey, come in it already started. Just put it down.

ADRIANA: Don't you want a piece of pizza?

RHONDA: No, wait till this scene is over. You know how much I love this part. Sit down. [*To nurse*] Gladys, what? I told you I don't want to take the pills until after the movie. I'll fall asleep.

[*The phone rings.*]

Oh my God, it's Grand Central in here today!

[*She answers the phone.*]

Hello? What? No, my parents came by earlier, it was fine. Yeah. No look I gotta go. *Gladiator's* on. Adriana just walked in with a pizza. I'll talk to you tomorrow. Gotta go—Good-bye!

ADRIANA: He's so hot in that skirt.

RHONDA: He's like an animal. Get him!! Joaquin is such a prick in this. I love him. And he's cute, you know, even with the little scar. Ssssh . . . What? Gladys, I told you. Not now—good-bye— Hurry up Adriana . . . and action!

[RHONDA *snaps the imaginary scene chalkboard. Very professional. The two women play out this scene as it appears in the film. It is obvious they have watched it a hundred times.*]

RHONDA [*as Russell Crowe*]: My name is Gladiator.

[*She turns slightly in bed.*]

ADRIANA [*as Joaquin Phoenix*]: How dare you show your back to me? Slave! You will remove your helmet and tell me your name.

[RHONDA *mimes taking off her helmet.*]

RHONDA [*as Russell Crowe*]: My name is Maximus Decimus Meridius. Commander of the armies of the north. General of the Felix— GLADYSSS!!!! Loyal servant to the true Emperor Marcus Aurelius. Father to a murdered son, husband to a murdered wife. I will have my vengeance, in this life, or the next.

[RHONDA *puts her helmet back on and grabs the reins of her horse and starts to gallop with her arms.*]

Get him! Get him, Adriana!

ADRIANA: I got him. I got him!!! Ball and chain!

RHONDA: Eye of the tiger!!!!

[ADRIANA *lets out a battle cry. As the* Gladiator *music swells, she hurls the ball and chain and is victorious!*]

[*Lights shift exuberantly into . . .*]

ADRIANA: It is two weeks before Valentine's Day and after five eternal months in ICU, Rhonda is now well enough to be moved to the rehab hospital. She can now have living plants and flowers in her room because they are no longer afraid of her dying of an infection. I can't wait to decorate her new room, do a little feng shui, make it homey . . .
She tells me that . . .

RHONDA: This is going to be a very different place. I'm gonna be taking pottery making classes and occupational gardening therapy and the best part is that I'm not going to have to wear this stupid hospital gown anymore. And as soon as I get out of here, we are going to the beach to bring Yemaya her white roses and tell her thank you. I can't wait!

ADRIANA: I am feeling good too! I have been off bread and sugar for three weeks. I am doing my anger work every day, my healing sounds and abdominal massage every other day and I have decided to forgive my parents . . . so, I'm feelin' good.

I get off the elevator, turn the corner and I see a group of nurses rushing in and out of the room at the end of the hall carrying bloodied dressings. I know that has to be her room. This is a rehab hospital. This is where people come to learn how to walk again. So what the hell is going on down there and why is there so much blood? I just want to turn around and run. I don't have it in me to walk through that door and smile, no matter what I see, again. I don't realize that while I am thinking of a way out—my body has carried me right to her door, until one of the nurses says . . .

NURSE [*heavy Korean accent*]: Ohhhh you musta be ha friend . . . Adriana . . . she expecting you.

ADRIANA: She snaps off her bloody gloves and I think I am going to be sick.

[*Lights shift.*]

Rhonda's been in rehab now for the past month. Her schedule is so crazy, I have to make an appointment to see her. She barely spends any time in her room. She is shuttled around to an endless array of therapies by a wheelchair that costs more than most cars, several times a day. They start the day by strapping her to a tilt board and forcing her to stand upright at varying degrees, for hours, which is excruciating. Then she is shuttled off to the weight room to strengthen her upper body. After that, she is shuttled back up to her room, to have her wounds scraped . . . to keep activating new skin growth. I am asked to wait outside her door whenever they do this. Her screams are horrifying and I dread being invited back in when it's over.

RHONDA [*heavily sedated, dry mouth, hands shaking*]: Is this what they saved me for? I can't take any more of this . . . I wish I had died.

ADRIANA: A rush of reasons of why she should be here . . . how great she's been doing . . . how it's a miracle flood my head, but I stop myself from speaking them. I want her to be able to say what she feels and not be talked out of it.

[*Pause.*]

ADRIANA: I'm glad that you're here. I love you.

RHONDA: I feel numb.

[*Pause.*]

Will you stay with me until I fall asleep . . . no one else is coming today.

ADRIANA [*hides checking her watch*]: Sure honey.

RHONDA: Will you give me lovies on my arm?

ADRIANA: Like this?

RHONDA: With your nails . . . hmmm . . . Will you tell me a story?

ADRIANA: OK . . . uh . . .
   I've told you about my grandmother . . . well during one of my last visits with her, she was ninety, we had just gotten home from seeing Luis Carbonell, the famous Cuban monologist. He recites stories and poems to these intoxicating Cuban rhythms . . . so Abuela can't stop dancing all around her tiny apartment in Queens . . .

ABUELA [*singing "La Comparsa"*]: *Mira la que linda viene. Mira la que linda va . . .*

[*She laughs.*]

ADRIANA: Abuela dances over to her altar. Which is an ocean of perfume bottles, each saint had their own fragrance.

RHONDA: Which one was Yemaya's?

ADRIANA: I think it was Tommy Hilfiger.

Anyway, I am expecting some kind of an ancestral legacy to be bestowed on me. She hands me a canister of Midnight Musk talcum powder by Avon. She swears that it will drive Brian crazy. Apparently she had read in the tea leaves that we weren't doing so well in that department. Then she opens her lingerie drawer, she reaches softly into a sea of silk and takes out a see-through scarlet red nightie. She hands it to me with such reverence and says,

ABUELA: Here, *amor,* you enjoy this. Just put this on with a little powder *por aqui* [*gesturing between her legs*] y prannn prannn!!

ADRIANA: She boasted that when she'd go for her monthly checkups with her handsome GP, El Doctor Fox, or when she'd make her occasional visits to St. John's Hospital she always put on new lingerie. She claimed that she got better care,

ABUELA: *Porque nadie quiere ver una vieja con la narga pa fuera . . .*

ADRIANA: . . . because no one wants to see an old lady's ass hanging out. Then she showed me the new nail polish she was going to wear to her next appointment with El Dr. Fox, called . . .

ABUELA: *Secretos de Ceresas.* De secret of cherries.

[*She laughs.*]

ADRIANA: And then she laughed her laugh. The one that felt like a sunset after a long day at the beach.

[*Beat.*]

It never occurred to her that she was old or that parts of her body used to live in other places. Better places. It never occurred to her that she wasn't more desirable at ninety then she was at twenty. It never occurred to her, so she was.

[ADRIANA *fixes* RHONDA's *blanket and kisses her on the forehead.*]

RHONDA [*half asleep*]: I love you.

ADRIANA: I love you too. Goodnight.

I fill her water glass and say a prayer that she sleeps through the night. I hate leaving her, but these long visits are hard. I mean I go to the hospital with the intention of staying no more than two hours, but something always comes up and I don't know how to leave, so six, seven hours later I am tired, but as long as I can walk out of that room on two legs . . . what right do I have to be tired?

ADRIANA [*on cell phone*]: Hey, babe . . . it's me . . . pick up . . . pick up . . . hello . . . hello . . . are you there? [*Surprised*] I guess you went out. Baby, look . . . I . . . I know I promised we'd spend some time together tonight . . . Rhonda wasn't doing well and no one else—I just needed to stay . . . I'm sorry . . . I—I'm on my way home.

[*She slams her cell phone shut. Lights shift. A hot Latin beat is playing.*]

ESPERANZA: It's nice to make the party. To bring the presents. To bring the glitter. To bring the cha cha. *Pero ja nena.* Enough. It's time to wake up and smell the doughnuts! When was the last time you had coochie with Brian? Ah? When was the last time you wanted coochie? Like Doctor Phil says, *ay* he's so cute with his little bald head, "How's that working for ju?" Ju remember Mami? In and out . . . in and out . . . in in in . . . out out out . . .

[*She dances off. Lights shift.*]

ADRIANA [*inspired*]: It's mid-June and the streets of New York are decorated with smiling young graduates and the fragrance of lilacs and peony from the corner stores. I went on my first audition since 9/11 and I got the part. Parts actually . . . it's a play . . . a calypso version of *The Odyssey.* I play twelve parts in it and rehearsals have been a bitch, but it feels so good to be working again. I've been spending less time at the hospital. I feel bad not being there as much . . . and . . . a little relieved to have a legitimate excuse. I am on a break between rehearsing the Helen of Troy scene and the mermaid ménage à trois with Odysseus, he's really cute, when I get a message from Rhonda . . .

RHONDA: Adriana. I did it. I walked. I took five steps all by myself. I did it. Can you come by the hospital tomorrow? I want you to see me walk.

ADRIANA: So I go to the hospital early the next morning to see her physical therapy session. I am so excited. I meet her in the therapy room. She wheels in wearing an oversized Bon Jovi T-shirt that one of her doctors had given her from his rocker days and a homemade black wrap skirt . . . velcroed in the right places. She has state-of-the-art custom-made boots, to prevent the bones in her legs from shattering, when she puts her weight on them.

[*As* ADRIANA *recounts this, she reenacts* RHONDA's *physical actions simultaneously.* RHONDA's *movements are slow, sourcing her strength through excruciating pain.*]

Her wheelchair is pulled up between the two parallel bars. Two therapists help her get to her feet. She shakes as she grips fiercely onto the bars . . . slowly they let go of her. Her torso is hunched way over and I keep waiting for her to straighten up. She draws her right foot out from under her. She inches it forward . . . right . . . left. She repeats the motion . . . right . . . left . . . I notice drops of blood dripping onto the floor . . . right . . . left . . . More blood. Her physical therapist tells her to stop . . . right . . . left . . . blood starts gushing . . . trailing a red path behind her . . . right . . . left . . . right . . . left . . . right—her therapists scoop the wheelchair under her, forcing her to stop.

[*Beat.*]

I stare at the blood-soaked floor. It looks like a murder scene. As they wheel her past me she asks . . .

RHONDA [*out of breath, victorious*]: Did ya see that? I did it. I walked.

[ADRIANA *tries to share this moment of* RHONDA's *triumph, but inside it is clear that it is going to be a long time before* RHONDA *will go home. Lights shift. A bizarre mambo is being played on a harpsichord as* ADRIANA *mimes squeezing into a skintight spandex dress. She hops about throughout the scene as she is unable to move her legs in this dress.*]

ADRIANA [*excited*]: I'm on Tenth Avenue, in my mermaid costume from *The Odyssey* trying to get a cab. I decided to give Rhonda a thrill. I sneaked out the back door of the theater right after the matinee so the stage manager wouldn't see me. I have on a tight green spandex dress that trails a long tail of fishnets and sea shells . . . I have long green hair . . . I'm covered in silver glitter. And I'm having a hard time getting a cab! I am rushing to the hospital between shows to help Gabi give Rhonda a facial and do her hair the day before her big magazine interview. I am exhausted, but I know Rhonda's gonna love this. Taxi!

I enter the room and Rhonda and Gabi are deep in discussion about none other than Hillary Clinton, who had come to see Rhonda the day before and left her with a mega dose of star fever . . . Hillary this and Hillary that . . .

RHONDA: . . . and Oh Gabi you remind me so much of Hillary. You're always doing something exciting in the world that you believe in and I so admire that. I told her that if she runs for president she can count on my vote—Adriana, what are you wearing???

ADRIANA: My costume from *The Odyssey.*

RHONDA: Oh. Huh. Anyway, do you want to see the pictures of me and Hillary?? She's so much prettier in person. She had on the most beautiful jewelry . . .

ADRIANA [*to herself*]: Well screw you, madame. Maybe Hillary should be giving you this facial. I am exhausted, on my dinner break, standing here squeezing blackheads and exfoliating ungrateful skin . . . and not even a thank-you.

[*She squeezes a blackhead out of* RHONDA's *nose.*]

RHONDA: Ow! Adriana, what is wrong with you? You're so quiet.

ADRIANA: Nothing, nothing, really. Do you want "Viva Las Vegas" or "Sandcastle" for your nails?

Gabi is making me sick. She is just standing there in her Birkenstocks, acting helpless, while I do all of the work . . . [*Spoken in a flurry of out-of-breath effort as she progresses . . . trying to do it all.*] Can you get me some water? Sure honey. Can you fix my pillows? Of course. Will you massage my arms? OK. Will you wash my hair? Right away. Will you get me more juice? Absolutely. Will you hand me the phone? You got it. Will you straighten that up? That and more. Will you get me a fresh gown? How 'bout the pink one? Will you help me put it on? You betcha. Stay for my PT session? I'll coach you on the breathing! Be here when the doctor comes? With a pen and a pad!! Stay until I fall asleep? What are friends for?!!!!!!

[*Lights shift.* ESPERANZA's *Latin beat.*]

ESPERANZA: E'cu me *nena*, but we hab to talk becuz *come dice* Whoopi Goldberg in my favorite movie *Ghost*, "Ju in danger girl!" [*Music fades*] Ju know it's funny because ju criticize all the fringe friends, but let me tell ju sonsing, they are all a lot smarter than ju, because they all still hab a life. Oh jes they hab a life. Nobody gave up everything for Rhonda. Nobody but ju. An what does that get ju? Tell me? Because who the hell are ju? An what planet did ju fall from to think that ju can make it all better? Pleaaasssse. Been there done that. Let me tell ju sonsing. Ju want to be a goddess? Ju think it's jus dancing, eating chocolate, and wearing no panties?

[*She lifts her skirt.*]

No *Mamita* . . . it's work. Because ju have to have the courage to destroy. Ahh jes . . . jus as ju have the courage to save, and to birth, and to create, ju have to have the courage to walk away and let sonsing fall. Can ju do that? Can ju walk away and let her fall. Because she has to learn how to e'stand on her own two legs, an if they don't work anymore, that's her problem. Not jours. Ju didn't cripple her. And ju can't save her.

[*Music returns.* ESPERANZA *dances off. Lights shift.*]

ADRIANA: Ten months have passed and they have started to significantly decrease the morphine. Rhonda is becoming nasty and unrecognizable. She is now sixty pounds heavier from all of the medication and her beautifully chiseled face has receded into a bitter and angry scowl.

   I try to bury myself in the doing, like before, but there is nothing to do. I don't even know what to talk about. How do I complain about menstrual cramps, a lousy audition, or the few pounds I gained from the Fourth of July BBQ I went to?

   I make my way toward Rhonda's bedside to greet her. She scans me from head to toe.

RHONDA: Those pants don't flatter you. Ya gained a little weight?

ADRIANA: I move closer to the door, take a bite of the lunch I brought, and say, "Maybe a little."

[*Awkward pause.*]

RHONDA: Would you hand me my tweezers and my mirror?

[RHONDA *proceeds to pluck her eyebrows with shaky hands. She looks up.*]

Are you wearing a bra, 'cuz from the side your tits look really saggy?

ADRIANA [*flustered*]: No . . . I'm not wearing a bra.

RHONDA: You know you really shouldn't talk with your mouth full.

ADRIANA: What?

RHONDA: I said you shouldn't talk with your mouth full. It's disgusting.

ADRIANA: Disgusting?

RHONDA: Yeah. That's what I said. Disgusting. Hand me my water—

[*Loaded pause . . .* ADRIANA *pours a glass of water.*]

ADRIANA: I hand Rhonda her water, I close my mouth, and I chew. I chew my rage. I chew my hurt. I chew my hope of how I couldn't wait till they took her off the heavy drugs because, as I understood it, that meant that more of Rhonda was going to come back. Right? That's what the doctors kept saying . . . more of her was going to come back . . .

I can't do this. I can't. I don't know how to be in a room with her anymore, or home with Brian, or anywhere. I mean I was ready for a sprint. You know? Drop everything because Rhonda might die—no, she's going to be OK—no, she might die—gotta get down there—no, she's OK—no, she might die . . . run-run-run!!! Well I've dropped everything for the past year and even though she's not going to die anymore, I don't know how to pick it all back up.

I need a break . . . please. I just need a break . . . to catch my breath . . . and then . . . maybe . . . I can come back and bring something in the room that's alive again . . .

So I tell Rhonda that I need to take a couple of weeks off. OK, I can't bring myself to say that to her face. So I write it in a card. A beautiful hand-painted card with mermaids and unicorns on it. I tell her that I love her. That I have some things I need to work out and when I don't hear from her, I think she is OK with it.

A couple of weeks pass.

[*She catches herself.*]

OK, six weeks pass and I am feeling better. Gabi and I are having lunch. She has been spending more time with Rhonda and I appreciate the updates. We are at my favorite Greek place, Nikos, and somewhere between the hummus and the spanakopita she says . . .

[*Beat.*]

GABRIELLA: Rhonda's getting out of the hospital tomorrow.

ADRIANA: What?

GABRIELLA: Yeah. She's going home tomorrow.

ADRIANA: Why didn't she tell me?

GABRIELLA: She doesn't want you to know.

[ADRIANA *is speechless.*]

I know it's just her pride talking. Look there's going to be a party for her and some TV show is going to be there to film it. We're all going and I think you should go too.

[ADRIANA *shakes her head in disbelief.*]

Adriana, she's hurt. She says you just walked out on her.

ADRIANA: And what did you say?

[*Silence.* ADRIANA *slams down her money.*]

That should cover my share.

I walk out of the restaurant pounding my feet into the pavement down Broadway. I can't believe she doesn't want me there. What kind of bullshit is that?? I bet all the little feel-good fringe friends will be there right?? Funny how when the TV cameras are there people manage to show up!

Fine. I'm not even going to watch it. What am I going to see? These jackasses smiling while the TV show milks the moment of her "loyal friends" all around her. Makes me sick. Why don't they show her screaming and smelling and looking like a witch on TV? Huh? Why don't they let America see what that looks like. No let's just see the pretty picture of the crippled girl going home.

I should just go down there right now and say you know what, bitch?? I'm here. You can't get rid of me with your little sleeping beauty act. That's right the wicked fairy is here. Taxi!!!!!

NURSE: Excuse me . . .

ADRIANA: The head nurse says . . .

NURSE: You're not allowed to go in there.

ADRIANA [*ridiculously kind*]: Oh no . . . don't worry she's expecting me.

I walk into Rhonda's room and she's sitting there like the Queen of Sheba, eating ice cream, and watching *Survivor* . . .

[*To* RHONDA] So you don't want me to know you're getting out of the hospital tomorrow huh? What kind of bullshit is that??

RHONDA: I've got nothing to say to you. Get out of my room.

ADRIANA: No I'll get out of here when I say what I came here to say. Now, you tell all these morons that haven't been here to come and share this day with you, this day that we have dreamed about for a fucking year and shhhh don't tell Adriana because I don't want her there. How ungrateful can you possibly be?

RHONDA: How ungrateful? Adriana, you just checked out. You walk out on me, I have no idea what's going on. You send me a stupid little card and you expect me to be fine with that? Well I'm not fine with that. And since you've been gone other people have been here and they've been good to me.

ADRIANA: So six weeks cancels out a year of me being here???? Where were all your little migratory birds then huh? I was here when every fuckin' body wasn't. All right Mike was here, I'll pardon him, he did his best. But everyone else came when it was convenient, when they could squeeze you in. Do you know the things I've put on hold to be here with you?!!!

RHONDA: Lower your voice. You're makin' me sick. I didn't ask you to make me your little patient. I didn't ask you to try to save me, I had doctors for that! I thought you were here because you love me, but obviously you had other reasons for being here.

ADRIANA: What? Have the drugs left you with amnesia with a capital A? Who was by your bedside when your life was hanging in the balance, praying over your body, putting talismans and charms in your room, calling in supernatural help so you'd survive? Who loved you and fed you and caressed you when these so-called other friends were too scared to come in here and see you near death, or smell your shit, or listen to you scream??? I was here and I know you're alive because of me.

RHONDA: Nobody saved me . . . and the reason why I am getting out of this hospital tomorrow is because of me. I'm the one that got myself up every morning. I'm the one who stood on these two legs no matter how much it hurt, no matter how much I was bleeding. I'm the one who did the work to get the hell out of this hospital and get the hell out of this bed, so don't you try to pretend that you had anything to do with that because you know what??? I saved myself!!!! Now get the hell out of my room. I don't want you here.

[*Pause.*]

ADRIANA: I never had that conversation with Rhonda. The taxi never made it to the hospital. Instead and I don't know why, I got out of the cab at Ground Zero.

[*Lights shift slowly as beautiful music plays very softly . . . supporting this moment without being sentimental.*]

I get out and walk all the way up to the footprints of the Towers. All the way up to the makeshift fence surrounding the quiet earth. Space. So much space. This hole . . . this empty tomb . . . I am standing there pressed up to the fence just taking it all in, when some idiot tourist pushes me out of the way [*music ends*], so that he and his oblivious little group have more room to take their picture. They are all just standing there grinning like they are in Times Square on New Year's Eve.

And then I see them. Double-decker buses. Tourists disembarking, disembarking to cross the street and stand in front of the gated fence and take pictures at Ground Zero like they are standing in front of the Statue of Liberty or the Empire State Building and they are all smiling. And to the right of them is a vendor, with a little program that has the Towers burning on the cover and it says "Day of Tragedy" . . . five dollars. Day of Tragedy . . . five dollars. Day of Tragedy . . . five dollars??? Next to the souvenir program are neat little stacks of "I've Been to Ground Zero" T-shirts in small, medium, and extra large. I want to know what you do with a T-shirt from Ground Zero. I want to know what the hell that means, because I don't understand how it is that in our country we don't have a way for people to mourn . . . like do you remember after it happened, St. Paul's church right across the street from Ground Zero had that fence that went all the way around four city blocks and people spontaneously came down here with their flowers, T-shirts, cards, their candles . . . stuffed animals and rosaries . . . baseball hats . . . symbols that meant something to them, whether they were people who knew someone that was lost, or just a stranger coming here from some faraway place, because they had to. I mean how did we get from that to . . . Day of Tragedy . . . five dollars . . .

I march right up to the Grey Line Bus and I yell . . .

"Do you know where you are? And what the fuck are you smiling at??"

I root myself into the wounded earth, determined to stay here and prevent any more idiots from smiling, when I hear a voice say . . .

EDDIE [*older Puerto Rican man*]: It's OK, mama. They don't understand.

ADRIANA: I look to my left and standing there is my own white-haired Puerto Rican version of Clarence, from *It's a Wonderful Life*. He has on a wide-brimmed Panama hat, a starched white linen guayabera, and a smile as open as the sea. He hands me his sandalwood-scented handkerchief and says . . .

EDDIE: I come here every day.

ADRIANA: He takes a beat-up old camera out of his shirt pocket. He kisses it and says . . .

EDDIE: This will be with me until the day I die. Can I show you sonsing?

ADRIANA: He takes some pictures out of a worn envelope.

EDDIE: I almost died that day. I was e'standing right here when the towers was burning. I took these pictures while I was trying to get away. I was choked by the black smoke when the building collapse . . . I was trying to get away. That's all I can remember until I woke up inside di ambulance and dis big strong young Latino man was punching me in the chest saying . . .

"C'mon, Papi. C'mon, Papi. You're not going to die on me. You breathe. C'mon, Papi. C'mon. Breathe. Breathe." And as I was watching him, I thought he was my son. I don't have a son, but if I had one, I thought, that's what he would look like.

And all of a sudden, I e'start to breathe.

And my new son scream, "You're alive, Papi! You're alive!" And I was alive! So I looked him up a few weeks later because I wanted to tell him thank you. And you know what he say to me, "No, Papi, thank you. You're my hero, because the one life that I was able to save that day . . . yours . . . somehow helps me get through all this."

ADRIANA: I am still holding onto his handkerchief when he asks . . .

EDDIE: Would it be OK if I take your picture?

[ADRIANA *nods. He raises the camera up to his eye.*]

And it's OK if you smile.

[*Flash. Lights shift. The sound of soft ocean waves crashing.* ADRIANA *comes downstage.*]

ADRIANA: I am at the sea. I come here often to bring Yemaya her white roses and to thank her. It has been over six years since Rhonda and I last spoke, and even though we haven't had any contact, I do know she is alive, and for that I give thanks.

I have notebooks full of things I would like to say to her. I've spent a lot of time imagining what it would be like if we ever saw each other again. Like what would happen if we bumped into each other on a street corner . . . or on a subway . . . or . . . my favorite . . .

[*She vividly paints the scene.*]

. . . I would be on an airplane, in first class, sinking into the large leather seats, wondering why the windows are the same size as coach—I'd be listening to ABBA on my computer. I'm a huge fan. I'd look up and see . . . Rhonda. Dressed to the nines. And like a geisha that's had a little too much sake, she'd walk down the aisle and take the seat next to me . . . I'd notice that she smelled like Rhonda again. After a long pause I'd say . . .

ADRIANA [*softly*]: Hi.

RHONDA [*distant*]: Hello. You changed your hair.

ADRIANA: I did.

RHONDA [*warmer*]: Looks nice.

ADRIANA: Thanks.

[*Back to audience*] I'd hold the left earpiece of my headphones up to Rhonda's ear and slowly, as if against her better judgment, she'd accept it . . .

[*Singing . . . softly at first*] You can dance
You can jive

RHONDA [*singing like a bad cruise ship singer*]: Having the time of your life
Woo woo woo

ADRIANA: See that girl

RHONDA: Watch that scene . . .

ADRIANA [*exuberantly*]: We'd grab hands and sing "Dancing Queen" as the plane lifts off into the sky—

[*She catches herself.*]

But I don't want to live in imagined endings anymore. I want to live in what is.

[*Beat.*]

So . . . what is? Brian and I broke up. I left New York, moved to Los Angeles, and I learned how to drive. Which is a big deal for a New Yorker!

What is? A couple of months ago, I heard a man, Dr. Michael Bernard Beckwith, talking about forgiveness. He said until you are grateful to the person and the experience that caused you pain, you haven't forgiven. And in that moment, I realized I had only accepted what happened, but I hadn't really forgiven Rhonda. So the next morning, after holding onto the phone for nearly two hours . . . praying, rehearsing speeches, and lighting candles, with my heart racing . . . I called Rhonda. I got her voicemail and I told her that I love her and I was grateful for what we had shared. And that I didn't want one of us to leave the planet without her knowing that.

What is? That I now know that love isn't doing, love is being . . . being real . . . being brave . . . being myself . . . and my heart . . . which I have spent most of my life protecting, is the strongest muscle I have in my body, and every time I use it, it just keeps getting stronger, and stronger, and stronger.

[*Music plays as* ADRIANA *gathers water from the bowl and releases it onto the center of the playing area, closing the circle.* ADRIANA *moves to the music . . . grateful for what is . . . as the lights fade to black.*]

BLUE SUITE

Mildred Ruiz and Steven Sapp

PRODUCTION HISTORY

An earlier version, titled *Eyewitness Blues,* was commissioned and produced by New York Theatre Workshop and developed by Talvin Wilks
in 2004. The play was directed by Talvin Wilks, with music by Antoine
Drye, Carlos Pimentel, and Paul Jonathan Thompson; scenic design by
Narelle Sissons; lighting design by Heather Carson; sound design by
Darron L. West and Bray Poor; choreography by Adesola A. Osakalumi;
flamenco movement by Jaime Coronado; and production stage management by Antonia Gianino.

Duende (Muse) .... Mildred Ruiz
Junior McCullough .... Steven Sapp
Musicians .... Antoine Drye, Paul Jonathan Thompson

The Goodman Theatre Production, August 11–19, 2006, titled "Blue
Sweat," was directed by Chay Yew, with music by Maurice S. Turner III,
Paul Thompson, and Carlos Pimentel; scenic design by Narrelle Sissons;
lighting design by Heather Hershey; sound design by Ryan Rumery; fla-
menco guitar by Enrique Lopez; and production stage management by
Heather Hershey.

Duende (Muse) .... Mildred Ruiz
Junior McCullough (Soul) .... Steven Sapp
Junior McCullough (Body) .... Maurice Turner

CHARACTERS

Duende (Muse)
Junior McCullough (Soul)
Junior McCullough (Body)

DUENDE [*singing/flamenco movement*]: *Aaa Aaa iii*
   Aaaaa iii
   A iii, A iii
   Que ganas tengo que llegue, aaai
   El músico e mis amores
   El músico e mis amores
   Yo voy a ser, la guitara
   Pa su trompeta e dolor, aaai
   Su trompeta de dolores
   Su trompeta de dolores
   Soy Duende aunque no lo quiera
   Soy Duende aungue no lo quiera
   El hará lo que yo le diga
   Ay si quiere verse a mi verá
   Le re le
   Le le re le re le
   Le re le
   Le le re le ra
   [*Addressing the audience*] Let me introduce myself.
   My name is Duende.
   But you can call me
   Duende.

   I was the one
   who sparked the secret love affair
   Between the hidden,
   Aching spirit of Spain,
   And that haunted
   Bleeding soul of jazz.
   Many a night I spent drunk
   On a pyramid wall with two Mexicans
   There, I battled the sun
   Every morning
   And set it down to sleep at night

   Ai me vestí de luto

   Every night
   I play chess with death

And drink skin-melting acid
To celebrate each pawn lost
and each pawn won.
So I keep coming back for more
Keep coming back
To pose naked in portraits

Duende
You can find me
Between fingertips
On the Sistine Chapel,
That's where I hide,
between the paintbrush bristles
As crimson drops
Drip on my white canvas skirt
Finding possibilities
Everywhere you choose to look.

Duende
Should you really choose to look,
You can find me
On the horn man's tongue
As he licks his mouthpiece
ready to blow
You can find me in dancing feet
Spilling out of tear ducts,
My hair tangled
Around strangled
moaning vocal cords
In the slightest
movement of the wrist
In the deepest moment of thought
In the ether of dreams
and nightmares
It is there that I exist

Yet, I was crafted
Molded

Seasoned by your very hands
La receta esta perfect
So sop me up with a biscuit
'Cause I taste
just like you want me to
There would be no hallelujahs,
if not for me
You need me

But you don't call me anymore
Now I have to make house calls going door-to-door
Like I'm selling Skin So Soft
and makeup to ashy
desperate housewives
I am inspiration in a bottle
I love my job
But I hate it too
If you haven't noticed
I have issues
Is that possible?
You see, I am lacking inspiration
Starting to lose the passion
For sparking passion
But that's another story
A long one
And there is no intermission tonight

A duende's work is never done
Tomorrow,
My workload will be just as heavy
I have scheduled an uninspired
airport lounge A
passionless illiterate karaoke bar
And an entire university,
a school of higher learning nothing
But, tomorrow is tomorrow,
tonight I still have time
for one more

Streetlamps flicker
rhythms push at my feet
And play loudly
Car rolls by demanding to be heard
All bass
All drum
Graffiti hugs the walls
like old lovers
Bodegas are like shrines
There are no brownstones here
Section Eight housing Coats the block
with welfare and *cupones*
Young upscale white, wannabes
Post up on the corners
Whistling sweet nothings
To thick-thighed *mamas*
And heavy-chested *mammitas*
Not understanding
That this is where you don't come
If you ain't from around here

[DUENDE *pushes a door open.*]

Ay Fo!
Aquí apesta
What's that smell?
Smells like somebody's career
just died in here!
All I know is that, that smell
had better not get in my hair
Me lo lavé con el shampoo de leche
de Mirta de Perales
Ay, ay, ay,
This cannot be the right place. I'm a have to double-check
this address
'cause this cannot be it.
Damn
I think this is it.

Cómo va ser?
Shit,
now I look like the fool
Overdressed and all hooked up
Emprejila
Con las tetas en el cuello
Y a dónde está la fiesta?
This used to be the spot, you know
Everything here was on point
back in the days
This place was spotless
The lights were bright
The attire was tight
And the music was on and popping
I remember
when I used to come here
Ella stood there
on this very spot
Scatting language into art.
And Duke,
sat in a chair right there
As she serenaded him.
Bambatta put his turntables
and crates near the front
Tito Puente
set up his timbales in that corner
And Dave Valentin
is scheduled to meet me here
Next month,
at my request.
This room once heard it all
I use to come here
And inspire them to play
Now
the walls are aging
Layers of decrepit posters
Play the role of wallpaper

They fade
Music stands lean.
The best seat in the house
faces the door
And red velvet ropes
hold back no one
The ghost light is still on
Even though the house is open
And the house
is light
tonight
Some of the audience
is at the bar
The rest are out back smoking
And a few stand in the back
of the room
when they arrive

[TRUMPETER *enters and sits on chair.*]

And this
is my newest project
I'll call this one
"the end of the day"
Sitting backstage
far away from the audience
In his trusted chair
With his personal flask
for his personal stash
Waiting for his set to begin
Backstage
the lights are dim
His suit looks cheap
His posture relaxed
He profiles for no one back here
This one looks like
he's not gonna be easy
Looks like

he's been wearing that suit
For far too long
He looks like
he has issues too
He looks,
Muerto!
Ay, ay, ay
You don't even know,
Today,
I'm gonna pull you out of your
flatline
Singing
Clear!

Passion!
Clear!

Inspiración!
Clear!

Till I hear pulse
Till this heart beats
Till rhythm rhymes
And trumpets speak
You
Are a new breed,
Bronx Child,
A fusion of everything
You've ever heard,
Ever seen,
Ever done
And here you are
Accompanied by yourself
A split personality of sorts
Confused
Don't know your place
in the timeline;
Your role in the traditions of

Louie, and Miles.
But even if your body
was to make a sound
It's your soul that must resound.
Time for a *dos* of Duende
You are Junior McCullough
Y yo

[*Singing*] *Soy Duende aunque no lo quiera*
Soy Duende aungue no lo quiera
Y harás lo que yo te diga
Ay si quiere verte a mi verá
Le re le
Le le re le re le
Le re le
Le le re le ra

[TRUMPETER'*s soul enters.*]

JUNIOR: Who the fuck are you?
And where do you
think you're going,
dressed like that?

DUENDE: Let me introduce myself
I am Duende

JUNIOR: Who?

DUENDE: I, add the detail
of that blue haze to Harlem
I,
breathe the scent
into singing gardenias

JUNIOR: WHAT the hell you talking about?

DUENDE: I came to find you.

JUNIOR: Find me?
I didn't know I was lost.
Well, here I am!

DUENDE: Yes,
   here you are
   Playing for nobody
   Out of shape and out of breath
   Lost
   Just waiting to be found.
   You know, I found your picture
   on a milk carton the other day

JUNIOR: My picture?
   Did they get my good side?

[*He shows her his backside.*]

DUENDE: I liked it better
   when it was not so ugly
   When it was innocent
   Before your face was drawn
   Before your eyes were sunken
   Before you became the you
   You chose to lose

JUNIOR: Where do you think I went?

DUENDE: Where I couldn't reach you
   Dug yourself into a hole
   And sat in the dark for days
   Drowning in a bottle
   Drugged up to stupidity
   Te fuiste pal carajo?
   And I'm still trying
   to pull your ass out

JUNIOR: Come on now
   I don't have time for nobody's
   bullshit but mine!

DUENDE: You know I'm the one
   who sits in the pit of your stomach

JUNIOR: You must be my ulcer.

DUENDE: I'm the one you dreamt of
   The one who woke you up
   wet from the night

JUNIOR: Ah, my wet dream.

DUENDE: I witnessed your first kiss with
   Tina.

JUNIOR: How did you know that?

DUENDE: Your first orgasm with Sheila.

JUNIOR: What?

DUENDE: The time you fell, crossing
   Delancey
   I was there while the old man
   cleaned the blood off your knee
   I was there
   when your baby teeth fell out.
   Remember, how you couldn't
   hold the trumpet against your lips?

JUNIOR: I was there.

DUENDE: I was there
   And so were you.
   We both know
   you've been tooting your own horn
   For a long time.
   But it's been a long time
   Since you simply stopped to blow.

JUNIOR: Blow the horn?
   Been blowin' the horn
   Stay blowin' the horn
   I just played yesterday
   Played yesterday
   and the day before that
   And the day before that

And the day before that
And the day before that
And the day before that
And the day before that
And the day before that
Stay blowin' the horn
Early mornin'
Blowin'
Like a crackhead getting a hit
Blow
Middle of the day
Gotta go all the way
Blow
Gotta get my get right at night
Blow
And now I sit in my backstage cage
Ready to blow.

DUENDE: Your attitude blows
You don't even realize
That passion stopped dripping
from your horn's spit valve?
What did you do?

JUNIOR: I don't know . . .
I lost it . . .
I'm lost.
Maybe I should go look for myself

DUENDE: Whatever it takes

JUNIOR: Is that what you want?
Will you leave when I'm done?

DUENDE: You'll be done if I leave

JUNIOR: Then I'll go look for myself
If I should return
By the time I get back
Please ask me to wait

DUENDE: Then make it quick baby boy
   'Cause you can go
   brain dead in seconds
   If you don't catch your breath.

JUNIOR: I can't remember the last time
   I took a good deep breath

DUENDE: What is it that makes one breath
   Any different than the other?

JUNIOR: I can't remember

DUENDE: Did you ever stop to hear one breath?

JUNIOR: I can't remember
   I can't remember
   When

   the begin began

DUENDE: In the beginning,
   Buddy Bolden laid his head on my lap
   Seeking rest from mental chaos
   His breath became the beginning
   and you, the child of that creation
   In the beginning
   I held you in my arms.
   Junior, son of Satchmo
   Who breathed into my ear
   Son of Miles
   Whose breath caressed my belly
   Brother of Wynton
   Who nightly blows
   along the slope of my neck
   And Arturo
   Who just blows and blows
   till you and I remember
   That Jazz
   is your beginning

And Jazz
will be your end
Your breath is older
Than even you can comprehend

JUNIOR: You sure love to hear yourself
talk . . .
Then tell me Angel
Am I gonna fly too close to the sun
tonight?
Am I gonna burn what little wings I
have left, tonight?

DUENDE: I simply want you to remember
Tell this tale in the same vein
Of every other once upon a time
And remember all those you forgot
to forget
Do you remember?
Your first breath was filled with
fluid!

JUNIOR: Can't forget!

DUENDE: Painful and scary, wasn't it?

JUNIOR: Should not forget
'Cause if I don't tell it, it may never be told
Secondhand music notes
Still hang in the air from the
other pipers
Who have played before me
Clinging to the walls
Like graffiti that won't come off
No matter how hard you scrub
To some, it's vandalism

DUENDE: To some, it's art

JUNIOR: To some, it's dead
And some

want to keep it . . .
Same as it ever was

DUENDE: Same as it never was

JUNIOR: Same as it ever was

DUENDE: Same as it never was

JUNIOR: Am I Ishmael?

DUENDE: On a journey.

JUNIOR: Am I Odysseus?

DUENDE: Lost.

JUNIOR: Am I Ellison's Invisible Man?

DUENDE: I
    can see you, portrait of an artist trapped
    between
    The art and a hard-ass place

JUNIOR: I only wanted to live life
    Happily ever after

DUENDE: The answer's in the breath

JUNIOR: Gave up my right to remain silent
    So anything I say,
    Can and will be held against me
    So don't push me,
    'cause I'm close to the edge!
    Tell me,
    Am I the trumpet player
    Playing the role
    of the trumpet player?
    The trumpet player,
    the late-night Dark Gable
    the music is a shot of hot Cognac
    mixed with honey
    sliding down your throat

an old rhythm gyrates in your ear
and you like it
the trumpet player
howling at the moon
but the moonlight
is just another spotlight
The trumpet player
waiting for the last call
for alcohol before he
Goes down forever
I'm drowning in music notes
and vodka
The trumpet player
looking for another vein
to shoot that trumpet solo in
to keep me going
But I'm playing
and I'm living
and I am
I, feel like a Raider
of this lost art
Another archaeologist
passing through
with all these ghosts around me
And they come round me
like they understand
like they know me and shit
like we speak the same language
like they know the secret handshake
call me brother
like we brothers
like they momma tuck my daddy
like my momma tuck they daddy
But they don't respect my voodoo
like they don't respect me
don't respect my music
talking

talking
loud
loud
loud
like they scared
scared they gonna hear the truth
coming out my music
hear the truth
coming for they soul
coming round the mountain
coming for they soul
like me
Like my music
Soul music
like they understand my music
like it's that easy
some call it jazz
call it
call it
like it's gonna answer the phone
call it hip-hop meets jazz
call it
call it
don't you hear the phone's still
ringing
call me a progressive
postmodern
urban
contemporary
future aesthetical
musician
that's what I am
that's what I do
like the label's gonna mean
something
like it's gonna make me,
me

like anybody's qualified
to tell me
who me is
Except me
like I wasn't here the whole time
Like I just took a vacation
Left me alone
by myself
to ponder the ramifications
of me being me
And then
I returned back to me
Refreshed
rested
and rejuvenated
to continue this journey
with me
on my never-ending search to find
me

DUENDE: That's why I am here.
    To search and rescue
    Let me hold your breath
    so I can take you back

JUNIOR: With all the frustrations and
    expectations?

DUENDE: Let me hold your breath

JUNIOR: All the traditions and
    contradictions?

DUENDE: The only way
    To find your way
    Is to journey back

JUNIOR: I was fine till you got here!

DUENDE: Really?

JUNIOR: Where were you when I needed you?
    I waited hours for your call
    Now you bring your ass here,
    'round midnight,
    Ready to knock me from the ladder
    Seduce me,
    into your stream of consciousness
    Le le le le le le
    Le le le le le le la
    But where the fuck were you
    When I needed you?
    Well
    I'm not ready for submission,
    bitch
    Ain't no room for that in my
    aesthetic.
    So go somewhere else
    Amuse someone else
    Make a potion
    Cast a spell
    Go sleep with Zeus
    Go conquer hell
    Go and do whatever Duendes do
    And I doubt
    they do much of anything anyway.
    Just go!
    But before you do, understand this,
    You cannot "hold" my breath
    Because I no longer have it
    I lost it
    Winter stole it
    one cold night,
    The night that you were gone
    The same night the fire burned
    The night the smoke was blinding
    Ashes to Ashes
    Blue Black

like Miles!
And what did you ever do for him?
Miles Davis

Arthritis
Car accident
Cocaine use
Diabetes
drinking
Drug-induced delusions
gallstone operation
hallucinations
heart palpitations
heroin habit
hip operation
larynx nodes
liver infection
police beating
got himself shot
or did he shoot himself?
sickle cell anemia
stroke
throat operation
ulcer
But his death certificate said
he died of cardiac arrest
due to respiratory failure
Respiratory failure due to
pneumonia
And where were you
Were you out,
"holding his breath"?
Were you the one?
Did you knock Bunk Johnson's
front teeth out his mouth?
Did you make his trumpet bleed?
What did you ever do for that man?

How 'bout Clifford Brown
Good brother
Died young in a car crash
Did you put him to sleep
in the back of that car?
Booker Little,
died young
Fats Navarro,
Tuberculosis killed him
Or was it you
Spitting up blood
Tuberculosis and narcotic addiction
And where were you?
Nah, Don't come here
trying to do me no favors.
I was fine till you got here!
Ashes to Ashes
I Lost!
I Lost!
And where the fuck were you
When I needed you?

DUENDE: You have the nerve to ask me
where I was?

Newport Jazz Festival

I was there
Lookin' hot
I wore a red dress
And you,
Wanted to wear the lady
On the corner table.

Bard College

1989
Wadada Leo Smith
Held a horn in your hand

I was there
You said you loved my scent
Lilacs
Always lilacs

Lincoln Center

out of doors

You saw me,
there,
In the reflecting pool
Gdańsk, Poland

I wore a raw amber necklace and nothing else
It went so well with your horn
Zeus was furious
That was the first time
You looked reality in the eyes
As they called you "nigger"
to your face
And I'm the one
with the scars to show for it
Dark deep blue varicose veins
The veins grow bluer
The wrinkles deeper
Darker
As the critics
try to kiss you good night

And you asked me
where I was
I was there when you were four
As you picked up your first trumpet
Remember that?

[*Pause.*]

Spine straight
Feet flat

Shoulders back
Relax
Spine straight
Feet flat
Shoulders back
Relax

JUNIOR: Why are you doing this?

DUENDE: So you can remember

JUNIOR: What are you trying to do?
Seduce me?

DUENDE: I already have,
Let's go

DUENDE AND JUNIOR: Spine straight Feet flat
Shoulders back Relax
Spine straight Feet flat
Shoulders back Relax
Spine straight

Feet flat
Shoulders back
Relax

[TRUMPETER *plays scales.*]

JUNIOR: Spine straight Feet flat
Shoulders back Relax

[TRUMPETER *keeps playing throughout.*]

DUENDE: I can hear you,
Tunin' up
Playin' horn was your game
Born with a silver trumpet
in your mouth
You'd play the horn
before you talked
Born,

On the after beat
You patted your foot
before you walked
When you tuned up
I could hear you
Clean across the river
I could hear you
Clean across the river
You woke up the workin' people
And kept the easy, living
I can hear you callin'
I can hear you callin'
I watch you
I watch you
You're callin' your flock now
You're callin' your flock now
Here you come

JUNIOR: I came home late, one night
    after a Yankee game
    and found my father

[TRUMPETER *plays pan piper.*]

    sitting in our living room
    listening to Miles Davis's
    Sketches of Spain.
    I think it was,
    my father
    crying like a baby
    so I stop
    and look
    I don't say anything
    just looking
    now, if you know my father
    tears don't just fall for anything
    keeps that stuff close
    like he only has so much to spare

so I'm looking
almost afraid to move
don't wanna spoil his moment
but I also can't turn away
it was almost beautiful
and I realize I'm not breathing
so I take a breath
and he sees me
and he just stares
eyes full of tears
and me
Miles joins in
making the moment almost corny
and then
my father says
"Do you hear that trumpet?"
tears rolling
"Isn't it beautiful?
Do you hear that?
And don't just listen
I want you to hear it"
so I didn't listen
I just shut up
and heard it
heard that trumpet cry
and laugh
and testify
and scream
and holla
seduce
and preach
and I heard it
and I cried
from somewhere deep
and private
cried like I was supposed to
so there we were

Crying
and we never said a word
to each other
started to look at the trumpet
a little different after that
I knew I could never come to it
without having something to say
so when you play
you have to play
like it's your last time
a one-time moment
that never happens again
no matter how hard
you try to re-create it

[TRUMPETER *stops.*]

DUENDE: You're only born once

JUNIOR: Yeah,
I was born in St. Francis Hospital

[DUENDE *sings Andrés Eloy Blanco's poem "Píntame Angelitos Negros" over-lapping* JUNIOR's *following speech.*]

To my mother, Puerto Rican
my father, black
my momma said,
that at the time I was born
the nurses were surprised
that this Puerto Rican woman
was having this
black boy
from this
black man
didn't like,
this black baby boy
born before his time
premature
half black

baby boys
didn't fit in,
back in those days
but my momma,
didn't care if the world was ready
or not
it was my turn

I grew up an only child
guess my momma didn't want
the world to have
another half-and-half from her
but I didn't mind being alone
sitting in my room
creating a world all my own
like kids are supposed to
invisible friends
dreaming
about what it would be like
grown up
and I wanted to be a baseball player

to be a Yankee

like Reggie Jackson

DUENDE: Mr. October

JUNIOR: Yeah,
   doin' it
   listening to the crowd
   I didn't live too far from Yankee
   Stadium
   so some nights
   I would just go
   and feel the atmosphere
   the energy
   nothing like the rush
   that wave of excitement

when all those people are there
pulling together

can you hear it?

DUENDE: Yes

That was just a dream then
something you think about
but nobody's around
to show you how to really get there
anyway,
music was something else to do
something that my parents
could understand
my father gave me a trumpet
when I was young

[TRUMPETER *practices "When the Saints Go Marching In."*]

but it was just like anything else
a child would get
a toy you play with
for a couple of days
after that it becomes
just another thing in your room
an island of misfit toys

[TRUMPETER *stops playing.*]

Like bows and arrows,
cowboys and Indians,
parachuted men,
plastic soldiers,
and G.I. Joes

JUNIOR: Yeah . . .
My father went to Vietnam
Ain't much good come from that.
It only taught him 'bout death.

[TRUMPETER *plays "Reveille."*]

In World War II,
Only fifteen to twenty percent
of combat infantry
Were willing to fire their rifles.
In Korea,
About fifty percent,
In Vietnam,
ninety percent
He didn't talk about it much

Didn't talk about it much
But when he did . . .
We'd run physical training
in the morning
And every time
your left foot hit the deck
you'd chant,
"Kill, kill, kill, kill"
Drilled into your mind so much,
that if it came down to it
It didn't bother you
Everyone that you know you killed
And then there are
your stages of killing
The concern 'bout killing
The actual kill
The exhilaration
Remorse
Rationalization

DUENDE: And

[TRUMPETER *stops playing.*]

the acceptance

JUNIOR: Yes

DUENDE: You accepted your first trumpet
    as a gift from your father

JUNIOR: Told me stories
    about his friend Gates,
    music man
    Could tell you
    who recorded what and when
    He was a regular jukebox
    Played trumpet
    Could run down all the players
    And their styles
    Carried a trumpet in his bag
    Kept him sane.
    He said,
    "Couldn't play no horn in the bush
    Ain't no good sound gonna come out."
    The horn will reveal all . . .
    If you let it.
    My father always said . . .

DUENDE: "You should know the horn
    like you know a woman's body"

JUNIOR: Gates would just pull out that horn
    And just look at it

DUENDE: Run his fingers along the valves
    And the slope of the neck

JUNIOR: Would say,
    "you gotta know this horn
    Like you know a woman"
    One day
    Gates didn't come back
    from the bush
    They didn't find him

DUENDE: Found his horn

JUNIOR: And my father gave it to me

DUENDE: And how well do you know your horn?

JUNIOR: Like I know a woman's body

DUENDE: Have you found its G-spot?

JUNIOR: A, B, C, D, E, F, and G

DUENDE: That many?
    I'm lucky
    I even got one the last time
    You found "my" G-spot
    when you played "Blue Sweat."

[TRUMPETER *plays "Blue Sweat."*]

    Remember that?

JUNIOR: I don't think about that anymore.

DUENDE: Hot and Sweaty
    Mnun
    What inspired that?

JUNIOR: Daddy told me
    'bout how he met my momma
    Puerto Rican girl
    from Spanish Harlem
    She loved him
    He loved her
    With all her broken English.
    He helped her put it together
    And in between hidden kisses
    And heated exchanges
    She practiced them words.
    They hid from a world
    That wouldn't understand
    Their mixed-up love.
    What would her momma say
    'Bout this *moreno*

Some dark-skinned man
That America was afraid of.
Too much trouble for a family

DUENDE: "*Que no habla ingles.*"

JUNIOR: And for this black man
    Who couldn't bring
    his little *mammita* home
    What would his momma say
    'bout her son
    Who didn't bring home a black girl
    went out tippin'
    and fell at the feet
    of the first *mira mira*
    he crossed paths with
    so they hid it
    Deeper than any Spic
    or Nigger remark could touch them
    They just fell in love
    He knew he was hooked
    As soon as he heard
    the sound of her hips
    Rubbing against
    her flower-print dress

DUENDE [*as Mrs. McCullough*]: I wore
    a flower-print dress
    Made me feel so

JUNIOR [*as Mr. McCullough*]: Pretty.
    Now, that ain't a word
    a man like me would use much
    But that dress . . .
    She just looked so pretty and

DUENDE [*as Mrs. McCullough*]: Cute . . .
    you couldn't tell me
    I didn't look

very cute in my dress.
my flower-print dress
hangin' on me just right
Hugging me
in the way
a flower-print dress
is supposed to . . .
I knew he was looking
Because I was looking.

JUNIOR [*as Mr. McCullough*]: Hot.
it was always so damn hot.
you know?
that evil type of hot
That
get off me
don't even look at me
type of hot
but there she was

DUENDE [*as Mrs. McCullough*]: There he was . . .
looking.
you know? . . .
in that way that men be lookin'
wanting to know everything too fast
Except all the right things
at the right time

JUNIOR [*as Mr. McCullough*]: And it was the right time
to make a new friend
'cause all I was looking for was . . .

DUENDE [*as Mrs. McCullough*]: a good time.
and I was gonna have
a good time too.
I was always looking
too good not to . . .
So I make my way over to his way . . .

JUNIOR [*as Mr. McCullough*]: I eased up next to her
　And waited

JUNIOR AND DUENDE: For my song to come on

[TRUMPETER *stops playing.*]

DUENDE: That's why you wrote "Blue Sweat."

JUNIOR: "Blue Sweat."
　I forgot about "Blue Sweat."
　Well,
　that one's for my parents
　and I was happy
　then
　playing what I knew
　And it felt good
　Felt like it's supposed to feel
　When you come to the Music
　Honest
　Raw
　And real
　Or the music won't work
　It just won't act right
　Like a child
　Who you tried your best to raise
　But every now and then
　You've got to put it in its place
　But the critics
　didn't know my parents
　Didn't care
　that this moment was for them
　Said things like,

DUENDE: "Junior McCullough,
　Jazz man
　Reputation unstable,
　Music ideas unfocused
　Chaos in Cadence

What the hell is he trying to say?!
We liked it better when he was
brash arrogant
and bold
He should leave the
sentimental stuff to Kenny G."

JUNIOR: It was the first time
    I started to think about
    the shit I was playing
    Overthinking it
    I mean,
    I feel it,
    I play it,
    just like that
    The way I hear it
    And let it lay
    The way it's gonna lay

DUENDE: After that,
    You started thinking
    more about your image
    brash
    arrogant
    and bold,

JUNIOR: Why not?!
    I realized
    and reimagined myself
    Inside of myself
    Learned how to play the game hard
    I didn't just cross the line
    I snorted it
    Fucked it in every position
    you can't think of
    That line between love and hate
    luck and fate
    And you know that line is thin

Tryin' to get as far away
from that baby boy
my momma knew
My daddy knew
just another one of the
puff puff pass people
passing through life in a fog
at all the right parties
Making the right connections

For all the wrong reasons
but here I come
Here I am
So I blow
and blow
Can't you hear the crowd

And blow
and blow
and blow
They love me
And blow
and blow
And I'm blowin' it
I'm blowin' it
Lost in the sauce

Surrounded by all these people,
And if I can't dazzle them
with my brilliance
I will baffle them with my bullshit

Tryin' to make them like family . . .
My Family

DUENDE: But your family wasn't a happy one

JUNIOR: No.
Daddy came back from the war,
came home different

DUENDE: But your parents,
    They loved each other very much
    I could smell
    the scent of their passion,
    when you used to play "Blue Sweat."

JUNIOR: Maybe what you smell
    is my daddy
    Holding a dead man's horn
    in his hand
    And he gave it to me

DUENDE: Your momma didn't let you blow
    that horn in the house, did she?

JUNIOR: She said
    I should get a job
    workin' for transit
    Said,
    "There's always a steady gig
    in transit."
    Life could have been
    a much easier ride

DUENDE: Not in transit

JUNIOR: Daddy came home
    Unable to see his own eyes in mine

DUENDE: Momma's baby.
    Poppa's maybe?

JUNIOR: To belong or to replace

DUENDE: Man of the house?

JUNIOR: Only one can survive

DUENDE: How did you survive?

JUNIOR: In music notes!
    and I come home different every day.

DUENDE: You see your mom and dad
  in the work you create
  don't you?

JUNIOR: No,
  I don't anymore
  But if I did,
  My dad would have to be
  the Jazz I play
  And my momma
  the Blues I do

DUENDE: What's your religion?

JUNIOR: I'm a devout musician

DUENDE: In the church of denial

JUNIOR: Always strugglin' to survive
  the trial and tribulation
  set before me

DUENDE: Your mother died
  after you ran away . . .

JUNIOR: I don't want to talk about that.

DUENDE: People think you're going crazy,
  Say they see you
  talking to your horn.

JUNIOR: That's my private conversation
  with God.
  A back-and-forth conversation
  The highest level of improvisation
  But I ain't got nothing to say
  to him right now

DUENDE: You talk to God?

JUNIOR: Yeah
  Sometimes.

And he talked to me
Once.
In the voice of an old man
Who lived on my block
Chillin' on the corner
Playing chess by himself
He said
"Hello,
How are you now?
My name is Amadou
That's what everybody calls me.
When I first came to this country
I was excited
about all the things
that I could do,
The simple things
that people here take for granted.
So, when I would listen to people
talking
about the everyday things they did,
I would say,
I'm a do that
Yes
Yes, I'm a do that
So people just started calling me
Amadou
Yo, Amadou
How do you do, Amadou?
What's up, Amadou?
And the name just stuck Amadou,
yes,
I like that

[*As if turning to see* JUNIOR]

Hello, Junior.
How are you doing, boy?
I must say

You are not looking very well
It's because you walk
to different drum
I always want to play that drum
with you
But you keep drum to yourself
Your journey,
begins with me
Story is simple
One everybody knows
back where I come from
A ritual of self-definition
and preservation
At home,
When a woman is pregnant,
She goes out into the wilderness
with a few friends
And together
they meditate until they hear
the song of the child.

[DUENDE *hums lullaby like moan.*]

Every soul has its own vibration
Unique flavor and purpose
When the women attune to the song,
they sing it out loud.
And return
to teach it to everyone else.
When the child is born,
The community sings the song.
Later,
when the child goes to school
The village chants the song again.
When the child reaches adulthood,
The people come together and sing.
And at the time of marriage,
the grown child hears their song again.

Finally,
when the soul prepares to pass
from this world,
Family and friends
gather by the grown child's bed,
Just as they did at their birth,
and sing them into the next life.
I told you,
just like that Junior,
You may not have grown up
in my tribe
And maybe no one
sang your song to you
But life is always reminding you
When you are in tune with yourself
And when you are not
And the only way you are gonna be
Everything you are supposed to be
Is if you go and find your song
And your song

Is sitting farther that your ears can hear
Far past this neighborhood
Who only hear
what they want to hear
Past your friends
Even past your family
Yes
Even your family
If you do not go now
The rhythm that plays in you
will stop
The fire that burns
may not burn as bright
And your soul
will not look at the world
with wonder

Only contempt
I have heard you play your trumpet
And it cries for more
You cry for more
In the end, hopefully,
You will find your song
and sing it well.
And now
you know I don't have much money
But when you give
It always comes back
Like I know you will
take this."

And I said nothing
Stood up tall
And said nothing
But as I walked away
You heard all
that needed to be said
In the rhythm of my step.
And I'm a do that
I'm a do that
I'm a do that
Yes
I'm a do that
And I left

[TRUMPETER *plays Kenny G.*]

DUENDE: You left to do that?

JUNIOR: The night I left
    I gave my mother my laundry to wash
    So she wouldn't suspect
    Laid at the foot of my mother's bed
    Like I use to do as a child
    Until she fell asleep
    And then sat up late with my father in silence

As he listened to his soul
waste away inside his old records
By the time the morning came
I was already gone
Gone to find the rest of myself
And I found me
In late-night jam sessions
And bullshit jobs
to keep my pockets wet
And in bands
looking for a trumpet player
who could keep time
And the older cats like
Clark Terry
Who would
take a moment in between sets
to drop a little knowledge on you
To give you a little bit
To make it through another day
And I didn't leave
any bread crumbs behind
And I didn't look back
And I made a name
for my newfound self
Bad young trumpet player
on the scene
The underground whispers
turn up a little louder
Got me a record deal
Signed my soul on the dotted line
In blood,
Sweat, and tears
But I don't care
I've got something to say
And I'm saying it and playing it
Some shit that's so old it's new
And the critics cheered

Heard shit
I wasn't even trying to say
And the phone won't stop ringing
Everybody wants to hear my story
And this is why
I ran away
To be this person
At this moment right now

[TRUMPETER *stops playing.*]

DUENDE: And the record didn't sell shit!

JUNIOR: Not enough of this
   Too much of that
   Not enough pop for the people
   But the masses are asses
   They only like what they can digest
   And it's gotta go down easy
   So I stopped being me
   And became one of them
   Playing whatever makes them happy

DUENDE: What about the drugs?

JUNIOR: What drugs?

DUENDE: You didn't think
   I was gonna skip the drug issue
   Did you?
   Even Miles went into a barn
   and kicked

JUNIOR: The Drugs,
   The Drugs
   It's so cliché
   The drugs
   I only dibbled and dabbled
   Some people dibble more than they
   dabble with their doobies,

But I didn't
Let me tell ya,
I blame it all on the titi
A brand new baby
Gets that first taste
of mother's milk
Bang Zoom
On a mission
for a little sunshine ever since.
From milk
To candy
To soda
Wine coolers
And malt liquor
Cigarettes
To weed
Vodka and cocaine
Just that social gat fly
Tryin' to get in
when you fit in
doin' as the dummies do
hoping I could find the flavor
of that first fix
So I blame it all on the titi
From my first step,
I've been on a journey
Have walked with the low down
and dirty
Sat in the lion's den
Watched them inject
And reject themselves
Trying to get higher
and higher
Had to learn the double talk well
You can go crazy
if you ain't got no interpreter
Had to confront

Educate
And stimulate the dragon
Had to learn
that you can't always
destroy the dragon
He's been around long before me

DUENDE: That's right
I've been around a long time

JUNIOR: I saw the dragon
in a child one time

DUENDE: Not a dragon.
You saw me.

Málaga 1997

JUNIOR: I was there
Me
Sitting in a flamenco class
Writing music for a student recital
For a woman I was trying to impress

[TRUMPETER *plays.*]

Finesse
And undress
Funny how the promise
of some good loving
And a check
Could make a man
do almost anything
And in the middle of all that
Just happy to be here
Juvenile energy
There was this one little girl
Kinda hiding in the back
Her steps were careful
Almost apologetic

You could almost miss her
Behind the others
Other woman dancing
She followed
A half-step behind
Trying to keep up
The moment growing and swirling
And so did she
Stronger
With every three count
And then
She
Ten years old
Transformed
Riding on flamenco rhythms
Dancing with spirits
Flying on an unrehearsed symphony
Little girl
So old
Caught up in this holy dance
With the Holy Ghost

DUENDE: Duende

JUNIOR: Her Dragon
Eyes closed
Body wailing.
I have yet to feel so free.
And I hate her
All that she is
All that she's gonna be
And I hate me
And all that I'm not
All that I use to be
I see the dragon in her
Ten years old
But where is mine?

DUENDE: Lorca understood it

JUNIOR: Duende
    That deep song

DUENDE: mysterious
    Cante jondo

JUNIOR: I could see it

DUENDE: Lorca knew

JUNIOR: I can't explain it

DUENDE: I can!
    Duende only comes
    when you surrender to the fire
    It's a struggle
    Can't find it in the throat.
    Climbs up inside you
    From the soles of the feet.

JUNIOR: Flamenco
    Jazz
    It's all blues
    It's all blues
    Flamenco
    Jazz
    It's all blues
    It's all blues
    All blues
    They all got that,
    Deep song

DUENDE: It's not a question of ability
    but of . . .

JUNIOR: Duende

DUENDE: Yes, true living style,

JUNIOR: Jimi Hendrix,
    voodoo child
    screaming through a purple haze

with a guitar string
wrapped around his throat

DUENDE: Of blood,

JUNIOR: Robert Johnson,
crossroad preachin'

DUENDE: Of ancient culture,

JUNIOR: Miles,
You could see it all over his face.

DUENDE: Spontaneous creation.

JUNIOR: Monk, drank it

DUENDE: Straight no chaser

JUNIOR: Bird LIVES in it

DUENDE: In me

JUNIOR: Billie took a bite from that fruit
So did the man who stands
Second tenor from center
on my grandma's church choir,
So did the sax player
who stands in the number-two train tunnel
Collecting change in a bottle,
so did the junkie on the corner
Who conducts a daily orchestra
collecting sound bites
as life bites him in the ass
so did my momma
so did I
Bit a bite
and found you
Duende

[DUENDE *performs footwork.*]

DUENDE: Duende rises through the body
   Burns through the souls
   of a dancer's feet
   Duende

JUNIOR: Courses through the blood
   Breaks through a poet's back
   like a pair of wings
   Smokes through the lungs

DUENDE: Duende

JUNIOR: Scorches the voice
   Gives life to words
   Blows fire through the horn

DUENDE: Duende

JUNIOR: It is risky and deathward leaning
   And I have yet to feel so free

   Most of us are gone
   by the time we hit fifty
   If we're even lucky
   to reach that age. I am black,
   and a horn player,
   I expect very little
   from my life expectancy
   They warned me
   that if I took up this instrument,
   I'd prove a high insurance risk
   Yet my insurance is this horn
   I'm not cursed
   to push a rock up hill
   I'm cursed to carry this

[TRUMPETER *stops playing.*]

DUENDE: Cursed?
   Cursed?
   It was a gift from me.

[*The following dialogue overlaps.*]

Cursed!
I'm the one who's cursed
Cursed to keep on giving

JUNIOR: Cursed to find salvation
nowhere else but in its metal

DUENDE: Giving legacies
To those who do not want them

JUNIOR: Cursed to see my reflection
in its polish

DUENDE: Voices to those who will not sing

JUNIOR: Cursed to spill
all my last breaths
into its chamber

DUENDE: Trumpets to those who will not blow

JUNIOR: Cursed to run
Cursed to hide
It's the curs-ed gift that keeps on giving.

[*Overlap ends.*]

DUENDE: I'm the one who's cursed
And tired of giving!
You have got the nerve
To look a gift horse in the mouth.
I no longer stand here
for pure pleasure
I'm fighting to survive
I'm a thing of myths and legends
I have stared Medusa in the eyes
I came to you, per your request
I'm well prepared
to play with death
I have use for you

And I know,
that you have use for me
Look into "my" eyes,
Now,
Tell me what you see

JUNIOR: You can keep
your fucking Duende!

DUENDE [*singing*]: *Rosa Blanca*
que cae en el río
Que a su rama ya no ha de volver
Desojada por un mal cariño
Que ha dejado morir su querer
Tan hermosa que ella se veía
Y en su rama guardaba su amor
Pero ahora esta triste y sombría
Pobre rosa, perdió su color.

JUNIOR: How do you know that song?

DUENDE: *Si la hubiesen visto en aquel tiempo*
Cuando el aire del río la asotaba
Cuando llegaba la noche hermosa
Su rocío de amor la llenava
Pero hoy, que a pasado aquel tiempo
De esa rosa ya no queda nada
Solo el recuerdo perdido
De una rosa en el río sepultada
Solo el recuerdo perdido
De una rosa en el río sepultada
Si es que ustedes aman mucho
Como la rosa del cuento
No lloren por un cariño
Voten sus penas riendo
Alegres vivan la vida
Y olviden ese querer
Que unos se van y otros vienen
Trayendo bellos placeres

Que les hará comprender
Que el primero no es amor
Tan sólo es una ilusión
Que nos hace enloquecer

Que el primero
no es amor
Tan sólo es una ilusión
Que nos hace enloquecer
Pobre rosa que se ha muerto

[TRUMPETER *begins to play "Momma Had a Suitcase."*]

Que se quedó en el olvido
Por culpa de un mal querer

JUNIOR: If Momma had a suitcase,
    Then she kept that suitcase from me
    Played the part of Momma well,
    Even after the curtain went down
    Never looked for applause,
    That just wasn't her way.
    But my momma could sing,
    Had her way
    of singing them songs
    In that Hallelujah praise the lord way
    Use to wrap herself
    Round a song
    Make the song do like she'd say
    Sing a song
    Till it can't be sung no more
    Could hear her soul
    come jumping through them songs
    Like you could hear my soul
    Come jumping through my horn
    And if Momma had a suitcase,
    She kept that suitcase from me
    Never let me see them dreams,
    Never knew

who she wanted to be
Never knew
who she was suppose to be
My momma,
Strong,
Raised me
Strong
And beautiful
Wanted what all mommas are suppose to want
When they become mommas
For her baby boy to be happy

But she didn't have to give up
them dreams for me
Didn't have to become
What mommas become
When they become mommas
Gave up her breath
so I could breathe
Spoke another tongue
Had so much to say
She was happy then
The times she sang
The times I played
I've never felt so
Sounded so
Horrified
And Beautiful
In my life

DUENDE [*singing*]: Your momma had a suitcase
    Full of papers in the house
    Your momma had a suitcase
    Hidden deep beneath the couch
    She'd lock it and unlock it
    Only for her eyes to see
    But one day I watched her closely
    And at night I stole the key

Little did you know
That your momma had no choice
That she used that little suitcase
As a prison for her voice
Wrote her words
on all types of paper
From coffee napkins to bamboo
Chose a blue suitcase for a reason,
'Cause the truest truths are blue
She sat at her window
Once that suitcase was gone
But I spoke to her daily
Trying to find her new song
She tried to release me

Tried to set Duende free
But I'm cursed to keep giving
Gave her new songs to breathe
And here you are her mirror image
Drowning Duende in blues
I see death at your doorstep
Time has come to pay dues

[TRUMPETER *stops playing.*]

JUNIOR: Stop singing . . .
I don't wanna hear that . . .
Hear her . . .

DUENDE: *Ven aquí Junito,*
Ven a la ventana

Desde aquí se ve todo
Aquí, puedes respirar

JUNIOR: Momma
Momma
My mother

[TRUMPETER *plays* soleá.]

Nosy Mrs. McCullough
Sits at the window
Eyes empty
Vacant
Void
Elbows nailed to a pillow
Always watching
Lookie Lookie Lookie
Look-a-here Look-a-here Look-a-here
Wannabe everybody's momma
Big momma bird in the nest
Always listening
Every day
To that park percussion
Laughter,
Hand claps
And finger snaps
Nosy Mrs. McCullough
Momma
All up in the Kool-Aid and don't
know the flavor
All up in my ass
and don't know shit
What she lookin' for?
What's she starin' at?
Just sits there
Minding everybody's business
Every day

DUENDE: While Mr. McCullough

JUNIOR: Daddy

DUENDE: Sweeps

JUNIOR: Starts at seven

DUENDE: And sweeps

Early morning
Cleans and sweeps

And dumps it in black Hefty bags
Big black Hefty bags
All by eight forty-seven

JUNIOR: Every day

DUENDE: Your daddy
Eyes vacant
Does his duty
Sings Bob Dylan songs
Learned in Vietnam
Knock, knock, knockin'
on heaven's door
Did his duty
Tour of duty
For the red, white, and blue
Washes away
Melted snow cones
And crack vials
Red, white, and blue
Sweeps the trash talk
Of hollow hoop dreams
The leftover words
Of street-taught deceivers
Who promise flying lessons
in the eye of a needle
The sound bites of
photo op hunting
One-stop shopping politicians
Who just
Promise
Your daddy
Cleans and sweeps
All the forgotten smiles
From family reunions and cookouts
All the spit and stories
Swapped by part-time lovers
and old friends
Who made the park come alive

JUNIOR: But the park is alive
   With death

DUENDE: Yes

JUNIOR: Dry brown blood

DUENDE: Yes

JUNIOR: Somebody was bleeding blood
   "Oh no, Not my baby!"

DUENDE: Yes

JUNIOR: Cops and robbers play the bang bang

DUENDE: Yes

JUNIOR: Play it till the final curtain

DUENDE: Yes

JUNIOR: Watch the people duck, dodge, and die

DUENDE: Yes

JUNIOR: Caught up in the crossfire
   at the crossroads

DUENDE: Yes

JUNIOR: And so Daddy

DUENDE: Mr. McCullough

JUNIOR: Sweeps

   Every morning

DUENDE: All the sadness

JUNIOR: Red-brown blood

DUENDE: Madness

JUNIOR: Sweeps

DUENDE: Red, white, blue

JUNIOR: Used condoms

DUENDE: Jawbreakers

JUNIOR: And now or later

DUENDE: Gladness

JUNIOR: And packs it
     in big black Hefty bags

DUENDE: All by eight forty-seven

JUNIOR: Every day

DUENDE: And then there's Junior

JUNIOR: That's me
     I was born in seven months
     Not nine
     Came two months too soon
     So the world always seemed
     two steps behind

DUENDE: Could walk in eight months
     real good
     Learned his ABCs right after

JUNIOR: And my mommy swore
     I wouldn't be no hood
     Wanted to keep me on Sesame Street
     Not running the streets
     With every and anybody
     'Cause I was gonna be
     Somebody
     So Mommy's little Dudley-Do-Right

DUENDE: *Que no*

JUNIOR: Can't do nothin'

DUENDE: *Dije que no!*

JUNIOR: To school and back
     Is how he interacts

DUENDE: No parties?
    No secret hallway kisses?
    No chillin' on the corner?
    No last-second
    basketball game misses?
    Just your room

JUNIOR: And my music

DUENDE: *Y tu ventana*

JUNIOR: And my window

DUENDE: Like your momma

JUNIOR: Like my momma
    And I had
    that caged bird complex in effect
    I wanted out
    Wanted to take a long slow drag
    off life
    Breathe it in deep
    But I couldn't get a puff
    And my jones was coming down
    And I started to sweat
    And the world was calling
    Calling
    Calling
    Calling
    Calling

DUENDE [*singing*]: I can hear you calling

JUNIOR: Calling
    Calling
    Calling
    Calling
    I sat
    Listened
    Waited
    Calling

Calling
Calling
Calling

DUENDE [*singing*]: I can hear you calling

JUNIOR: Calling
Calling
Calling
Calling
One day I
stopped
And answered
"Yes!"

DUENDE: Mrs. McCullough
Calling
Junior!

JUNIOR: Calling
Calling
Calling
Calling

DUENDE: "Junior!"

JUNIOR: Running
Running
Ran
Going Going
Got ta get gone

DUENDE: "Junior!"

JUNIOR: See him
Saw him Spot him
Got him
Gone

DUENDE: "Junior,
You come back here, boy!"
"Junior!"

JUNIOR: But I never came back

DUENDE: "You, Come back!"

JUNIOR: Never came back

>   Home
>   You know,
>   some say I'm dead
>   Found me dead
>   in that park
>   Some say I'm Livin' life long
>   And some say something different
>   Every day
>   Different situation
>   Different ending
>   Moral lessons
>   Urban lessons
>   For the people
>   by the people
>   Need our lessons
>   Learn our lessons
>   Painful pill to swallow

DUENDE: Junior!

JUNIOR: Urban Legend
>   That's why
>   My daddy Mr. McCullough

DUENDE: Junior

JUNIOR: Cleans and sweeps
>   And my mother
>   Nosy Mrs. McCullough

DUENDE: Junito

JUNIOR: Sits and Waits
>   Every day

DUENDE: So what are you waiting for?

JUNIOR: I'm not waiting.
   I'm already here
   Trapped
   In the biggest concert of them all
   Where you're forced to play
   That same old shuffle-along song
   Steppin' and fetchin'
   Your way to the top

   So take a seat
   People
   People
   People
   Is everybody in?
   Is everybody in?
   Is everybody in?
   The ceremony is about to begin

   Have the libations been poured?
   The chicken bones gathered?
   The spliffs
   ah, the mighty spliffs
   rolled to perfection?
   No,
   go get Jehovah
   Allah
   Jah
   Olodumare
   Or whatever you call him
   Or her
   Who knows?
   Could be?

[*Singing.*]

   Who knows?
   Could be?
   The Almighty
   Alpha and Omega

The Supreme Being
Get him on the line
Tell him that I am here.
From the birth to the earth
The cradle to the grave
land of MTV
And the modern-day slave
From the womb to the tomb
It's so old it's new
And now the moment
you haven't been waiting for

It's the new coon review.

See it all
Take a picture
Get a good look
It's a coming-out party baby
The gloves are off
The doors are wide open
I got all my skeletons behind me
Ready to bring the ruckus
To all you motherfuckers
Are the lights focused?
All the cues written?
'Cause this is gonna be live
No second takes
No do-overs
If I say it
I said it
Don't like it
Dead it
'Cause when it's on
it's on
And there is no room
for half-stepping
So no names will be changed
to protect the innocent

OK, OK,
I hope all the people are
comfortable
Seat belts fastened
'Cause sometimes, the ride
can get a little bumpy
Please turn off all cell phones
Pagers
And any other type of shit
that makes noise

I'm gonna be up here
Trying to tap into some deep shit
In front of a room full
of strangers
As we get to know each other
on this special one-night stand.
Let me be the nightmare
you've always wanted
Slippery Scary
Sexy
Just enough but not too much
The one your daddy warned you about
Guess who's coming to dinner
Shit,
I'm just trying
to put a little paint
where it ain't
I hope you like me
Are intrigued
about the possibilities
Think that I am deep
And of course
want to tuck me.
'Cause somebody's gonna get tucked,
up in here tonight.
Sex! Don't be scared

It's just another form of
inspiration
And I'm always looking for
Inspiration

DUENDE: I'm right here baby

JUNIOR: Let's get it out in the open.
    Sometimes when a musician's
    onstage
    On the bandstand
    On display
    The moment's right
    The energy is flying
    You're there for the ride
    Sometimes
    The moment promises
    You answer
    You can look out
    The audience looks back at you
    Caught up in the moment too

    You can see promise
    And promise can see you.
    I have promises to keep,
    And Miles to go
    before I sleep
    But the reason
    we are gathered here today
    Is to be entertained

    And you want to be entertained,
    don't you?
    Ain't that what this is all about,
    Entertainment?
    Entertainment!
    OK, OK . . .
    How many trumpet players does it take
    To change a lightbulb?

DUENDE: How many?

JUNIOR: Five.
One to change the bulb
And four to argue
About how Louis Armstrong
would have done it
Ohhhh I gotta a lot-a-more
a lot-a-more
What's the difference
between a trumpet player and God?

DUENDE: What?

JUNIOR: God
Knows he's not a trumpet player.

Yes! Entertainment
We have to stay away
from the obligatory
black cliché references

There will be no collard greens
Watermelon
Or black-eyed peas
to go with my Condoleezza Rice,
today
No gratuitous hip-hop
crotch grabbing
There will be no recourse,
discourse, or intercourse
Over the use of the word Nigger
There will be no hanging ropes,
Burning crosses
Or water hoses to illustrate
past transgressions.
No scantily clad
big booty women
will parade across the stage

Damn!
Shaft Super Fly
Puffy or Snoop Dogg
Will not
be making guest appearances
And yet,
will this still be authentic
black expression?
Let's send out an email blast
CC: it to Bell Hooks
Skip Gates
Stanley Crouch
Cornel West
Nelson George

My boy, Greg Tate.
The black intelligentsia
The Niggerati
The ones that are called
to decipher this dilemma
Make it easier to digest
You want the definition to be clear
It should sound like this
Talk like this
Dress like this.
Will I still be a monkey,
if I don't wear the monkey suit?
Shit, I'd rather be sharp
than a B-Flat
But I gotta play it straight
Show the folks that you educated
That you got some smarts.
Is that what you want?
Is this how it's got to go down
for me to be down?
Maybe die young
and leave a good-looking corpse
I can see it now

I'll be leaving a taping
of Russell Simmons's new show
Def Jazz Jam
Hosted by Savion Glover
Making Jazz
"By and for the Hip-Hop generation"
Noisier and funkier
for a "New Audience"

Suge Knight will be waiting for me
in his car on the corner
Trying to buy the rights
to my sweet bad-ass songs
I too,
will get in the passenger's seat,
Deja vu!
And a black '57 Chevy
With tinted windows
And twenty-two-inch rims
Will be easing on down the road
right behind me.
Wynton Marsalis

Will be riding in the back
While his consigliere
Stanley Crouch is driving
Ken Burns is riding shotgun

Camera in hand
Shooting his latest film
Death of a cool:
Niggers gone wild
While we stop at the traffic light
The '57 Chevy
rolls its windows down
And with Louis Armstrong
blasting through the speakers
Pulls up next to us
And with tears in his eyes

Wynton "The Lion King" Marsalis
Trumpet in one hand

Gun blazin' in the other
Screams "Real Jazz, Motherfucker"

At the funeral
The congregation will be crying
As Al Sharpton is singing
"If I were the king of the forest"
Bill Clinton will be waiting on the side of the stage
Wearing a Harlem Renaissance
T-shirt,
With his Sax,
ready to play a stirring rendition
of "Black and Blue."
Dianna Krall sits in the other room
Resisting temptation
To run out of town
with Billie's gardenia
But Abbey and Cassandra stand like guardians
Tall majestic oracles
she'll never pass
Colin Powell,
just fired from his reality show
"The spook who sat by the door"
Sits quietly
By the door
Talking with Cornel West,
Who is still in his Matrix costume,
About whether he should take
the blue pill or the red pill.

Norman Mailer's "White Negroes"
Amiri Baraka's "Blues People"
Afrika Bambaataa's "Zulu Nation"
And the children of the off-beat
generation
Have all come to pay their respects

It will be rainy and foggy
with a whisper of danger
and eroticism
And a slight scent of weed,
in the air
A procession will be led
down every back alley
Where the cats and crows
used to know me
There, you'll find
my family and friends
Believers and Deceivers
Beat Makers and Heart Breakers
Lovers and Liars,
Writers and Exciters
Trendsetters and Bed Wetters.
The bad-ass
Ass kickers
Ass kissers
Assholes
And the ones who love them

My Niggas
Spies
Chinks
Guineas
And Kikes
The Fags
Old Hags
Bitches
Hoes
And Dikes
The Wannabes
The Gonnabes
The if I Coulda Wouldabes
The Twelve Steppers
The Ho' tepers

The Muthafuckers
The Down on They Luckers
The Poets
The Ho-ets
The not afraid to show it's
The Liberators
Agitators
Motivators
And masturbators
All, God's children,
Black men and white men,
Jews and Gentiles,
Protestants and Catholics,
Will all join hands together
And sing the words
to that old Negro spiritual

"Ain't no stoppin' us now,
Ain't no stoppin' us now
We're on the move
We're on the move"

And finally,
My tombstone will say
"I told you I was sick,
A Mutant Restless,
Neurotic,
Psychotic,
Insane in the membrane,
A slacker,
A junkie,
A trumpet-toting flunky,
No plan
Inspiration choked in my hand
I believed in everything
And nothing
I was musician,
black

Sociologically programmed
to self-destruct
I told you I was tucked
Cause of death

JAZZ

DUENDE: Behold
The plight of the black man

Behold
How he holds his own breath
in his hand
Everything you said,
is true
But you've placed
a tag of blame on everyone
But you forgot
to place the tag on you
You wanted it all
But gave it all up
Ended up with nothin' Colorless
A black-and-white sketch
Of the masterpiece
you used to be
Why did you destroy what we had
I gave you everything
I gave you my best years
I gave you a handkerchief
to dry your brow
And you don't even wear it
Did you forget?
Or are you just stupid.
I am furious
That you don't see
that every option is open
I wish I had hands
to hold that brass the way you can.

I hate that my lips
Cannot taste the metal
on that mouthpiece
Or taste even a piece of flesh
On your lips.
You have a gift
You don't appreciate
I'm tired
of you coming in late
Or not coming in at all
Tired of picking up after you
Tired of slaving away
trying to make you feel
your own rhythm
while you just sit
and drink
And stink of laziness
Scratching your balls
While blaming the world
for all your ills
I wish
I had the skills you have,
to find music in everything
you hear
I hate
That you can't hear the music
in me.

I need you . . .
To wake up . . .
To put your song together
To catch your breath
To take this stage
And fight me,
Duende
till the death of you and me

Do you remember?

Do you

JUNIOR: I remember

DUENDE: Do you remember her

JUNIOR: Yes.
My mother

DUENDE: Junior!

JUNIOR: I remember
she remembers
Dreaming
Of her body moving
and her voice wailing

DUENDE: Junior!

JUNIOR: She was made for the big stage
The bright lights
Billboards
But a star isn't always born

DUENDE: Junior!

JUNIOR: She remembers the pain
Before the joy
Found joy,
in singing a tune for her baby boy

DUENDE: Junito!

JUNIOR: Mommy remembers
Loneliness
Her man was gone
Even when he came back from the war
different
She once felt strong beside him
Could conquer the world beside him
But he was gone

She raised a child alone
Baby boy
took Poppa's place, in her eyes
And she just watched
Sat at her pillow
With dim eyes
Her dreams had changed
From the window,
she saw war
On TV she saw the war
Her man, embodied war
And war she remembers well
Launched her own war
Drug war
Looking for me
In the eyes of the civilians
Who live around her
Looking for me
But have given into the darkness
Of that drug profession
And they all look like me
Same age
Like me
Her Junior
But they are not me
And they won't stand for this
nosy woman
Called the cops
Trying to be everybody's momma
So they just gonna burn it down
Burn my parents' house down

Mommy
Burning
Burning
Burning
Engulfed

Killed
Wednesday morning
Fire
Still looking for me
Fire
Left to find music
Fire
The roof
The roof
The roof is on fire
We don't need no water
Let the motherfucker burn

DUENDE [*singing*]: *Desde el cielo*
Ella te ve y te perdona
Pero tu tratas en vano
Y no te dejas perdonar
[*Spoken*] Your mother
With a bundle of young man's clothes
A bundle of sadness
By the side of her bed
Believing you would come home
Like you promised
She could see you
in those clothes again
Walking in her kitchen
Snatching that extra piece
of chicken from her plate
Napping on her lap
as she watched her novella
She hoped you would come home
and wear them
So she could simply wash them all
again
Instead
she pressed her nose
against your shirt

Tried to feel you
against her cheek
Trying to find you
Downy fresh
Her little boy
Soft
Rejecting that you were not there
Denying you would never come home
So she waited
for nothing

JUNIOR: And what happened to my father?

DUENDE: Sat alone
In a burnt-out
shell of an apartment
And instead of listening
to Miles Davis's
Sketches of Spain
Puts on "Blue Sweat"
Your music
Feeling your mother in every note
She ended up getting laid out
in the kinte cloth
her man laid on her pillow,
And a soft *mantón*
Was draped over her shoulders
to keep them warm.
She was an Army of one
With no medals of honor or valor
Just those won for her by her man
In Vietnam

JUNIOR: And I was
always on the run
My father remembers
My mother remembers
I remember

How I chose to go blind
Chose not to see
what I had seen too often
So I
Ran away to the world of
And the land of
Made love to
Gave it all to
Found God in
Found my song in
Mother's song
Father's war
I hear voices

DUENDE: Not anymore
Blow again
So that you can live
You've got to believe in something,
Junior
So you might as well believe in me
[*Singing*] You've got to believe in something
So why not believe in me
You've got to believe in something
So why not believe in me

JUNIOR: Run home for a long time
Come on run home for a long time
Run home for a long time
Come on run home for a long time

[*Repeats throughout.*]

DUENDE: Oh, Tell me have you ever
I bet you will say never
Come on tell me have you ever
Have you ever held a horn player's
Breath in your hand?

Tell me have you ever
I bet you will say never

Have you ever held a horn player's
breath in your hand?
Have you ever held a horn player's
breath in your hand

JUNIOR [*spoken*]: When passion first hits you
    It's like a runaway train
    An orgasm so strong
    it puts you back
    to the beginning of time
    Joy so pure it scares you
    It asks a question
    and gives you the answers
    at the same time
    Why am I here?
    To do this thing? Add another piece
    to the puzzle
    And if I gotta explain it
    Then I'm already
    two steps past you to the left
    Running and jumping
    like a freedom suit
    Composed by revolutionaries
    Comrades of the cool
    Gangsters of that good God almighty
    righteousness
    Can I feel it again?

DUENDE [*sung*]: Oh, don't you wish
    you could have been there
    I say it was my handkerchief
    That nightly dried
    old Satchmo's brow
    In his smile I left my kiss

    Oh, just because his hair was curly
    Just because his teeth were pearly
    Oh, just because
    he always wore a smile

And he liked to dress up,
in the latest styles,
latest styles
Oh, just because,
he was glad to be livin'
Or because,
he took his troubles with a smile
Mmm
Just because his color's shade
Don't make a difference
He was my Louie all the time

JUNIOR [*spoken*]: This is my yes
In a chorus of maybes
Who slept with no
and had a baby named I can
And I can hear it
loud and clear
I'm a do that
Do that Boom bap bap
Da Boom bap
I'm a do that Again
I'm a do that
I hear my voice now
The same voice as I
left my house
and greeted my neighbors
The voice as I
asked the clerk for gas
The voice as I
turned on the car radio
As I flipped
from station to station
As I rolled down the window
to adjust the mirror
In front of the corner store
Around the corner

At the front door
In every step I took to get here
tonight
My voice
that's the best sound
I've ever heard
Best sound I've ever heard

DUENDE [*sung*]: Yeah, I know you're the one baby
    With that Archangel breath
    I know you're the one
    With the sound I most miss
    I seek to find my Junior
    in the horn that you kiss
    I know you're the one
    With that revelation style
    I know you're the one
    And I ain't seen you in a while
    I have no plans for leavin'
    I'm revealin' your style
    I can tell you stories
    about trumpets before you
    And you might not believe me
    But they've
    been through the same shit too
    I have no plans for leavin'
    I have plans for you
    Believe me when I tell ya
    I sat in a barn with Miles,
    Held a horn in his hand,
    Kickin' habits Breaking styles
    I have no plans for leavin'
    I'm revealin' your smile

    Zup dup ta
    dudapda duraburaba
    Zap da ru rap da
    Zup dup ta

dudapda duraburaba
Zap da ru rap da
I have no plans for leavin'
It's time to start believin'

JUNIOR AND DUENDE: I've got to believe in something
So why not believe in me
I've got to believe in something
So why not believe in me me me

JUNIOR [*prompting the* TRUMPETER]: Play

[TRUMPETER *plays.*]

HOME/LAND
A THEATRICAL JOURNEY

Albany Park Theater Project

PRODUCTION HISTORY

Home/Land premiered on January 20, 2012, at the Laura Wiley Theater, the home space of Albany Park Theater Project. The original production ran for thirty-three performances through April 28, 2012.

Home/Land is based on more than two dozen interviews that Albany Park Theater Project conducted in Chicago between December 2010 and July 2011. The text and staging were devised by the ensemble and directing team. The artistic director was David Feiner; the directors were Colby Beserra, David Feiner, Mikhail Fiksel, Stephanie Paul, Maggie Popadiak, and Rossana Rodríguez-Sánchez. The production had sound design by Mikhail Fiksel, lighting design by Jeremy Getz, scenic design by Scott C. Neale, costumes by Mieka van der Ploeg, original songs by Rossana Rodríguez-Sánchez, and choreography by Stephanie Paul and Maggie Popadiak. The stage manager was Samantha Symon.

Ensemble .... Lesley Albarran, Osbaldo Antuñez, Marilyn Carteño, Stephanie Castrejon, Randy Dang, Lilia Escobar, Ely Espino, David Gauna, Gissela Gualoto, Jaime Lopez, John Paul Marquez, Nichole Martinez, Jose Mata, Kimberly Mayo, Vincent Meredith, Luis Millan, Bladimir Orduño, Jacqueline Ovalle, Stephany Perez, Paloma Reyes, Raul Rico, Jalen Rios, and Kyra Mae Robinson.

CHARACTERS

From early in the process of devising *Home/Land*, we thought of the piece as an act of witness. We imagined a family twenty or thirty years in the future looking back on our present moment in history and memorializing the cruelties of a bygone immigration system, while retelling a people's history of the grassroots resistance that brought humanity to immigration policy in the United States. We thought of *Home/Land* as an act of people's history with our teen ensemble as its authors.

We extended this conceptual idea into the staging of *Home/Land*. As the audience arrived, they were greeted by our ensemble members—not as the characters they play, but as themselves. The opening song of the play takes us to that family a few decades from now, as the rest of the ensemble gathers round to listen to the song, very much as themselves.

As the song ends, specific stories and characters begin to emerge from the ensemble. Throughout the play, actors travel from role to role, assuming various identities. It matters little how the roles are divided; what is significant is that all the performers always carry with them their underlying identity as artists bearing witness to the stories of the people around them and recording those stories as a people's history.

STAGING

In the original production, the main playing space was a long and narrow alley stretched between two small end stages, with audience seated on both long sides of the alley, facing each other, and very close to the stage. Action flowed from one end of the stage to the other, at times crossing the space on one of four rolling platforms, with one scene frequently setting up or starting before the previous scene finished, and no blackouts or extended transitions. While the play is structured thematically into three acts, there were no pauses in the action.

As the audience arrived, ensemble members greeted them. The play began with a welcome by the artistic director or an ensemble member, with the entire company spread throughout the space. And then, without a fade to black, and with the ensemble all bearing witness . . .

ACT ONE

Crossings

[*Song: Three* CHILDREN, *a brother and his younger sisters, from a better time in the future. Accompanied by two guitarists, they play and sing a lullaby that remembers how the audience got from its time to theirs.*]

BOY:
Mis niñas, niñas bellas hermanitas
yo no se si saben bien
El cuento de aquel árbol de hoja dulce
que se enraizó en la tierra en que creció

El árbol reventó de una semilla
que vino de muy lejos hasta acá
calló desde una rama con raíces
al otro lao del borde, más allá

Los hombres asustados con el árbol
Trataron de arrancarlo de una vez
Y el árbol se abrazó mas a la tierra
creciendo y dando frutos de comer

Y tanto quizo el árbol a su suelo
Que los hombres no lo pueden arrancar
Y es hoy bajo la sombra de este árbol
que te cuento la historia una vez mas.

GIRLS:
Brother brother, tell the story
Share the tale I've heard you tell
The story of the sweet leaf tree
That in this ground did grow so well

The tree grew from a traveling seed
A seed that came from distant lands.
It crossed the border on a breeze,
Into this ground where now it stands.

When hateful men all filled with fear
They tried to tear it from its roots
The tree held stronger than before
And soon gave birth to sweeter fruits.

Today the tree stands tall and brave
It overcame those fearful men
And now beneath its gentle shade
We share its story once again.

[*Movement:* RAMIRO *emerges from the children's past, our present. He leaves home and begins the journey to a new land. He struggles against seemingly insurmountable obstacles—represented by the bodies of two anonymous ensemble members—forces that block his way forward, pull him backward, knock him to the ground.*]

[RAMIRO *is left kneeling on the floor, hands above his head.*]

RAMIRO: I was arrested the first time in Costa Rica. One of the cops told me, *Open your hand.*

[RAMIRO *keeps his fist closed.*]

Show me what you have in your hand.

[RAMIRO *opens his hand, revealing a small toy duck.*]

I used to criticize people that left for the U.S. Then my daughter was born. Having your own children is magnificent—to feel her hand grow bigger in your hand each day. But no matter how much I worked, I couldn't put food in my daughter's mouth. And so the time came for me also.

I flew from Ecuador to Panama. From Panama, I crossed borders, hiding at night, sleeping under the rain, smelling bad, bathing in rivers. But the worst was the memories of my daughter.

One day, I was getting a pair of shoes from my bag, and a toy duck fell out. I called my wife and asked her, "Who put a duck in my bag?" *Tatiana did.* It seems that when my daughter realized I was leaving, she put this little toy of hers in my bag.

What is that! the cop asked. "It's a toy." What's inside of it? Do you have drugs!

"Nothing. It's just a toy."

The cop knocked it from my hand.

[*An ensemble member knocks the duck from* RAMIRO'*s hand, flinging it across the stage.*]

[*While standing, crossing, and picking up the duck:*]

"You know what? That's a personal thing. I'm not harming anyone, I'm not stealing, I'm migrating. You can detain me, but you don't take these things from home, that belong to my children."

The duck was my company the whole trip, all the way to Chicago. I lost everything but my little duck.

[*Lights and sound take the audience to very early morning, a secret dock on the rocky shore of a great big ocean. A large group of* IMMIGRANT PASSENGERS *board a boat.*]

RAMIRO: From Costa Rica, I traveled through Nicaragua, then Honduras, to Guatemala. To go from Guatemala to Mexico, we took a boat on the ocean. Twenty-five of us—parents with their children, brothers and sisters, friends, strangers—on one tiny boat.

[*The* IMMIGRANT PASSENGERS *have crowded onto the small boat. The boat sets off. The boat and* IMMIGRANT PASSENGERS *sway in the gentle waters near the shore. A young girl, overcome with fear, tries to jump from the boat toward the disappearing shore. Another* PASSENGER *catches her. The disruption sends a ripple through all the* PASSENGERS. RAMIRO *searches frantically for the duck, which he fears has been taken from him. An even more forceful ripple passes through the boat, disrupting its fragile equilibrium. The boat is now in deep water. One of the* PASSENGERS *sees a fierce wave coming their way. The* PASSENGERS *prepare themselves for disaster. The* PASSENGERS *meet the fierce wave. Their boat is consumed by the water . . . but it emerges! They survive. The boat arrives in Mexico. The* PASSENGERS *debark, standing once again on solid ground.*]

RAMIRO: We traveled on that boat for twelve hours. We got to Chiapas. After half an hour in Mexico, they caught us again—and sent us back to Guatemala.

[*An overwhelming force pulls all of the* IMMIGRANT PASSENGERS *back across the ocean—back to where they stood before they boarded the boat. From the huddle of* IMMIGRANT PASSENGERS, *a new character emerges:* YOUNG AHLAM, *a precocious eight-year-old. She carries a small carrying case for dolls.* YOUNG AHLAM *removes a teddy bear from her case and tries to sell it to a* CUSTOMER, *played by an ensemble member seated in the audience.*]

YOUNG AHLAM: Now let's see what I have for you. How about a bear. "Roar!" No, really, this bear is very gentle, see?

[*She cuddles the bear to her* CUSTOMER.]

And white like the snow. Oh, I can see that you two like each other. So, how much? How much for Mr. White Teddy?

CUSTOMER: Five dinar.

YOUNG AHLAM: Five dinar!? Did I mention Mr. Teddy was a gift from my grandma? She got him for me at Entertainment City, which is the best mall in Kuwait. The woman said he came all the way from Alaska—in America. My family was very rich when we lived in Kuwait, which I'm not supposed to say because it's not polite to boast, but still it's true. My mother is Palestinian, born in Jordan, grew up in

Libya. My dad is Palestinian, born in Palestine, grew up in Jordan. I was born in Kuwait, but I'm still Palestinian even though I never went there. Now we all live in Jordan. But soon we are going to America. [*Back to business*] I think Mr. Teddy is worth a lot more than your five dinar. At least fifteen.

CUSTOMER: Eight.

YOUNG AHLAM: Eight! What's that, Mr. Teddy?

[*She holds the bear up to her ear.*]

An insult, I know. [*Back to* CUSTOMER] Twelve.

CUSTOMER: Ten.

YOUNG AHLAM: OK, ten, but only because Mr. Teddy looks so happy with you.

[YOUNG AHLAM *pulls another doll from her case and makes a real member of the audience her next customer.*]

YOUNG AHLAM: How about Rainbow Brite for you? Do you want to know her story? I got her for my sixth birthday. My mom took me to Kids "R" Us, the big one in Farwaniya that was the best toy store in the world. It got burned down when Iraq invaded Kuwait in 1990. People said it was Palestinian kids who burned the store, but really it was Iraqi soldiers. They only blamed us because Yasser Arafat sided with Iraq, and since he's the Palestinian leader, the Kuwaitis decided all Palestinians were bad. That's why they kicked us out of Kuwait and we lost everything except the clothes on our back.

So how much for Rainbow Brite? After he stole Mr. Teddy from me, I don't think I can sell her for less than twenty dinar . . .

[YOUNG AHLAM *improvises in response to the audience member/customer. Eventually, she sells Rainbow Brite.*]

YOUNG AHLAM: OK, you can pay me later. I'll remember.

[YOUNG AHLAM *removes a princess doll from her case.*]

YOUNG AHLAM: Next we have this princess with her very pretty dress. Her name is Princess Ahlam, which is just like my name. When we moved to Jordan, Mom got Princess Ahlam for me because I was very sad to leave Kuwait. She said I shouldn't expect lots more dolls because dolls are expensive and the situation in Jordan is really bad. I was supposed to be asleep, but I heard Dad tell Mom we either stay in Jordan and starve, or we sell everything and buy plane tickets to America.

So, who wants to buy Princess Ahlam?

[*Lights shift to* LUCA *and his* FATHER, *who prepares the young boy for their imminent journey across the border.*]

FATHER: Did you thank your mother for breakfast?

LUCA: Yes.

FATHER: Did you finish everything?

LUCA: Yes, and my stomach kinda hurts.

FATHER: Did you wash?

LUCA: Yes. I even cleaned behind my ears, see?

FATHER: Teeth?

[LUCA *flashes dad a smile.*]

Do you remember what I told you last night?

[LUCA *nods yes.*]

What's your name?

LUCA: Luca.

FATHER: No, Luca! Your name is Jose Garcia.

LUCA: Jose Garcia.

FATHER: Keeping saying it until it's you.

LUCA: My name is Jose Garcia. My name is Jose Garcia.

FATHER: Where are you from, Jose Garcia?

LUCA: Chicago. Chicago. My name is Jose Garcia and I'm from Chicago.

FATHER: Why were you in Mexico, Jose Garcia?

LUCA: Visiting my *abuela* because she is really sick.

FATHER: Don't say it like a Mexican. Say it like an American. Don't you want to be an American?

LUCA: I AM an American.

FATHER: You ARE an American. Good. What are your favorite things about Chicago, Jose?

LUCA: School. Friends. Sears Tower.

FATHER: Good. Now keep saying it.

LUCA: School. Friends. Sears Tower. School. Friends. Sears Tower. My name is Jose Garcia and I am from Chicago . . .

[JOSEFINA *enters, in a rush, carrying an enormous cardboard box. She speaks directly to the audience.*]

JOSEFINA: Sorry I'm late. I was on a job this afternoon—people hire me to take pictures: weddings, *quinceañeras.* Today, a new baby, their first, a girl. *Una nena preciosa!*

　　I come out of the house, open my truck, there are two guys inside, robbing me. They look at me, I look at them—*Que chingados creen que estan haciendo!*—They take off. I run after them, three blocks, don't catch them—they learned a lesson. So I stopped at home, took a shower, cleaned up, you know?

[*She calls offstage*] *Mijos, Santa llegó temprano con una caja de juguetes!*

[*A group of* CHILDREN *dash onto the stage, dig into the box that* JOSEFINA *delivered, pulling out toys and playing with them joyfully—and loudly.*]

[*To the* CHILDREN, *in Spanish*]: *Mijos! Calladitos por favor, El Padre está hablando por teléfono y yo estoy hablando con esta gente tan amable . . .*

So: welcome to la Misión Nuestra Señora de Guadalupe. Is this your first time at our church? No, of course, you came to interview El Padre. This is our little chapel, where we hold our Mass, and this other room is where we have lawyers deal with people's cases, and where we counsel them—we give them hope, and we help each other through. El Padre told you this used to be a bar, yeah? When there's a march or press conference, the whole church is full with people painting banners. On Sundays, the doctor comes for our clinic. People donate food, clothes, toys—I don't mind telling you, La Misión is my Sears.

I guess I should start at the beginning, my first crossing. I have come here three times, always illegally. What other way is there for us? The first time, I was fourteen, I ran away from home. Because of poverty. I didn't have a clue about the U.S. I heard that people who came here returned with many green bills, so I thought maybe I could get some too.

I arrived at five in the morning, and by eleven that night I was working at a factory.

When I was seventeen, I met my husband, and God has blessed us with three wonderful children. I always tell my kids to study. Even the kids on the street, I tell them, "You should be reading a book." They say, "Doña, please don't start with the sermon," but they respect me.

[*Directly to the audience*] It's so important to meet people like you who want to hear our stories.

[VICTOR, *one of the* CHILDREN, *dribbles a soccer ball across the stage, picks it up, throws it to* NATANIEL, *another of the children. This begins a game of the* CHILDREN *passing the ball back and forth.*]

VICTOR: Nataniel! What do you think El Padre is doing in there with the *polimigra*?

NATANIEL: I don't know. They've been in there forever.

DANIELA: Are they arresting him?

MATIAS: They can't arrest El Padre. He has super power.

EVARISTO: El Padre gets arrested all the time.

RODRIGO: They arrested him last month at *la marcha,* I saw.

NATANIEL: But he got out right away. The *polimigra* can't keep El Padre.

LINA: Maybe he hypnotizes the guards, and they have to let him out.

RODRIGO: Or he turns invisible and sneaks out.

AMILCAR: Or he melts the prison bars with his eyes!

MATIAS: Not that kind of super power. Power from God.

CHILDREN [*looking up to the heavens*]: Ohhhhhhh.

MARIANELA: My *abuela* says El Padre's strength comes from what happened when he was a kid.

DANIELA: I heard his parents died.

RODRIGO: I heard that, too. They were playing *fútbol*.

NATANIEL: They weren't playing, they were watching.

DANIELA: Do you know the story?

NATANIEL: My *tío* came from the same village as El Padre, in El Salvador.

DANIELA: Will you tell us?

NATANIEL: It was the time of the civil war in El Salvador. The village was called El Salitre, like the breeze of the sea, salty and warm. The village was very small, and all the people were *campesinos*, farmers. When El Padre was a little *chavo*, nine years old, they had a big *fútbol* tournament in El Salitre.

[*The* CHILDREN *become the* fútbol *tournament. Four kids play the* fútbol *match; the others chant and cheer.*
The sound of the cheers turns into boots marching.
And then gunfire.
One child falls to the ground, dead.
Another.
More.
NATANIEL, *as* EL PADRE, *runs and hides.*
Quiet.
NATANIEL *returns.*]

NATANIEL: Dead bodies paved the dirt roads. El Padre found the bodies of his mother and father.

LINA: Why did the army kill all those people?

NATANIEL: It was the government army, and the government of El Salvador was ruled by a dictator.

MATIAS: The dictator was backed by U.S. imperialists, Ronald Reagan, and the CIA.

CHILDREN: What?

MATIAS: That's what my parents said.

NATANIEL: El Padre escaped from the army and into the mountain, to live in the jungle.

[*The* CHILDREN *turn on their bellies and crawl through the jungle.*]

MARIANELA: My *abuela* says the jungle is where El Padre gained all his strength.

AMILCAR: How did he survive?

NATANIEL: He met *la guerrilla.*

MATIAS [*as a* guerrillero]: Welcome, *camaradas.* This is the people's jungle. Here, we all take care of each other, and we fight the government's army to take back our country.

MARIANELA [*as a* guerrillera]: You have lost your parents, so now you are everyone's children. Come with us, we will keep you safe.

[*The* CHILDREN *follow the* guerrilleros *deep into the mountains.*]

NATANIEL: El Padre got used to living in the mountains. His only possessions were a pair of shoes, a pair of pants, two shirts, and a plastic sheet he slept on with another comrade. When it rained, they covered themselves with the plastic.

[*They pull a clear plastic tarp from the box of toys* JOSEFINA *brought earlier. Shaking the tarp in the air, they create the sound of a storm . . . or is it a battle?*]

One day, not long after El Padre's tenth birthday, two comrades came to the children from El Salitre.

MATIAS: Our *columna* needs to leave the camp, to go on a mission.

MARIANELA: You can't stay here, the army will find you and kill you.

MATIAS: You need to come with us.

MARIANELA: It's going to be dangerous.

[MARIANELA *hands an M16 to* NATANIEL, *who reluctantly takes it.* NATANIEL *becomes* EL PADRE. *The* CHILDREN *have become a* columna *of* la guerrilla; *they cautiously make their way offstage and into battle.*

ANDRES *enters, looking for someone. From a hiding place on the far other end of the space,* ADELINA *dashes across the stage and into* ANDRES's *arms. Immediately, it is as if they are dancing. Whenever these two are together, even when they are perfectly still, they dance.*]

ADELINA: I did it, I did it, I ran away! Oh, I felt guilty as I was leaving. Papi isn't a bad man, he just got angry because you brought all your friends when you came to ask for my hand—and because they'd been drinking. And Mami . . . Mami will be sad, but we'll get married, and they'll forgive us.

ANDRES: Even me?

ADELINA: Even you!

[ADELINA *breathes for the first time.*]

Is this really happening? Am I really here? Are *you* really here? Tell me our story, Andres, tell me how this happened, tell me how we happened, tell me so I believe.

ANDRES: We met at a dance.

ADELINA: We met long before that dance.

ANDRES: We grew up together—

ADELINA: *guaches* from the same town—

ANDRES: your family's ranch over there—

ADELINA: and your family's ranch over there.

ANDRES: You called me *empolvado*—

ADELINA: Because you always were, dust all over yourself.

ANDRES: And you hated to get even a speck of dirt on your dresses.

ADELINA: You still have that same soothing face, the one that says, "Don't be angry, don't be worried."

ANDRES: And you still have the same big brown eyes that always say, "I'm listening."

ADELINA: You left for a while, to the U.S., to work. You came back a couple times, but—

ANDRES: Never nothing.

ADELINA: We got old, twenty-two and twenty-three.

ANDRES: And then—

ADELINA: I hadn't been to a dance in a while.

ANDRES: It was outdoors, really beautiful, decorated with palm trees and hanging lights. All the women sat together on benches.

ADELINA: And the guys stood behind us. You came as a group and asked us to dance.

ANDRES: You got to choose.

ADELINA: You looked at me with a face that said, "Give me a chance."

ANDRES: Your fingertips touched the back of my neck.

ADELINA: Your neck was so warm—

ANDRES: And your fingertips were so cold.

ADELINA: Your friends kept asking, "Aren't you going to share?" And you just held me tighter.

ANDRES: At the end of the night, you got into your brother's car—

ADELINA: You held the door, kept it from closing, you took both my hands, looked me in the eyes and asked, "Will you be my girlfriend?"

ANDRES: You laughed.

ADELINA: You said, "I'm serious."

ANDRES: You said, "I'll think about it."

ADELINA: *If you really want me, you'll wait.*

ANDRES: *Till when? I can't wait forever.*

ADELINA: *Till Tuesday. In the plaza, when I come to buy tomatillos and chiles.*

ANDRES: You wore a white dress.

ADELINA: You weren't dusty.

ANDRES: *So judge, what's the verdict!*

ADELINA: *Yes, of course I'll be your girlfriend. We'll get to know each other.*

ANDRES: That was a month ago.

ADELINA: Twenty-nine days.

ANDRES: My father will make a wedding for us. We will be married.

ADELINA: And then?

ANDRES: I want a kid, and I'm going to spoil the heck out of him.

ADELINA: How about three kids and we'll spoil the heck out of all of them?

ANDRES: Three kids is too much money.

[*Silence.*]

ADELINA: When you went to America, was it hard to get there?

ANDRES: Half the time, you don't know where you're going. The other half, someone else is leading you, and you don't know if they know the right way, or what they might do to you, or how much extra money they're going to demand.

ADELINA: But it was worth it.

ANDRES: I want a son.

ADELINA: You don't get to pick.

ANDRES: You can hope. You can always hope.

[ANDRES *and* ADELINA *begin their journey toward the border, toward their new home.*]

ADELINA [*singing*]: *Cariño, cariñito mio*
cuéntame el cuento otra vez
de como dos guaches
cruzaron a pie
la frontera en su luna de miel

De como soñaron cariño
Con los niños que van a tener
y como con besos los consentirán
lo mejor del mundo les darán

Cariño, cariñito mio
Cuéntame el cuento otra vez
De como Dos guaches
cruzaron a pie
y al final, todo salió bien

[ANDRES *and* ADELINA *are joined on the stage by more and more* IMMI-GRANTS, *each on their journeys, each moving slowly but determinedly toward an unknown but necessary future, each carrying a suitcase.*]

ACT TWO

A Demonic System

[*As the* IMMIGRANTS *near the promised land, a monstrous sound interrupts* ADELINA's *song. Helicopters. Spotlights. Border Patrol. The* IMMIGRANTS *flee. One* IMMIGRANT *is trapped in the searchlight of a helicopter as* . . .

Reveille. Music: Up-tempo "God Bless America." LADY LIBERTY *enters—the Statue of Liberty meets Dallas Cowboy cheerleader, sporting her signature turquoise-patina colors and seven-star crown, holding a torch/flashlight in her right hand and a set of color-coordinated pom-poms in her right.* ROBERTITO MARRÓN *enters with her, and together they set the stage for "Who Wants to Be an American," the most popular game show in some not-too-distant, not-too-far-away America. The stage includes a giant, life-size game board of a series of stars leading toward a land of opportunity. Music continues as the introduction begins.*]

ANNOUNCER: Bienvenidos, Youkoso, Bienvenue, and Welcome to "Who Wants to Be an American?" The game where huddled masses yearning to breathe free and wretched refuse from teeming shores try their hand in the land of opportunity and play for equality and prizes galore! Now, here's your host—Bob Whiteman!

[ROBERTITO *encourages, even bullies, the audience to clap.*]

BOB WHITEMAN: Hello! Hello, everybody! Thank you! Thank you so much . . . [*Applause fades.*] Welcome to "Who Wants to Be An American?" I'm your host, Bob Whiteman. Before the fun and games begin, please give a warm welcome to my indispensable assistant, Robertito Marrón!

[*Applause.*]

ROBERTITO: Bonjour, amigos! Chao ong! Kamusta ang buhay? [*Arriving at* BOB WHITEMAN] Hola, mon ami!!

BOB WHITEMAN: This show would be impossible without your help, amigo . . .

ROBERTITO: Oh, stop it.

BOB WHITEMAN: . . . Well, today, as always, we've got a fantastic, fun show in store for you all—another undocumented immigrant competing to become a real naturalized citizen by proving his mettle and earning his stars and stripes. Let's start out by meeting today's lucky contestant! Lady Liberty, if you please . . .

LADY LIBERTY: His name is Marcos Medina!

[*The* IMMIGRANT *in the searchlight now finds himself a contestant in a spotlight:* MARCOS MEDINA.]

ROBERTITO: He was born in Mexico.

LADY LIBERTY: Then, he was brought across the border at the tender age of nine.

ROBERTITO: Marcos enjoys our inalienable rights of life, liberty, and the pursuit of happiness, despite the fact that he's an illegal alien.

LADY LIBERTY: But, time is running out . . .

ROBERTITO: . . . and, if this young man wants to stay in the States, he's gonna have to pass all of the tests provided to anyone—

LADY LIBERTY, ROBERTITO, AND BOB WHITEMAN: . . . who wants to be an American!

BOB WHITEMAN: Hello, Marcos. Welcome to the show.

MARCOS: How did I get here?

ROBERTITO: He said, "Welcome to the show!"

MARCOS: Thanks for having me, Mr. Whiteman.

BOB WHITEMAN: Please, call me Bob.

ROBERTITO: Call him Bob!

MARCOS: OK, Bob.

BOB WHITEMAN: Thanks, Marcos. Now, Marcos, if you ask me, this land should be your land just as much as it is my land. But, from California to the New York Island, there are some people who disagree. So, to keep things fair, every contestant on the show must compete against a real, live natural-born American citizen. Let's select a volunteer from our studio audience.

[*Music: Up-tempo "This Land Is Your Land."*]

If you were born in the US of A and have the birth certificate to prove it, then—"I WANT YOU!"—to be our next contestant on—

BOB WHITEMAN, ROBERTITO, AND LADY LIBERTY: "Who Wants to Be an American?"

ROBERTITO: C'mon, Americanos! Throw your hands in the air like you just *do* care!

BOB WHITEMAN: Lady Liberty, who's it gonna be?

[LADY LIBERTY *shines her torch/flashlight around the crowd.* ROBERTITO *selects the* CONTESTANT, *brings him/her to the stage.*]

BOB WHITEMAN: Hello, what's your name?

CONTESTANT: [*States his or her name.*]

BOB WHITEMAN: Wonderful. And how are you tonight, [*insert* CONTESTANT *name*]?

CONTESTANT: [*Answers question.*]

BOB WHITEMAN: Great. And are you an American citizen?

CONTESTANT: Yes.

BOB WHITEMAN: Do you have a birth certificate to prove it?

CONTESTANT: Yes.

BOB WHITEMAN: Do you have it with you?

CONTESTANT: No.

BOB WHITEMAN: Well, I don't need to see it. I trust your face. You just look so American.

ROBERTITO AND LADY LIBERTY: You do. You look *so* American.

MARCOS: What does that MEAN?

ROBERTITO: You know *exactly* what that means.

BOB WHITEMAN: OK! Without any further ado: let's get the game underway!

[*Drumroll for a cheer from* LADY LIBERTY.]

ROBERTITO: *Fantástico!*

LADY LIBERTY: Marcos, Marcos, be all that you can be
Just follow the path to the land of the free.

BOB WHITEMAN: Lady Liberty, tell us today's first challenge.

[LADY LIBERTY *opens a suitcase to reveal "the deck." The first card reads, "Musical Chairs."*]

LADY LIBERTY: Musical Chairs!

BOB WHITEMAN: [*Insert* CONTESTANT *name here*], your objective in this challenge is to defend the rights and privileges you hold so dearly and take for granted every day. You can also ensure that the taxes you pay aren't monopolized by people who have never even contributed to the system.

MARCOS: I pay taxes.

[*"Buzz!"*]

BOB WHITEMAN: Marcos, your objective is just to get your own piece of the pie. Any questions?

MARCOS: We're just playing musical chairs, right?

[*"Ding!"*]

BOB WHITEMAN: That's correct. When the music starts, you march in a circle around the chair. When the music stops, you try to take a seat. Whoever gets there first, wins the round! It's that simple.

MARCOS: Got it.

BOB WHITEMAN: Good. Maestro! Music, please . . .

[*Music: Hyper-fast "My Country, 'Tis of Thee" or another patriotic song. It plays for a while, then stops.* ROBERTITO *hip-bumps* MARCOS *to the floor and assists* CONTESTANT *to the chair.*]

ROBERTITO: *Que fantástico!*

[BOB WHITEMAN *escorts* CONTESTANT *back to audience.* LADY LIBERTY *brings him/her a lemonade and a Hostess Apple Pie.*]

BOB WHITEMAN: [*Insert* CONTESTANT *name*], since you won this round, you can go relax in the Land of Opportunity while Marcos sweats it out. Because, when all is said and done, you don't really care about your government's immigration policy, you just want to make sure that your job is safe and your property taxes don't increase.

ROBERTITO: Enjoy yourself, gringo/a. You get to chill.

BOB WHITEMAN: Marcos, now that [*insert* CONTESTANT *name*] has reached his/her goal, it's just you against the deck. Do you *comprende, amigo*?

MARCOS: Yeah, I get it, Bob.

ROBERTITO: Watch it.

BOB WHITEMAN: And the next challenge is . . .

[LADY LIBERTY *displays a card from the deck.*]

LADY LIBERTY: School!

BOB WHITEMAN: Good one, Marcos. Out of curiosity, [*insert* CONTES-TANT *name*], where did you go to high school?

[CONTESTANT *answers.*]

BOB WHITEMAN: Were you the valedictorian?

[CONTESTANT *probably answers "No." "Buzz!"*]

What a disappointment for your family. How about you, Marcos?

MARCOS: I got straight A's . . .

[*"Ding!"* BOB WHITEMAN *pushes* MARCOS *forward one star on the game board.*]

BOB WHITEMAN: Uno!

MARCOS: I took Advanced Placement classes in every subject . . .

[*"Ding!"*]

BOB WHITEMAN: Dos!

[MARCOS *moves to the second star.*]

MARCOS: I was president of the National Honor Society . . .

[*"Ding!"*]

BOB WHITEMAN: Tres!

[MARCOS *moves to the third star.*]

MARCOS: And senior year, when my girlfriend and I had our baby boy—

[*"Buzz!"*]

BOB WHITEMAN, ROBERTITO, AND LADY LIBERTY: Oh, Marcos!

ROBERTITO: *Que horrible!*

BOB WHITEMAN: I'm afraid teen pregnancy is an automatic penalty.

MARCOS: But wait, I—

ROBERTITO: *Vámonos.*

[ROBERTITO *lifts* MARCOS *and carries him back to the first star.*]

BOB WHITEMAN: Sorry, Marcos, your indiscretion means you're back at square *zero.* So, what's it gonna be, you can cut your losses and head for the hills or stick to your guns and try to do this right . . .

MARCOS: Are you kidding me? I love my son. I'll tell you exactly what I'm gonna do.

[*He advances one star with each triumph.*]

First, I'll get myself a fake ID.

[*"Ding!"*]

I'll work this part-time job slingin' fast food to support my family and raise my son . . .

[*"Ding!"*]

. . . and I'll do that job so well they'll hire me to run the place . . .

[*"Ding!"*]

. . . and I'll use that experience to become manager of a currency exchange . . .

[*"Ding!"*]

. . . and then the owner will promote me to be general manager of his entire chain of businesses . . .

[*"Ding! Ding! Ding!"*]

. . . and with the little bit of money I can save, I'll take classes at the local community college . . .

[*"Ding!"*]

. . . and I'll pay cash because I don't qualify for financial aid, since I don't have my green card . . . YET.

[*"Ding! Ding! Ding! Ding! Ding! Ding!" Applause!*]

ROBERTITO: *Que fantástico!!!*

[*Drumroll for a cheer from* LADY LIBERTY.]

LADY LIBERTY: Marcos, Marcos, you've come so far
The home of the brave is just one more—

BOB WHITEMAN: Wow, Marcos! Unbelievable. Since you did so well with this challenge, you get a bonus space. Move up one more star!

[MARCOS *clearly sees that a Penalty Star lies in front of him.*]

MARCOS: But, Bob . . .

ROBERTITO: Move it!

[MARCOS *steps onto the Penalty Star.*]

BOB WHITEMAN, ROBERTITO, AND LADY LIBERTY: Oh, Marcos!

BOB WHITEMAN: Don't look now. You've landed on a Penalty Star.

ROBERTITO: *Que horrible!*

BOB WHITEMAN: And the penalty is . . .

[*Sirens and searchlights!*]

BOB WHITEMAN: Marcos, what a shame. It's every illegal alien's worst nightmare: *TRAFFIC STOP!*

ROBERTITO: License and registration, baby!

BOB WHITEMAN: That's right, Robertito, the four words every illegal alien dreads, when a routine traffic stop lands you in the hands of Immigration and Customs Enforcement.

ANNOUNCER: At this point, Marcos might be feeling the urge to give up on his quest to earn our Grand Prize—the Green Card, and his path to American Citizenship. If so, he can always choose Voluntary Departure. Voluntary Departure grants Marcos the privilege to exit the country without an order of removal, avoid possible detention, and return to apply for legal residency without fear of censure.

BOB WHITEMAN: It's up to you, Marcos, get back on the boat to Mexico or stay and fight an uphill battle against the legal system.

MARCOS: I'll stay and fight, thank you very much.

BOB WHITEMAN: All right, you heard him, folks. That means it's time for the Cook County Lightning Round!

ROBERTITO: Hear ye, hear ye! It's the Lightning Round!!

[BOB WHITEMAN *and* ROBERTITO *descend on* MARCOS, *circling him like vultures.*]

BOB WHITEMAN: Marcos Medina, how did you come into this country?

MARCOS: Well, my—

BOB WHITEMAN: Who helped you? Why didn't you just come here legally?

MARCOS: We t—

ROBERTITO: Are you on welfare?

MARCOS: Wh—

BOB WHITEMAN: Why should our taxes pay for your kid's education?

MARCOS: I—

ROBERTITO: Why should we let in foreign workers when we don't have enough jobs for ourselves?

BOB WHITEMAN: Do you have family here?

ROBERTITO: Who are they? Where do they live?

MARCOS: Are y—

BOB WHITEMAN: What's the name of your employer?

ROBERTITO: Are there other immigrants working there?

[MARCOS *can no longer contain his frustration and rage.*]

MARCOS: What would you do if your family was starving and you lived in a country with no opportunity? Or a land decimated by war? Or a place where speaking your mind would get you executed? What would a border mean to you then, Bob? Robertito? Lady Liberty?

BOB WHITEMAN: Whoa, the nonnatives are getting restless!

MARCOS: Do you know how impossible it is to immigrate to the U.S. legally? Penalty Star, Bob.

BOB WHITEMAN [*to* ROBERTITO]: Help me out here, amigo.

ROBERTITO: I'm Samoan, Bob. Kiss my ass.

[ROBERTITO *exits.*]

BOB WHITEMAN: Lady Liberty?

[LADY LIBERTY *drops her pom-poms, high-fives* MARCOS, *and exits.* MARCOS *and* BOB WHITEMAN *are alone.* MARCOS *approaches him gently, humanly.*]

MARCOS: Maybe the whole idea of borders is morally wrong, Bob. Can't we sit down and talk about this? This isn't a game, Bob, this is my life.

[MARCOS *is interrupted by a seventies-style La Cucaracha car horn.*]

BOB WHITEMAN: All good questions, but that sound means we're out of time. Marcos, you did good. But not good enough. I'm afraid you haven't won the ultimate goal of American citizenship, but you will be getting this lovely consolation prize . . .

[BOB WHITEMAN *exits*.]

ANNOUNCER: It's an ankle monitor! Provided by our good friends at the Department of Homeland Security, it's a sturdy plastic construction that will last a lifetime and a fashionable black design that will go with any ensemble. Not only that, but it tethers you to your home electronically and allows Immigration and Customs Enforcement, also known as ICE, to keep tabs on your activities at all times. With compliments from all of us here at the show . . . and leaving you with the timeless question: "Who Wants to Be an American?"

[*Outro: Mournful version of "My Country, 'Tis of Thee." As the "Who Wants to Be an American?" set and props are struck, three* CHILDREN *have huddled together, happily watching an amusing TV program. Perhaps it's that popular new game show?* MOM *and* DAD *join them, see what they're watching, turn off the TV.* MOM *is* JOSEFINA, *whom the audience met earlier at La Misión. They bring their* CHILDREN *together for a family hug. This is the Jiménez family:* JOSEFINA *and* ISMAEL, *and their* CHILDREN, REBECCA, JULIAN, *and* LUCILA.
Early morning. The Jiménez home in Chicago. Morning energy.
ICE *at the door, in full tactical gear.*
ICE *enters the home, takes* ISMAEL, *wearing only an A-shirt and boxers, from his family.*
Everyone's wide awake now.
The CHILDREN *run outside after their father.*
JOSEFINA *runs into the house. She searches furiously for clothes for* ISMAEL.
ICE *pulls* ISMAEL *from the* CHILDREN.
Handcuffs. Chains.
ICE *drags* ISMAEL *away as if he was a criminal as . . .*]

LUCILA [*screams*]: PAPI!

[*And* JOSEFINA *returns with clothes . . .*
. . . and the family reaches for their father . . .

. . . but he is gone.
The CHILDREN *collapse, wither to the floor.*
JOSEFINA's *soul leaves her body . . .*
. . . but she must gather the strength to lift up her CHILDREN *and continue.*
Whistling. A song in the distance . . .
. . . The family knows that whistle and that song.
The whistle reanimates the family.
ISMAEL *is back—still wearing nothing but boxers and an A-shirt.*
The whistling becomes part of the score.
The CHILDREN *greet* ISMAEL *with hugging, tickling, and playing.*
JOSEFINA *greets* ISMAEL, *wipes his face, and helps him put on a shirt.*
The family is together.
BEEP BEEP BEEEEEP . . .
. . . a harsh sound interrupts the reunited family. It comes from a black box
strapped above ISMAEL's *ankle. An ICE ankle monitor.*
The CHILDREN *battle to see and touch the ankle monitor; they are kids, and*
it is a gadget.
JOSEFINA *disperses the* CHILDREN *and soothes* ISMAEL.
BEEP BEEP BEEEEEP.
Again, the CHILDREN *battle to see and touch the ankle monitor.*
Again, JOSEFINA *disperses the* CHILDREN *and soothes* ISMAEL.
BEEP BEEP BEEEEEP.
Now it's just irritating. The CHILDREN *cover their ears.*
JOSEFINA *quiets the* CHILDREN *and soothes* ISMAEL.
BEEP BEEP BEEEEEP.
The family is at wit's end.
BEEP BEEP BEEEEEP.
They can't take it anymore.
BEEP BEEP BEEEEEP.]

ISMAEL: ENOUGH!

[JOSEFINA *gives* ISMAEL *a pair of pants. He puts them on over the ankle*
monitor. The family cautiously gathers 'round him. They touch his chest, feel
the rhythm of his heart.]

JOSEFINA: And life kept going.

[*Life keeps going. The* CHILDREN *go to school,* ISMAEL *goes to work,* JOSE-FINA *is a* ruletero, *taking care of everything and everyone . . . The family is a machine, driven by the rhythm of* ISMAEL'S *pulse.*]

My children went back to school. My husband went back to his job, waiting tables at a hotel. And me, I came here, to La Misión.

El Padre has supported us fully in this process. And Marcos Medina—you met Marcos earlier—he volunteers here at La Misión, ever since El Padre helped him with his case.

I went to see many lawyers, but all of them told me no. Marcos found me the only lawyer that would take my case. I say my case because we are one. My husband is the father of my children. Anything that happens to him happens to me.

[*Life keeps going. The family machine intensifies.*]

Time was running out. My husband was going to be deported on the sixth of April. On April fifth, Marcos Medina took us to one last lawyer. God put him on my path. He made phone calls, got an emergency hearing, he went to court the same day. He called us that night and said, "I stopped the deportation. I need $2,500 for the court, right now."

[*Life keeps going. The family machine intensifies.*]

It's been money, money all the time. I get whatever work I can. People hire me to take pictures. On weekends, I sell *tamales* and *champurrado* out there, on the corner. I went to friends, my ex-bosses, *financieras.* Some gave me twenty dollars, some fifty, some five hundred. I'm in debt up to my neck, I must owe my soul already.

I started selling our things.

JULIAN: The TV.

LUCILA: The couch.

REBECCA: My bike.

JOSEFINA: It still wasn't enough. So I sold more.

JULIAN: My bed.

LUCILA: My bed.

REBECCA: My bed.

JOSEFINA: We have only one bed now, but we sleep happy.

[*Just as the family machine threatens to explode,* JOSEFINA *calms it and brings it to a place of rest.*]

I tell my children:
"*Mijos,* as hard as it is for us, it is just as hard for *Papi.* His future is not decided, he is worried, he is carrying the weight of the whole world on his shoulders. Let's see, how many little hands do we have here? If we take Lucila's two hands, and Julian's two hands, and Rebecca's two hands, plus my two hands, that's eight hands. What do you think if with all these hands, we help Papi carry all that weight?"

[*Together, the family carries the weight of the world.* ISMAEL *and the* CHIL-DREN *exit. We, the audience, are back in La Misión with* JOSEFINA.]

It's a slow process, a slow agony that wears you out. We have been fighting two years now. We have had three emergency hearings. Our last court hearing will be the first of June. The lawyer says that's the final one, when it will be decided if he stays or leaves. If he stays, it will be a miracle, but we have had many of those. If I don't win, I'll call you guys to say, "I lost, I'm leaving." But we will keep coming back, even if it is as wetbacks, I don't care. We will keep coming again and again.

The good thing is that we have a little joy to look forward to. My daughter turns fifteen next month, and *mis compañeras* here at La Misión are planning a *quinceañera* for her. And I hope you will join us. I would love to have you celebrate with us.

[*"Ding!" The attention signal over the intercom of an airplane.*]

FLIGHT ATTENDANT ONE: Ladies and gentlemen, welcome aboard American Airlines Flight 630 from Phoenix to Chicago's O'Hare International Airport. Please don't worry about the undocumented Palestinian woman now boarding and wearing a head scarf.

[*As* FLIGHT ATTENDANT ONE *continues,* AHLAM *boards the plane, talking on her cell phone and searching for her seat, very much in her own world.*]

AHLAM [*on cell phone*]: I don't think I can do this, Fatima . . . I'm getting on the plane now, but I don't think I can go through with it.

FLIGHT ATTENDANT ONE: Even if she starts bawling, or banging her head against the window . . .

AHLAM: This is me being calm.

FLIGHT ATTENDANT ONE: . . . or otherwise acting crazy, we promise she's been thoroughly screened by TSA.

AHLAM: Yes, of course they searched me. If my name and *hijab* weren't enough, I'm standing there bawling and shaking, I'm practically screaming TERRORIST ALERT.

FLIGHT ATTENDANT TWO: Prior to closing the main cabin doors, federal regulation requires the stowing of all carry-on luggage . . .

AHLAM: I'm telling you, I have to get off this plane. You have to turn around and come pick me up.

FLIGHT ATTENDANT TWO: . . . and the turning off of all electronic devices . . .

AHLAM: I know I said this is what I have to do.

FLIGHT ATTENDANTS ONE AND TWO: . . . including cellular telephones.

AHLAM: You think I don't know that my family is counting on me? That I don't know what my responsibility is?

FLIGHT ATTENDANT ONE [*to* AHLAM]: Excuse me, ma'am, I need you to turn off your phone and take your seat.

AHLAM [*to* FLIGHT ATTENDANT ONE]: Sorry. [*On phone*] I have to go. Yes, I know I'm doing the right thing. Yes, I am, I'm taking deep breaths.

[AHLAM *puts away her phone, takes her seat, and immediately begins rummaging in her backpack, earnestly looking for something.*]

FLIGHT ATTENDANT TWO: Once airborne, our flying time from Phoenix to Chicago will be three hours and twenty-two minutes, but it's going to seem a heck of a lot longer than that for one of our passengers.

[FLIGHT ATTENDANT ONE *approaches* AHLAM *and hands her a beautiful leather journal.*]

FLIGHT ATTENDANT ONE: Is this what you're looking for?

AHLAM [*taking the journal*]: Yes, thank you.

FLIGHT ATTENDANT ONE: My pleasure.

[AHLAM *writes feverishly in her journal.*]

> [*Over* AHLAM's *shoulder*] Oh, that's adorable, you're trying to write out your feelings. But don't you get angry just looking at that journal, remembering how your friend got to study abroad in Spain but you couldn't, because you're undocumented and you can't leave the country or you'll never get back in. Don't you get jealous, picturing all the amazing architecture your friend got to see, in Barcelona, Cordoba, Sevilla, Granada . . .

AHLAM: I'm sorry, what'd you say?

FLIGHT ATTENDANT ONE: Can I get you anything else?

AHLAM: Oh. Uh, no, thanks.

[*She goes back to writing.*]

FLIGHT ATTENDANT TWO: Air traffic control forecasts both physical and emotional turbulence this afternoon . . .

FLIGHT ATTENDANT ONE: You can make sure your belt is securely fastened by inserting the metal fittings one into the other and pulling on the loose end of the strap if you like . . .

FLIGHT ATTENDANT TWO: but it won't help:

FLIGHT ATTENDANT ONE AND TWO: Prepare for takeoff.

[*TAKEOFF! And* . . . *abruptly* AHLAM *is in a new place, she speaks with a different energy, a new urgency. The* FLIGHT ATTENDANTS *transform, visually becoming doppelgangers to* AHLAM. *They take her on a journey of memory and emotion, traveling rapidly from place to place and time to time, themselves becoming other characters in her life.*]

AHLAM: Arizona—

FLIGHT ATTENDANT ONE: Last night—

FLIGHT ATTENDANT TWO: Midnight.

AHLAM: Senator John McCain's office—

FLIGHT ATTENDANT ONE: The street corner—

FLIGHT ATTENDANT TWO: —beneath McCain's window

AHLAM: Three kids asleep, under an open tent, made from an American flag. Fatima whispers to me:

FLIGHT ATTENDANT TWO/FATIMA: "They're undocumented."

FLIGHT ATTENDANT ONE: You shout at them in your head:

AHLAM: *Do you know where you are!* This is Arizona, where the police can ask for your papers just because you look undocumented. This is Arizona, where highway billboards proclaim:

ALL: *"Stop the Invasion!" "Illegals Go Home!"*

AHLAM: This is Arizona and you're sleeping out in the open with nothing but an American flag tent to protect you?

[FLIGHT ATTENDANTS ONE *and* TWO *pull* AHLAM *into a new scene.* FLIGHT ATTENDANT TWO *becomes* FATIMA.]

FLIGHT ATTENDANT ONE: Chicago—last year:

FLIGHT ATTENDANT TWO/FATIMA: Congratulations, Ahlam, you got the job.

AHLAM: For real? Me? I got it? Yes! Can I hug you?

[*She hugs* FLIGHT ATTENDANT TWO/FATIMA.]

I'm not always like this, I mean, I'm not usually a hugger, but this is my dream job. I love everything about Inner City Muslim Action Network. I'm going to be the best communications assistant you ever had. No, I'll be the best employee you ever had. When do I start?

FLIGHT ATTENDANT ONE: We just need your ID.

AHLAM: My ID.

FLIGHT ATTENDANT TWO/FATIMA: For the paperwork.

AHLAM: I have my student ID.

FLIGHT ATTENDANT ONE: Birth certificate?

AHLAM: It's from Jordan . . .

FLIGHT ATTENDANT TWO/FATIMA: Passport?

AHLAM: Jordan.

FLIGHT ATTENDANT ONE: Social security card?

AHLAM: Yes! But . . . it says "not valid for employment."

[*Uncomfortable pause.*]

FLIGHT ATTENDANT TWO/FATIMA: You were teasing me.

AHLAM: Teasing you?

FLIGHT ATTENDANT TWO/FATIMA: You were the most qualified candidate.

AHLAM: Teasing you?

FLIGHT ATTENDANT TWO/FATIMA: I really wanted you for this job.

AHLAM: Teasing you?

FLIGHT ATTENDANT ONE: Chicago—last week:

FLIGHT ATTENDANT TWO/FATIMA: We need you in Arizona.

AHLAM: Arizona?

FLIGHT ATTENDANT TWO/FATIMA: I left my job. I'm registering voters in Arizona.

AHLAM: I don't understand.

FLIGHT ATTENDANT TWO/FATIMA: To overturn SB 1070. It's the law that requires cops to check your status if you "look" undocumented.

AHLAM: You were going to move to New York, to be with your fiancé.

FLIGHT ATTENDANT TWO/FATIMA: In Arizona they only see one face to the immigrant issue and it's a guy from Mexico picking apples who doesn't speak a word of English.

AHLAM: You should be earning big bucks at a fancy New York firm.

FLIGHT ATTENDANT TWO/FATIMA: It would be powerful to have your face down there.

AHLAM: You're a citizen.

FLIGHT ATTENDANT TWO/FATIMA: And I think it would be a good experience for you. Just for a weekend.

AHLAM: Not even for a day.

FLIGHT ATTENDANT TWO/FATIMA: Ahlam, you're my inspiration.

AHLAM: You're crazy.

FLIGHT ATTENDANT TWO/FATIMA: Architecture degree from University of Illinois, experienced web designer, fluent in English and Arabic. You deserved that job.

FLIGHT ATTENDANT ONE: Last year:

FLIGHT ATTENDANT TWO/FATIMA: You were teasing me.

AHLAM: Teasing you?

FLIGHT ATTENDANT ONE: That night:

AHLAM: I leave Fatima and the job that should've been mine. I take the train home, but I'm too embarrassed to face my parents. I go for a walk. I remember my father coming home from work at midnight and the two of us learning ABCs together.

FLIGHT ATTENDANT ONE/FATHER: "Education is our ticket out."

AHLAM: "Look, Dad! I got a ninety-three on this really big test."

FLIGHT ATTENDANT ONE/FATHER: "Ninety-three is OK, but . . . what happened to the other seven points?"

AHLAM: I walk and walk.

FLIGHT ATTENDANT ONE: The edge of a forest.

AHLAM: I look up into the dark sky.

FLIGHT ATTENDANT TWO: Snow falling.

AHLAM: This is America. Someone will fix this. They'll pass a law, and they'll fix this.

FLIGHT ATTENDANT ONE: Last week:

FLIGHT ATTENDANT TWO/FATIMA: This is America. When someone passes a law like SB 1070, we fight back.

AHLAM [*a string of excuses*]: My parents won't let me fly. I got a new restaurant job: more hours, better pay. I need to pay off my diploma. Someone's gotta put my brother through college. I can't just leave.

FLIGHT ATTENDANT TWO/FATIMA: You know, Ahlam, sometimes when life is calling, you just have to answer the call.

AHLAM: That's the corniest thing anyone has ever said to me.

FLIGHT ATTENDANT ONE AND TWO: Ring-ring! Ring-ring! Ring-ring!

AHLAM: Just for a weekend.

FLIGHT ATTENDANT TWO/FATIMA: Yes! Can I hug you?

FLIGHT ATTENDANT ONE: First night in Arizona:

[AHLAM *and* FATIMA *in a car.*]

AHLAM: Oh my God: Best. Day. Ever. Who would've thought registering voters in a Walmart parking lot would be so much fun? And FOX News was there. FOX NEWS!? And running away from the cops, and sneaking back, and running away, and sneaking back.

FLIGHT ATTENDANT TWO/FATIMA: You're a natural. The way you handled that one woman.

AHLAM: Oh, accent lady? "Good afternoon, ma'am, my name is Ahlam and I'm with Promise America and we're registering people to vote in the November—"

FLIGHT ATTENDANT TWO/FATIMA [*as accent lady*]: "I'm sorry, I have to stop you."

AHLAM: "It'll only take three minutes."

FLIGHT ATTENDANT TWO/FATIMA: "I just don't get it."

AHLAM: "What? Registering to vote?"

FLIGHT ATTENDANT TWO/FATIMA: "Well, you're A-rab, you're askin' me to vote, and you have this East Coast accent—"

AHLAM: "OK, first of all . . ."

TOGETHER: "It's a Chicago accent!"

FLIGHT ATTENDANT ONE: Traffic slows.

FLIGHT ATTENDANT TWO/FATIMA: Construction ahead.

AHLAM: Single lane.

FLIGHT ATTENDANT ONE: Traffic stops.

AHLAM [*scared*]: *Fatima.*

FLIGHT ATTENDANT ONE: Police ahead.

AHLAM: He's turning our way, he's coming toward us, he's looking at me.

FLIGHT ATTENDANT ONE: Red light. Nowhere to go.

AHLAM [*panicked*]: What do I say if he arrests me? Do I get deported right away? Do I get a phone call? Can't call my father. My brother: I call my brother, have him call a lawyer first, then my dad.

FLIGHT ATTENDANT ONE: Light turns green. Traffic moves.

[*Back on the corner, staring at the tent.*]

AHLAM: Arizona . . . Second night . . . Midnight . . . Street corner beneath McCain's office . . . three kids asleep under a tent made from an American flag.
Fatima whispers, "They're undocumented."
I shout at them in my head: *Do you know where you are!*

[*Back on the plane.*]

FLIGHT ATTENDANT ONE: As we begin our descent, please return to your seats and fasten your seat belts.

AHLAM: I look out the window of the plane: endless sky and rippling lake reach together toward a clear blue horizon. The Chicago skyline grows near, Hancock Building and Sears Tower reaching up, up, and away in the birthplace of the skyscraper. I chose architecture school because I wanted to make something tangible, something I could see and touch. I want to touch the thing that's holding me back. I want to see it and touch it and break it and burn it down to the ground.

[*One of the youth emerges from the tent: it is* YOUNG AHLAM.]

[*Seeing her younger self*] I used to be the biggest troublemaker. In our neighborhood in Jordan, there was a construction site with a huge pile of white rocks. I'd race the boys to the top, get there first, push the boys down, and throw rocks at them! I was a real smart mouth. My dad would call to me, "Hey, you!" I'd snap back:

ALL: "My name is not hey you . . .

AHLAM: *"My name is Ahlam."*

FLIGHT ATTENDANT TWO: Flight attendants, prepare for landing.

AHLAM [*drawn back toward the tent*]: I am done holding myself back.
Arizona—three kids—nothing protecting them
You know where you are.
This is Arizona—
This is America.
My name is Ahlam, I am undocumented, I am no longer afraid, and I do not apologize.

[*Transition: The flag tent comes down. Revealed behind the tent, taking it down, folding it up:* EL PADRE, *the priest the audience heard about from the* CHILDREN *of La Misión. Opposite* EL PADRE, *at the far end of the stage, a massive green metal door with a Plexiglas window: the visiting room of a detention center. An* OFFICER *stands at the side of the door.*]

EL PADRE: I was tired to be in this mission, because there is much to do, and sometimes you can't do anything for someone, and you get tired.

I wrote my letter to the bishop and said, "I'm resigning, I am going to take off." I walked outside to mail my letter, and a man comes to me: *Padre, I need you to help with my wife. She is in detention in Taylorville.*

And I said, "No, I'm resigning. I'm going to do something else now. I can't continue doing this."

Padre, por favor . . . our little boy needs to see his mother. She is still nursing him.

[EL PADRE *has folded the flag so that it is now a baby. He cradles the baby.*]

When we get to Taylorville, the officer says,

OFFICER: You cannot take the child inside.

EL PADRE: "This child is here to reclaim his mother. This child needs to eat. Are you going to take off your shirt and feed him?"

And they made a huge mistake: they allowed me to bring the child inside. I gave the child to the woman, and the child felt his mother—do you know?—his eyes grew big.

And after fifteen minutes the officer said,

OFFICER: The time is over. You need to take the boy out.

EL PADRE: "I'm not going to take this child from his mother."

OFFICER: You did this on purpose, you brought the child in here on purpose.

EL PADRE: "No, you are the officer, you said I could take the child in here."

OFFICER: You have to take the child.

EL PADRE: "And I am not taking the child."

OFFICER: I'm going to arrest you.

EL PADRE: "Arrest me. But if you have a child, you are not going to sleep tonight."

OFFICER: Yes, I have a child.

[*Pause.*]

Well, what can we do?

EL PADRE: "The boy will finish eating, and he will go to sleep. Then I will take him."

The mother didn't resist, but she was devastated when I took the baby from her.

When I was driving back to Chicago, I think I was at Harlem and Fifty-Five, I get a phone call from the officer. "Are you going to arrest me?" I ask him.

OFFICER: I want to tell you that I don't feel OK. I did my best. I talked to my supervisor, and we are able to grant this woman a humanitarian release. I have her in my car. You can pick her up at 10 P.M. at Congress and Clark.

EL PADRE: These are the sacred situations, when families are reunited, that remind us that we cannot give up our struggle. And if I ever take arms again to fight, it would be so I don't have to see those separations.

[*Visiting room at a jail.*
ADELINA *and* ANDRES, *separated by an impenetrable metal wall and the glass of a prison visit window.*
This is strange and impossible: they've never been separated before.
And they've never been this scared before.
They try to communicate—to speak, to touch, to dance, to love—through the glass.]

ANDRES:
How the hell could I let this happen? The cops just pulled over, picked me out of thirty of us on the street. Out of everybody, the cops took me—I don't want to see her right now. I don't want to see

ADELINA:
There's glass and I see him and he can see me and we see each other.

her in this place this CARELESS
STUPID HELPLESS!

It's kind of cold in here.
Is he cold? No he's not cold. He's
warm.

Adelina.
Adelina. Adelina. Don't bring our
kids to this place. My kids, my
Pablo, my Patricia. I need to touch
my kids, I need to see my kids, I
need to feel my kids, I need to
smell them, I need to feed them.

Our children. He's not going to see
our kids. And they're not going to
see their dad. They're not going to
see each other, they're not going to
touch each other, they're not going
to talk to each other, they're not
going to hold each other, they're
not going to kiss each other.

I can't hear her voice clearly.
Her voice is muffled. I can't hear
her. I can't hear my wife.

But I'm with them. I'm with them.
I'm here. I'm here. I'm still here.

But I want to be with him.

If I never see them again, how long
will my family remember me? How
long will they remember my face,
my voice, remember who I am?

I'm not going to be able to let go of
my children.

Remember who I am.

What's the worst that can happen?
The cops give me to immigration.
Immigration deports me.
I'll come back.
I'll come back.
I'll come back.
I'll come back.

What's the worst that can happen?
The worst?
The worst?
The worst?
He could die.
He could get deported.
He would try to come back to us.
He could die trying to come back
to us.

ANDRES:

This can't be happening. This can't be real. I need to get out of here. I need to hear her voice. I need to touch her skin. I need her to know that I will be fine, that I will come back, that I will keep her warm.

I need to see my son.

ADELINA:
That's the worst.
But that's not real.
Tell me that's not real.

You need to stop. Stop taking care of me. Stop being good to me. I can take care of myself. I can take care of our children. I will feed our children like I've been feeding them. I will love our children like I've been loving them.
And just for now,
I'll be you.
For our children.

I heard about a priest who helps people like us. I'll go tomorrow.

[*Time's up.* ADELINA *leaves.*
Days later? Weeks later?
ANDRES *is visited by his young son,* PABLITO.
PABLITO *yearns to touch his father.*
Glass separates them.
Still, the boy's need urges him toward his father.
Violently.]

ANDRES:

No, I'm not a criminal.

PABLITO:
Why are you here? Why are you here? Why are you here? Did you do something wrong? You go to jail when you do something

wrong. When you're a criminal. Are you a criminal? You're not a criminal, you're my dad. You're my dad and you belong at home. You need to be there for Mom. You need to be there for Patricia. You need to be there for me. For me. For me. For me.

This glass cannot be stronger than me. This glass cannot keep me from my own family that I can't touch, that I brought up by my own blood, sweat, and tears that I can't touch. How is this glass stronger than me?

This glass needs to go. We need to break through it, we're strong. Together we can be together we can break this glass we can be together. Me and you. Me and you. This glass needs to break right now in front of my face so I can touch my son.

You're supposed to be with me today. We're supposed to play together. Today is our day to play together. To go to the park. We're supposed to go to the park. We're supposed to have fun.

You're a man, Pablo. Pablo, you're a man, do not cry in front of me right now. Do not cry in front of me. Not now. You're a man. You are my son, the son of Andres. I dreamt about you since the day I married your mom. You're all I've ever hoped to come out of this world. We are strong, OK? This is important, this is important. They can't do anything to you or your sister. Because you were born here. You are my love. You are everything that I have ever hoped for. You are my future and you will be better than I am.

[*The glass does not yield.*
Father and son do not understand how the glass can be stronger than their need
to touch. ANDRES *and* PABLITO *collapse, exhausted.*
Guards remove PABLITO.
Time passes. ANDRES *removes his orange prison jumpsuit.*
ANDRES *returns to his family:* ADELINA, PATRICIA, *and* PABLITO. *The*
family is together—perhaps everything turned out OK?
A guard gives ANDRES *an envelope.* ANDRES *opens the envelope and reads*
the letter inside.]

ANDRES: "Dear Andres del Valle. You have been granted the privilege of
voluntarily departing from the United States of America. If you fail
to voluntarily depart by May 18, 2011, a removal order will be entered
against you."

[*The family sags, crumples, withers.*
Only PATRICIA *remains standing upright.*]

PATRICIA: Come here, *Papi, te voy a hechar la bendición:*
God, my father is a hard-working man, he takes care of us, he
loves us. Please, God, protect him from any harm he could suffer on
his way, give him courage to overcome despair, and strength to fight
any obstacles he might find. Put our love in his heart, so that he can
remember that we are waiting for him, that we need him here with
us. God, I know you love this family, and you want it to stay together.
Take my father by the hand in this journey. Bring him home safe. We
will pray for him every day, until the day he comes back to our home.
En el nombre del Padre, del Hijo, y del Espíritu Santo. Amén.

[ANDRES *leaves his family, his home.*
Searching for something to help her and her family survive, ADELINA *finds*
what she needs in the memory of a hopeful time: a reprise of her song from
earlier, but now out of time. In her voice, the audience hears ADELINA *simul-*
taneously quaking with fear and summoning new strength. PABLITO *and*
PATRICIA *light* veladoras, *candles to* la Virgen, *in prayer for their father's*
safe return.]

ADELINA [*singing*]: *Cariño, cariñito mio*
    cuéntame el cuento otra vez
    de como dos guaches

cruzaron a pie
la frontera en su luna de miel

[*In his soul,* ANDRES *hears* ADELINA's *voice calling him back to his family. He begins the treacherous journey.*
ADELINA *and* ANDRES *are two parts of a whole. When he falters, her voice lifts his legs. When her voice breaks, his stride fills her lungs with the air to sing.*]

De como soñaron cariño
Con los niños que van a tener
y como con besos los consentirán
lo mejor del mundo les darán

Cariño, cariñito mio
Cuéntame el cuento otra vez
De como Dos guaches
cruzaron a pie
y al final, todo salió bien

[ANDRES *returns to his family.*
Relieved but worn, ANDRES *is a different man. The family has changed too. There is love, but no levity.*]

ANDRES: Is this really happening? Am I really here? Are *you* really here? Tell me our story, Adelina . . .

[ADELINA *and* ANDRES *begin to dance. A familiar and beloved dance, but interrupted and altered by the realities of their life.*]

ADELINA: You will change your name. Our children will say that their father is in Mexico, that it's only me and them.

    We will tell them to lie—and, outside our home, they will act like you don't exist.

    I will use my maiden name. I will say that I'm alone, that my husband is not coming back until ten years have passed, that my brother is helping me, that I'm babysitting to make a bit of money.

    You will work, as a busboy, two jobs as always, with your new name. Other than work, the children will beg you to stay inside. You will hardly leave the house.

    We will always live with fear inside. That our children will forget and say something, that you will be caught, that you won't come home from work.

You will say that, if you get deported again, we will all leave and start from scratch over there. But we both know that I won't take them back, that the future of our children is here, that I will stay and support them, and fight for them, until they are big enough to stay here alone.

[*Singing:*]

Cariño, cariñito mio
Cuéntame el cuento otra vez
De como dos guaches
cruzaron a pie
y al final, todo salió bien

[*"Ding!" The bell signaling the start of round in a boxing match.* LUCA, *now age twenty-two, takes center stage in a tight arena that could be a boxing ring or a courtroom.* LUCA *has a* POSSE *of fellow activists who follow him onto the stage, among them* MARCOS MEDINA *and* AHLAM. *They bear witness to, and occasionally participate in, his story.*]

LUCA: The United States of America vs. Luca Rivera. Representing the defendant, Luca Rivera: Luca Rivera.

I come from a family of fighters. My mom was a fighter. She fought the fumes she inhaled from twelve years working in a windowless plastics factory. And even when the fumes infected her lungs with cancer, she continued to fight with chemo, after chemo, after chemo treatment. Hell, she survived twenty-five years of marriage to my father—now that's a fight.

My mom, my mom had hands like a fighter—callused and tough from graveyard shifts at the factory, yet tender to the touch—and quick with a slap if you talked back. She brought me up in a good way—taught me manners, to be respectful, to say thank you. She taught me to stand up against kids who chased me with rocks after school because I talked funny. She taught me to be strong, to keep my head up, and to always move forward, even when life kicks us in the ass here and there.

And my dad? My dad just likes to fight.

[ANTONIO *steps into the ring. A* POSSE MEMBER *helps* LUCA *into boxing gloves.*]

ANTONIO: Luca Rivera vs. Antonio Rivera.

[LUCA *and* ANTONIO *begin to box.*]

LUCA: Back in Mexico, my dad was a boxer. He came to this country for one reason and one reason only—to work.

ANTONIO: If your ass ain't in school, it better be looking for a job.

LUCA: Keep your head down, stay hidden, and shut up. My relationship with my dad—always been rocky.

ANTONIO: Black.

LUCA: White. I was fifteen when 9/11 happened. Went to my first anti-war protest.

ANTONIO: Go to that protest and you can look for a new place to live.

LUCA: Didn't stop me. I went, and the sight of vivid colored banners; the sound of amplified, opinionated voices; people sharing their stories— it activated me.

ANTONIO: What the hell do you have to say that needs hearing, boy?

LUCA: Although I didn't get my diploma from Benito Juarez High School, I learned about great figures in Mexican history—activists, artists, workers. People who took arms against oppression and demanded change.

ANTONIO: You want change? There's the door.

LUCA: I define myself as an artist. I look up to Diego Rivera and Frida Kahlo. They lived a political and artful life.

ANTONIO: Your mom is dying and you're out painting banners.

LUCA: I want to make the struggle more colorful.

ANTONIO: Black.

LUCA: White. I told my parents I'm gay. I didn't really tell them I'm gay—I mean, come on, they kind of found out. My mom didn't understand. My dad . . .

ANTONIO: Get out of my house.

LUCA: I was seventeen when he kicked me out. I found refuge in activism. A group of us started planning the first Coming Out of the Shadows Rally. On March 10, 2010, eight of us would come out as undocumented and unafraid at Federal Plaza in downtown Chicago.

My mom got sick again. I was with her for every chemo treatment. I was designing flyers and pumping people up for the rally, then at Cook County holding my mom's hand as they pumped her full of chemo. I knew the day was coming when my mom wouldn't be with me anymore. That day was January 23, 2010.

[ANTONIO *takes off his gloves in reaction to his wife's death and leaves the stage.*]

I gave myself a week break and I went full force.

POSSE MEMBER: Round One. March 10, 2010.

LUCA: We take to the streets and head for Federal Plaza. There are people strumming guitars, banging drums, singing, marching. The eight of us take the stage and, one by one, we come out of hiding. I take the mic and I share the story of a woman who worked endlessly surrounded by toxins to provide for her family; the story of a woman who censored her concerns about health conditions in the factory for fear she'd get fired; a woman who fled poverty so her children could eat; a woman who ducked factory raids; a woman who told me to stand up for myself; a woman who taught me to dream; a woman who died working in a land where she's considered a criminal and is buried in a land where she is still considered a criminal.

And when I finish, I step away from the mic and it hits me—I'm never going to see my mom again.

POSSE MEMBER: Final Round: Luca Rivera vs. Senator Harry Reid.

LUCA: There's nothing keeping me in Chicago, so I leave my job, leave my apartment, leave my boyfriend, and I go where the movement needs me. Maine, then Boston, then Washington, D.C., where we have a new target: the United States Senate. Our goal: make them bring the Dream Act to a vote.

We plan, we practice, we hire legal advisors, we are ready. We dress in graduation gowns and head to Capitol Hill and our targets . . .

[LUCA *is joined by his* POSSE. *They all dress in graduation gowns.*]

POSSE MEMBER: Barbara Boxer, Democrat of New York.

ANOTHER POSSE MEMBER: John McCain, Republican of Arizona.

ANOTHER POSSE MEMBER: Charles Schumer, Democrat of New York.

LUCA: And Senator Harry Reid, Senate Majority Leader, and Democrat of Nevada.

We march into the Capitol building. Group one spreads a banner and sits on the floor of the Capitol atrium. They get arrested within forty-five minutes. People spill out of their offices to see what's going on. There's no avoiding us. My group walks into Senator Reid's office and it's just like we rehearsed:

"My name is Luca, and I'm undocumented. We know Senator Reid has the power to bring the Dream Act to a vote. We're not leaving until Senator Reid gives us a vote on the Senate floor. Win or lose, we deserve the respect of a vote."

POSSE MEMBER: *For my people.*

ANOTHER POSSE MEMBER: *For my family.*

ANOTHER POSSE MEMBER: *For my education.*

ANOTHER POSSE MEMBER: *For my future.*

LUCA: *"For my America."*

Senator Reid's staffers don't know what to do with us.

POSSE MEMBER [*as a staffer*]: Why are you here? The senator supports you!

LUCA: "But he hasn't done anything for us."

POSSE MEMBER [*as a staffer*]: Well, make yourselves comfortable while I call the police.

[POLICE OFFICER *enters.*]

LUCA: We knew we would get arrested, we were not leaving until we got arrested. My group was there for six hours. But we came prepared: we wore diapers. We were not leaving that office for nothing, not even to go to the bathroom.

LUCA, POSSE MEMBER, AND OFFICER: First warning.

LUCA: Seven thirty comes and the Senate building closes.

ALL: Second warning.
Seven thirty.

LUCA: Now we're trespassing on federal property.

ALL: Third warning.

[*The* POLICE OFFICER *arrests* LUCA.]

LUCA: We're together and we're not scared, we're smiling. There are pictures of me getting arrested and I'm smiling.

At two o'clock in the morning they start releasing us one by one by one by one by one. I'm charged with trespassing. As I'm leaving the jail I hear singing. I look up to see hundreds of people—our people—camped out, singing, waiting, sitting vigil for us. I see the cameras—yes!—the press here.

I'm transported to the memory of the last time I wore this gown. It's my eighth grade graduation. My mom, my sisters, and I head to Cook County for another chemo treatment after my graduation ceremony. I remember her sitting in the chair, smiling at me, her eyes filled with love and pride. She looks at me and says, *Luca, Sigue Adelante . . . keep moving forward.*

When I'm back in Chicago, I sometimes walk by her work. That windowless plastics factory doesn't exist anymore. In its place stands a condo. That's when I remember how I got to D.C. in the first place, your honor. That's when I remember the reason I'm standing here in your courtroom today. I'm here to keep my mother from disappearing.

[*The stage is no longer a specific place. We are aware of the vastness of the space.* FAMILIES *and individuals enter, each in their isolated world, each with a suitcase. The suitcases seem to weigh them down, to demand their focus but also steal their energy.*]

Each individual or family rushes to a personal destination, unaware of the others. They open their suitcases, tearing out the clothes inside, desperate and fearful.
Then they begin to pack again.
The packing is laden with emotion, to the point of being unearthly.
Into this terrain arrive two Sisters of Mercy, SISTER HELEN *and* SISTER ROSE. *They are in or near their eighties, but they have an energy so vital that the audience is rarely aware of their age. They travel through the theatrical space, supporting each other, sometimes stopping to help put an item in a suitcase or just to touch a hand. The* FAMILIES *are not directly aware of the* SISTERS, *though their proximity seems to lend some comfort.*]

SISTER HELEN: It was January of 2007. The coldest day we ever had in Chicago. I can't tell you how cold it was. We arrived as the buses were bringing people in from jails and other centers. As we stood there, we saw families arriving, always with a suitcase, and they were—

TOGETHER: always running.

SISTER HELEN: They would run into the center. Minutes later, they would run out of the center.

SISTER ROSE: And they would be tearing stuff out of the suitcase.

SISTER HELEN: Here they are, losing their loved one, and they packed this wonderful suitcase. They'd run in again, then out again,

SISTER ROSE: because the officials tell them it's still too big, or too heavy.

SISTER HELEN: We said, "My goodness, we should be inside the center, to pray with those that are so afraid and worried." So we go up to the officer and say, "Well, we'd like to go inside and pray with those that are being deported." And they looked at us—

SISTER ROSE: like we had horns.

TOGETHER: *"You can't do that!"*

SISTER ROSE: I never knew two eighty-year-old Sisters of Mercy could be so frightening to a man with a gun.

SISTER HELEN: And when we got into the car afterward, we said to each other,

TOGETHER: "We have to be here every week."

SISTER HELEN: So we started going every Friday, 7 A.M., and it would be the two of us praying—

SISTER ROSE: and singing.

SISTER HELEN: And our other sisters started joining us. One of them said, "Oh, we're not going to sing!" Rose said,

SISTER ROSE: "Look around, no one will hear you!"

SISTER HELEN: Because the center is in the middle of an industrial area.

SISTER ROSE: Broadview, Illinois.

SISTER HELEN: Factories, warehouses, trucks and a lot of

SISTER ROSE: . . . noise.

SISTER HELEN: We knew many immigrants from the nineteen-nineties, when we made a public sanctuary for refugees from the conflict in Central America.

SISTER ROSE: Su Casa Catholic Worker House. We lived there six and a half years.

SISTER HELEN: We thought we were retired, but it bothered us that we couldn't get inside Broadview. We thought,

TOGETHER: "What are we being called to do?"

SISTER HELEN: So we telephoned the director of ICE,

SISTER ROSE: but he would never answer our calls. We thought wait a minute, these are human beings. They have human rights. They have religious rights. They deserve comfort and—

TOGETHER: we can't take no for an answer.

SISTER HELEN: Fred Tsao at the Illinois Coalition, he wrote a bill allowing access for religious workers to any detention center in Illinois.

SISTER ROSE: Maureen Fitzpatrick at the South West Organizing Project, she and I went down to Springfield to meet with Representative Dan Burke, to ask him to sponsor the bill. So we went down on March 17, St. Patrick's Day . . .

SISTER HELEN: . . . 2008 . . .

SISTER ROSE: . . . and there was Dan with his green St. Patrick's tie on, so I complimented him on that.

TOGETHER: It's politics.

SISTER HELEN: I bet we went to Springfield two or three times a week for months. They would call and say,

TOGETHER: *"You gotta testify tomorrow!"*

SISTER HELEN: The bill passed out of the house executive committee, thank God! Got on the house floor:

TOGETHER: Passed unanimously.

SISTER HELEN: Iris Martinez and Jacqui Collins agreed to sponsor it in the Senate. People said, "You'll never be able to get it through the Senate this session."

SISTER ROSE: Don't tell *us* never.

SISTER HELEN: We do what we have to do.

SISTER ROSE: Jacqui Collins said, "You need to convince Emil Jones,"

SISTER HELEN: the president of the Senate.

SISTER ROSE: It just so happened that Emil Jones is Catholic, and we know his pastor. His aunt is a Sister of Mercy.
I said, "Father Flynn, would you go with us to Springfield?"

SISTER HELEN: We pick him up at six in the morning and off we go. Twenty of us march right into the office, all different faiths: priests, rabbis, Muslims. I say, "Father Flynn is Emil Jones's pastor and he would like to see the senator."

SISTER ROSE: "Oh, Father, the senator is very busy."

SISTER HELEN: "You mean his pastor came all the way from Chicago and Senator Jones would not have the courtesy to greet him?"

SISTER ROSE: "Well, just a minute."

SISTER HELEN: So a different woman comes out in her high heels and suit:

SISTER ROSE: "I will take the Sisters and the Father and that's it!"

SISTER HELEN: Well, of course, all twenty of us went in. Straight down to the Senate floor.

SISTER ROSE: When Emil Jones saw Father Flynn, he said, "Oh Father, I haven't been to church in many Sundays."

SISTER HELEN: I said, "This bill has to happen now,"

SISTER ROSE: and Emil Jones was kind of nodding

SISTER HELEN: —and this part is notorious—

SISTER ROSE: I just went right up to him and said, "You have the power to do this." And he kind of backed up a little and smiled. And I said, "NO, you have the power to see that this is passed."

SISTER HELEN: The bill passed unanimously in the Senate. It was signed into law in December, and became law in June of 2009.

[*The* FAMILIES *close up their suitcases and carefully position them, as if handing them to a loved one. The suitcases form two rows: church pews. The* FAMILIES *kneel and pray.*]

SISTER ROSE: Come August, they still wouldn't let us in the detention center, even though it's a state law.

SISTER HELEN: So the Illinois Coalition asked would we be willing to be arrested.

SISTER ROSE: We talked about it and prayed about it and said—

TOGETHER: yes we would.

SISTER HELEN: So it was planned that we would lie down in front of the deportation buses. This got press. I mean, it got to Washington. They put in the news that these two elderly nuns were going to get arrested, and Rose said,

SISTER ROSE: "I don't mind you giving my age but *elderly?*"

SISTER HELEN: The director of ICE called on my cell phone and he said, "You'll be called Pastoral Care. You can come every week. You can see the women and the men. You can pray on the buses."

TOGETHER: Everything we asked for.

[*The* FAMILIES *leave the pews and form a vigil behind the* SISTERS.]

SISTER HELEN: We saw one hundred people the first day. I had nightmares about orange jumpsuits.

[DEPORTEES *enter, wearing orange prison jumpsuits, chained at the ankles and wrists, shackled together at the waist. They move in unison, in two regimented columns. They are like ghosts.*]

SISTER ROSE: We're the only humans they see besides the guards, because families can only visit on television screens, and only for half an hour a week.

[*The* DEPORTEES *sit on suitcases: the benches of a bus.*]

SISTER HELEN: We pass out an information sheet and a prayer sheet. We get the full name of every detainee, their E Number, their birthday, the jail number, the country they're from, the languages they speak, and the telephone numbers for a friend or a relation, somebody we could call.

SISTER ROSE: Their family might not even know where they are.

SISTER HELEN: If a person has under ten dollars in their commissary account, we put ten dollars in. At least they can buy toothpaste, stamps, or potato chips because they are—

TOGETHER: hungry a lot of the time.

SISTER HELEN: Outside, the deportation bus looks just like a regular coach. But inside . . .

[SISTER HELEN *and* SISTER ROSE *take their positions in the front of the bus.*]

SISTER ROSE: Plexiglas separates us from the men and women. And behind the Plexiglas, a metal grate. You can't walk down the aisle, can't just touch them on the shoulder to say good-bye.

SISTER HELEN: It's dark. You can't see them, they're just shadows. I don't know whether they can see us.

SISTER ROSE: You have to get down on your knees. There's a hole in the glass, and you get down on your knees to talk through that hole to speak to them.

SISTER HELEN: They call out to us.

DEPORTEE ONE: *Hermana, Hermana! Dígale a mi esposa que la quiero, y que cuide de los niños.*

DEPORTEE TWO: *Hermana, Hermana! Por favor, llame a mi mama y dígale que regreso a casa a Ecuador.*

SISTER ROSE: Please tell my wife I love her and take care of our children.

SISTER HELEN: Please call my mom and tell her I'm coming home to Ecuador.

SISTER ROSE: It's very fast, I'm not sure we have even five minutes. It's really only enough time for a prayer.

ALL: *Padre nuestro,*
que estás en el cielo.
Santificado sea tu nombre.
Venga tu reino.
Hágase tu voluntad en la tierra como en el cielo.
Danos hoy nuestro pan de cada día.
Perdona nuestras ofensas,
como también nosotros perdonamos a los que nos ofenden.
No nos dejes caer en tentación y líbranos del mal.
Amén.

[*In unison, the* DEPORTEES *rise, lift their suitcases, and exit. The* FAMILIES, *standing in vigil, watch and almost wave good-bye.*]

SISTER ROSE: The whole system is demonic. What exists is an evil, evil system. And we must continue to fight against it with all that we've got.

SISTER HELEN: People think we're kind of crazy, even within our own family and our Sisters. We're off doing these crazy things, but—

TOGETHER: they're not crazy to us.

SISTER ROSE: After a while, there are certain things you just don't talk about.

SISTER HELEN: And it's wonderful that God put Rose in my path because it's tough . . . to be alone and be crazy.

ACT THREE

Small Miracles

[*As the* SISTERS *exit,* LUCA *emerges from the vigil. He is preparing for a rally. It could be any rally anywhere in support of immigrant rights. He is joined by more and more activists. Dozens become hundreds become thousands become hundreds of thousands.*

Among the activists are people the audience knows—ADELINA *and* ANDRES; ISMAEL *and* JOSEFINA; MARCOS MEDINA; AHLAM—*and many more they don't know.*

There are cameras: Yes! The press is here! Suitcases in the set drop open revealing TV screens broadcasting footage from immigration rallies all over the United States as our rally continues onstage.

In our rally, there are no words and no banners. There is drumming, there are instruments, there is singing, there is marching, there is dancing.

There is anger and frustration. But overwhelmingly, there is desire, optimism, and the joyful expression of community and solidarity and resilience. It must be breathtakingly beautiful.

As the rally winds down, the audience finds themselves transported to another loving expression of community, another celebration . . . They are back at La Misión, for REBECCA's *quinceañera!*

ISMAEL, JOSEFINA, JULIAN, *and* LUCILA *enter. They are radiant.*

ISMAEL *plays with his two adorable* CHILDREN. JOSEFINA *welcomes audience members.*]

JOSEFINA: Thank you for coming to my daughter's *quinceañera* . . . We're so glad to have you here . . . It means so much to have you celebrate with us . . . Thank you for joining us . . . Wait until you see my Rebecca . . . Do you see my two little ones there with their father?

[*The women and* CHILDREN *of La Misión open suitcases to reveal decorations: corsages, boutonnieres, flowers to go in their hair, simple floral arrangements.*

REBECCA *enters—our* quinceañera *girl—glowing in her pink gown. Her parents greet her.*

EL PADRE *comes forward to stand with* REBECCA.

The rest of the ENSEMBLE *find spots throughout the theater.*]

EL PADRE: We are here to celebrate the *quinceañera* of our Rebecca. And we have much to celebrate.

We celebrate the safe return of our Andres—or shall I say, our "Manuel"—who survived the dangers in his path to return to his family.

[*Cheers and applause.*]

We celebrate our Women Divorced by ICE, who made this *quinceañera* for us to enjoy, and who truly do the work of *mil madres*.

[*Applause.*]

And Marcos Medina has informed me that we can now also celebrate Mexico's victory in today's *fútbol* match!

[*Wild cheers and applause!*]

We celebrate that Rebecca and her family are together, even though her father's case is not resolved. We celebrate all the triumphs of our struggle. The small victories in our fight for a better life.

At the center of every people's revolution, you will find God, with the poor, fighting, for peace, love, and justice. We are following the path of Jesus, a fighter and a subversive, who came to the oppressed towns to demand social change. We are following the path of the Jewish prophet Amos, a radical who denounced the abuse of power. We are following the path of Buddha and Mohammed, prophets who lived and walked among the people.

We all fight in hope that the seeds of our struggle will take root in the land, and grow into tall and proud trees that will glow with vibrant flowers.

Rebecca is one of those who believe that the world can change. And so Rebecca offers us a vision of tomorrow. A vision of a family sitting beneath an old tree. A vision of a brother singing a song to his two sisters. A vision of these children sharing the sweet fruits of their better world as they share the stories of how they got there: our stories.

[*A guitarist begins to play.* EL PADRE *smiles. He begins to sing and soon is joined by the two* GIRLS *from the beginning of the play.*]

BOY: GIRLS:

Amigos, mis hermanos, compañeros,
yo no se si saben bien
El cuento de aquel árbol de hoja dulce
que se enraizó en la tierra en que creció

El árbol reventó de una semilla   The tree grew from a traveling seed
que vino de muy lejos hasta acá   A seed that came from distant land
salió desde una rama con raíces   It crossed the border on a breeze,
al otro lao del borde, más allá   Into this ground where now it stand

De tanto que amó el árbol a su suelo   Today the tree stands tall and brave
los hombres no lo pueden arrancar   It overcame those fearful men
Y es hoy bajo la sombra de este árbol   And now beneath its gentle shade
que te cuento la historia una vez mas.   We share its story once again.

CHARENTÓN
OPERA BUFFO IN TEN FRAMES AND AN EPILOGUE
After the play *Marat/Sade* by Peter Weiss

Raquel Carrió

Translated from the Spanish by Caridad Svich

PRODUCTION HISTORY

Charentón premiered at Teatro Buendía in Havana, Cuba, in October 2005, in the Festival Internacional de Teatro de La Habana. It was awarded the Critics Choice for Best Play of the Year. It was also then presented at the Festival Iberoamericano de Teatro de Bogotá, Colombia; the Festival Internacional de Teatro Experimental de Quito, Ecuador; the Festival Latino-Americano de Teatro de Salvador de Bahia, Brazil; and the Goodman Latino Theatre Festival, Chicago, among others. The play is inspired by the play *Marat/Sade* by Peter Weiss, as well as other historic and literary texts.

The Goodman Theatre production was directed by Flora Lauten, and the cast was as follows:

Marat . . . . Leandro Sen
Sade . . . . Alejandro Alfonzo
Simone . . . . Ivanesa Cabrera
Charlotte . . . . Sandra Lorenzo
Roux . . . . Miguel Abreu
Toussaint . . . . Carlos Cruz
Marquesa . . . . Dania Aguerreberez
Napoleoncito . . . . Sándor Menéndez
Antonieta . . . . Indira Valdes
Juana . . . . Ana Domínguez
Sanson . . . . Miguel Abreu and Carlos Cruz

PHOTOGRAPH: Ensemble scene, photograph by Pablo Massip.

CHARACTERS

Marat, French revolutionary
Charlotte, provincial noblewoman, Marat's assassin
Roux, radical priest, Marat's friend
Toussaint, Haiti's liberator, imprisoned in Paris
Marquis de Sade, writer
Simone, Marat's lover, an opera singer
Napoleoncito, young delusional actor who thinks he is Napoleon
Antoinette, young delusional baker who thinks she is Marie Antoinette
Joanna, the madwoman-child who thinks she is Joan of Arc
Marquise de Sade, the Marquis de Sade's mother; she ministers to him in the asylum
Sanson, a hangman, an executioner, could be anyone
Chorus (of Marat*'s voices and hallucinations)*
Beggars and noblemen in tableaux
Musicians (of Toussaint's army)

SCENE 1

The Mask and the Mirror

[*Interior: Very faint lights illuminate the upstage area. Center stage is bathed in darkness. The actors are seen standing, in character, in front of mirrors. Each cell or dressing room (on both sides of the stage and in the background, upstage) is illuminated by a small light that reflects the actors' faces and/or parts of their bodies in the mirror. It is as if they were characters in a story about to be told.*

Upstage center, the figure of MARAT *is seen. To the right of* MARAT *is* CHARLOTTE's *cell. To* MARAT's *left are the cells of* ROUX *and* TOUSSAINT *(who is alone, in the last cell). Downstage right, close to the audience, is the* MARQUIS DE SADE. *On the opposite side of the stage is* SIMONE. *On different parts of the stage, in the background and foreground, are the choral figures* (NAPOLEONCITO, MARIE ANTOINETTE, *and* JOANNA) *and the* MARQUIS DE SADE's MOTHER. *The musicians are on the* MARQUIS DE SADE's *side of the stage; he is their conductor.*

The sound of bells. At the start of the show, light filters in slowly through the space until the entire basement of the Charentón Asylum is in full view. Upstage, in the background, veiled, the Ragged Curtain of The Petit Trianon is on display. (Note: The Petit Trianon alludes here not to the original one in the Palace of Versailles, but rather the theater buffo—burlesque or satire—that the MARQUIS DE SADE *has created in the basement of the asylum where the play is performed by the* ACTOR-INMATES.)

Music is heard: "The Spectre of the Rose" (text by Théophile Gautier, music by Hector Berlioz), followed by the sound of voices and laughter, accompanied by movement and gestures. Bells ring.]

[*The* MARQUIS DE SADE *addresses the audience. He is dressed in period costume, albeit somewhat ragged and undone. He is obese. He has clearly dressed himself for this occasion. He wears a wig and fine, if weathered, shoes. (Two panels separate the audience from the scene; they open and close as if they were the doors to Charentón Insane Asylum.)*]

ACTOR-MARQUIS DE SADE [*behind the panels*]: Esteemed spectators . . . once again, Charentón opens its doors!

[*Sound of fanfare, laughter, and voices.* NAPOLEONCITO, MARIE ANTOINETTE, *and* JOANNA *open the panels (as if they were doors). The cell doors*

open upstage. All the actors are dressed as INMATES *of the asylum. They wear clothes made of frayed, white linen.*
Each actor grabs objects that correspond and/or identify their character in some way: spoons, jars, pans, old medals, hats, swords, flags, knives. (Simultaneous actions.)]

ACTOR-MARQUIS DE SADE [*above the melee, to the audience*]: Who says crazy people can't put on a play?

[*Laughter.*]

ACTOR-MARAT [*upstage, walking out of his cell*]: Mister Coulmier [*shows puppet figure of Mister Coulmier*] . . . The director of this asylum, has just been . . . [*throws the puppet into the air; the puppet hangs; percussion punctuates the action, as if this were an act at the circus*] . . . murdered!

[*The* ACTOR-INMATES *run to grab Coulmier. Freeze.*]

NAPOLEONCITO [*to the audience, regarding Coulmier*]: So old, so worn out . . . in fact, he's from a time when the Revolution . . .

[*Percussion (drumroll).*]

ALL [*drawing the curtains in the background*]: triumphed!

[*Image of the revolution. Music is heard very softly, as if it were coming from a great distance. The tune cites "La Marseillaise." It is sung by the actors, who are on or above the cart. The cart serves as a makeshift altar, guillotine platform, and can be transformed to become the stands where the masses call out. The actions performed should suggest images in the memories of the characters. The cart slowly rolls in. As music and actions continue . . .*]

ACTOR-MARQUIS DE SADE [*to the audience*]: It's not difficult to travel back in time. We only have to release the ties of reason . . . and we are in France . . . in 1793!

[*The cart is now in the center. The stage is bathed in white, black, and red, as the characters in their white linen costumes with red sashes and black boots and hats come into full view.*
NAPOLEONCITO, ANTOINETTE, *and* JOANNA *leap off the cart.* MARQUIS DE SADE'S MOTHER *remains on the cart. She wears the mask of death (after Brueghel's* The Triumph of Death). *Behind her is* CHARLOTTE COR-

DAY. *On the sides, further upstage, stand* MARAT, ROUX, *and* TOUSSAINT, *with lit torches in their hands. Freeze.* MARQUIS DE SADE *speaks.*]

ACTOR-MARQUIS DE SADE [*to the audience*]: Who doesn't remember the bloody events of the Great Revolution that changed the world?

[NAPOLEONCITO *blows a whistle and sings "La Marseillaise" in the mode of a battle song, full of vertiginous rhythm. The actors run around the stage with the cart, going round and round in circles, as they shout:*]

MARAT [*torch in hand*]: Liberty!

TOUSSAINT: Equality!

NAPOLEONCITO: Fraternity!

MARAT: Long live the Revolution!

[*From the cart,* CHARLOTTE CORDAY *cries.*]

MARQUIS DE SADE [*to the audience*]: Someone once said that History repeats itself . . . [*indicates his* MOTHER, *the* MARQUISE, *who wears the Mask of Death*] first as Tragedy [*the mask smiles*] and then . . .

[*The* MARQUISE *turns around and reveals her nude back and buttocks.*]

MARQUIS DE SADE [*laughing*]: As Comedy!

[*Mad laughter. A fanfare erupts: a cacophony of spoons, jars, pans banged about in unison. The* MARQUIS DE SADE *stops the actions with a simple, singular gesture. He indicates that it is* JOANNA's *turn to speak the text of his play.*]

JOANNA [*with odd movements and a nervous tic that impedes the flow of her speech*]: But now . . . [*with difficulty*] . . . it's the children's turn to [*in a hoarse, broken voice*] . . . gesticcccculate . . . !

NAPOLEONCITO [*assuming his signature Napoleonic accessories: hat, boots, sword, tricolored sash. Speaks frenetically to the audience*]: This is what these remorseless . . . indignant . . . mad . . . children want to see . . .

[*Goes to* MARAT, *points sword at him.*]

How the great ones died . . . ! [*Laughing and lowering his sword*] And later, how the lesser ones . . .

[*He embraces* JOANNA *and* ANTOINETTE.]

NAPOLEONCITO, JOANNA, AND ANTOINETTE [*as in pantomime: they form a tableau reminiscent of a living statue*]: Rise!

[*Laughter. Freeze.*]

[*As the living statue remains on "display," the sound of more characters making their entrance is heard.*]

SCENE 2

The Characters

ANTOINETTE [*to* NAPOLEONCITO]: Introduce us already . . . we want to act!

NAPOLEONCITO [*stupefied*]: Act . . . ? Act in what?

ANTOINETTE: In the play de Sade wrote for us.

[*The* MARQUIS DE SADE's *musical theme is heard. The* MARQUIS *enters, on his chair. They present him.*]

NAPOLEONCITO: This is the Marquis.

ANTOINETTE: A man of letters.

JOANNA: Prisoner of the Bastille!

ANTOINETTE: Secretary of the Committee of pricks!

JOANNA: And he has lived in this crap-house . . . [*looks about the space*] for many, many years!

[*Laughter. Individual gestures from the* CHORUS].

NAPOLEONCITO [*returning to the play-text, the* MARQUIS DE SADE's *text*]: Although he has spent most of his life either in jail or in exile . . .

ANTOINETTE AND JOANNA [*aside, to the audience*]: He hasn't lost his talent in prison!

[*They open his cape: It is filled with papers hidden away in pockets and seams: pieces of folded letters, scribbled notes, etc.*]

ANTOINETTE: He hasn't stopped writing.

JOANNA [*aside*]: His books are banned.

MARQUIS DE SADE [*laughter, to the audience*]: But everyone here has read them!

[*They carry him away.*]

NAPOLEONCITO [*bringing things back to order*]: Attention, Ladies and Gentlemen . . .

[*Drumroll.*]

The actors who will perform for you today [*in the style of a pantomime*] don't have much experience [*very timidly*] and the little they do have, they have acquired here in this armory.

JOANNA [*from upstage right*]: Armory?

NAPOLEONCITO: Sounds better than asylum!

[*They all applaud.*]

After all . . . [*aside*] everything here is dynamite . . .

[*They draw near.*]

ANTOINETTE [*with rolling pin in hand*]: And for those that don't want to blast away . . . !

[*She hits* NAPOLEONCITO *on the head.*]

MARQUIS DE SADE [*playing with them*]: We've got . . .

ALL: A Xanax day!

[*Mad laughter. Fanfare.*]

NAPOLEONCITO [*continuing his prepared speech*]: Our enlightened age demands that we do not stoop to violence.

[*He pulls at* ANTOINETTE's *hair.*]

ANTOINETTE [*as part of the speech*]: Punishment or humiliation . . .

MARQUIS DE SADE [*joining them*]: But rather culture and recreation . . .

ALL: So that everyone can be healed!

[*Laughter. Sound change:* MARAT*'s theme is heard. As the music plays . . .*]

NAPOLEONCITO [*to the audience, gently, almost lyrically*]: Don't think this place is merely a room in a hospital . . . On the contrary. It's a timeless place unbound by geography . . .

[*He looks behind himself. The curtain of rags is drawn.*]

. . . here you will see Marat . . .

[SIMONE *enters with* MARAT*'s rolling bathtub and turns on the faucet.* MARAT *faints (after Jacques-Louis David's 1793 painting* The Death of Marat*).* SIMONE *holds him.* ANTOINETTE *and* JOANNA *circle about him with mirrors.* MARAT *is half-nude, covered only in some white linen. He has a bandage on his head. The following text is spoken very quickly, in concert with the movement.*]

SIMONE: Die in his bathtub!

[ANTOINETTE *circles* MARAT *with a mirror.*]

ANTOINETTE: As everyone knows . . .

JOANNA: One horrible night . . .

[ANTOINETTE *goes upstage with mirror, where* CHARLOTTE *is positioned near the cart.*]

ANTOINETTE: Charlotte Corday . . .

ROUX [*from his cell, shouts between the bars*]: Whore!

[*Mad laughter.* ANTOINETTE *places the mirror in front of* CHARLOTTE.]

ANTOINETTE: plunged a fiery knife into Marat's chest!

[CHARLOTTE *tosses flowers, which fall into* MARAT*'s hands.*]

NAPOLEONCITO [*on the stairs, behind* MARAT, *continues the play-text, in a grave manner*]: In the role of Marat, we have a patient who suffers from paranoia.

[MARAT *is in the bathtub.* SIMONE *circles him and changes his bandage. The* MARQUISE *paints stab wounds on his body.* ANTOINETTE *and* JOANNA *hold up the mirrors. Tableau.*]

[*As he moves*] His skin burns, sallowed by sickness.

[*Laughter. Simultaneous movement and gestures.* MARQUIS DE SADE *helps* CHARLOTTE *down from the cart and pushes her toward* MARAT. MARAT *feels her near him. He is almost blind. He confuses her with* SIMONE.]

MARAT: Simone! Simone! Another bandage, please!

[CHARLOTTE *waves her hands in front of* MARAT'*s impassive eyes. She walks away.*]

NAPOLEONCITO [*resuming his speech*]: Now his skin pains him, and only the cool water into which he is submerged can soothe the fever that consumes him.

[*The sound of "La Marseillaise" is heard faintly, in the distance.*]

ROUX [*from his cell*]: Long live Marat!

ALL: Long live Marat!

NAPOLEONCITO [*to the audience*]: The woman leaning over him is his wife Simone . . .

[SIMONE'*s theme is heard.* SIMONE *laughs, drinks, and twirls about the stage. Wine bottles hang from her neck. Applause from* ALL. *They mock her and bring her the cart so that she may stand and sing from it, as if it were a little stage.*]

She was once the most famous singer of our time!

[SIMONE *sings. She is drunk, but the song she sings is a beautiful song from her glory days, before she met* MARAT.]

[*Quite spirited*] After falling in love with her enemy . . . [*indicating* MARAT] . . . she lost her jewelry, her castle, and her lover!

[*Laughter. Mad applause from the* ACTOR-INMATES. SIMONE *weeps.* ANTOINETTE *and* JOANNA *cover* CHARLOTTE *in black nylon and drag her forward.* CHARLOTTE *resists, kicking and screaming. She doesn't understand her role in this play or why she is being represented in this fashion. As she kicks and screams . . .]*

NAPOLEONCITO [*to the audience*]: Now we will meet the woman playing Charlotte.

ANTOINETTE: She's from Caen. A noblewoman from the provinces . . .

[ANTOINETTE *takes off* CHARLOTTE*'s shoes and displays them with envy.*]

Would you look at her shoes?

[*Mocking laughter and improvised slurs.* CHARLOTTE *screams, wrestling within* ANTOINETTE*'s grip, pushing her. They wrap the black nylon around* CHARLOTTE *as if it were a straitjacket.*]

She suffers from depression and sleeping sickness . . . but when she wakes up . . . !

[CHARLOTTE *falls to the ground. Everyone shouts. Simultaneous actions and gestures.*]

[MARQUIS DE SADE *sounds the bell from above, interrupting the chaos below so that the show may resume.*]

MARQUIS DE SADE [*to the audience, quite loudly*]: I call Mister L'ouverture . . .

[*Bells.*]

. . . the Liberator of Haiti!

[TOUSSAINT*'s theme is heard. It is a song once sung by slaves who worked the plantations in Haiti.* SIMONE *sings.* TOUSSAINT *covers* CHARLOTTE*'s body, which is still on the ground, with a large basket. He covers her in smoke. He makes her rise. Drums sound. The sound of the drums swells. The* INMATES *dance and shout and contort themselves into odd positions. The scene becomes something akin to a dark ritual, not unlike that of a witches' Sabbath.* ROUX *speaks over the music and movement.*]

ROUX [*on the cart*]: Lechery! Lechery in Charentón! . . . Enough . . . !

[*Sound changes to* ROUX*'s theme. It is a slow, nostalgic tune that contrasts greatly with the violent nature of his character.*]

ANTOINETTE [*on the cart, behind* ROUX, *to the audience*]: That's Roux. The radical town priest . . . loyal to Marat till the bitter end.

[ROUX *descends from the cart and begins to offer bread to the poor, not unlike Communion.*]

ROUX [*chanting, as if at the pulpit, over the action*]: Gather up your arms, comrades. Marat will give us the signal . . . ! To arms, comrades . . . !

[*They surround him. Another tableau.*]

CHORUS: Gather up your arms, comrades. Marat will give the signal! To arms, comrades . . . !

[*The "to arms" refrain is repeated in crescendo, as voices alternate with simultaneous movements and gestures, until they reach a climax.*]

ROUX [*crazed*]: Marat will give us the signal!

[*The* MARQUIS DE SADE *gestures to the* MARQUISE. *She bangs the metal pot over* ROUX's *head (it is as if he were being electrocuted). They all shout and cover their heads. The* MARQUISE *drags him toward stage center. Freeze.*]

NAPOLEONCITO [*to the audience, trying to ingratiate himself*]: And here we have the mother of the Marquis!

SIMONE [*breaking the tableau*]: A drunk!

ANTOINETTE: A slut!

NAPOLEONCITO [*charmingly*]: And she's a marquise, too!

[*The* MARQUISE's *theme is heard: The Pierrot's Song. The* MARQUISE *cradles the* MARQUIS DE SADE *and caresses him. The* CHORUS OF INMATES *surrounds the mother and the* MARQUIS DE SADE *with their instruments. They sing with an air of extraordinary sadness—the kind of sadness that will not be heard until the end of the show.*
Instrumental music. ANTOINETTE, NAPOLEONCITO, *and* JOANNA *move forward with their weapons in hand: a sword, rolling pin, and a spoon and jar. They create another living statue, as they present the next scene.*]

ANTOINETTE, NAPOLEONCITO, AND JOANNA: An homage to Marat!

[MARAT's *area is illuminated.*]

SCENE 3

Homage to Marat

[*Dim light.* MARAT *and* SIMONE *are alone.* SIMONE *sings.*]

SIMONE [*singing*]:
    Four years have transpired
    Since a Revolution against our sires
    My love has deified me
    I've forsaken everything for Marat.

[*She embraces him.*]

    In four years I have seen
    More death than I desire
    But I don't regret a single thing.

[*The* ACTOR-INMATES *watch the scene from their cells. They make sounds with their feet; they clap, laugh, etc.*]

SIMONE [*hearing the sounds, singing*]:
    They left with the horses,
    The carriages and the goods.

[*They draw near.*]

    From the other side of France
    Émigrés insult me.
    Before: they had been my friends
    Before: they had applauded my singing.

[*They surround her and clap slowly.*]

SIMONE [*spoken*]: Yet, I don't sing alone,
    My voice is one with the poor, the hungry

[*She holds* MARAT *up.*]

    . . . and the lonely!

[*The* CHORUS OF INMATES *surrounds* MARAT. *They have their cups in their mouths. They squat in different positions.*]

TOUSSAINT: Marat, we don't want to dig our own graves.

JOANNA: Marat, we don't want to eat off the floor.

ROUX: Marat, you are a friend to the people!

ANTOINETTE: We are hungry, Marat!

MARQUISE: Marat, we don't have any bread!

NAPOLEONCITO [*from the stairs, to the audience*]: Let us listen now to Marat as he argues with de Sade. Who is right?

[*The circle breaks. The* CHORUS *bring* MARQUIS DE SADE'*s chair.* MARAT *and* MARQUIS DE SADE *are now center stage. The* CHORUS *surrounds the scene.* MARAT *does not respond.*]

SCENE 4

Marat–Sade

SIMONE [*very softly, to* MARAT]: Mister de Sade . . .

ANTOINETTE [*to* MARAT]: Mister de Sade . . .

MARQUISE [*authoritatively*]: Marquis de Sade!

TOUSSAINT [*as an order*]: Marquis de Sade!

[*They all exit.*]

MARAT [*awakening from his delirium*]: Marquis de Sade! . . .

[*He touches his body*]

I am ill . . . but, nevertheless, we should talk.

[*Gestures and movements of the* INMATES *in the cells: the sound of chains, footsteps, water, keys opening doors, etc. (*MARAT'*s aural hallucinations.)* MARAT *looks around, looking for the source of these sounds.*]

[*With effort*] I feel as if . . . what we need here . . . is to keep our wits!

[*The sounds increase in intensity.*]

. . . How are we going to finish the play if from the very beginning

[*He tries to look around.*]

   . . . everyone shouts . . . and screams . . . and makes strange gestures?

[*Simultaneous sounds, movements, and gestures from the* CHORUS.]

   Or am I merely imagining things?

[*Music is heard: The Merchants' Theme. The* CHORUS *moves the four panels, surrounding* MARAT. *From the cells, in different pitches and physical poses:*]

CHORUS OF INMATES [*singing*]: Who controls the market?
   Who sits on the throne?
   Who keeps us locked up in here?

NAPOLEONCITO [*singing*]: We live in a prison!

TOUSSAINT: Against our will!

MARAT [*in the center, speaking*]: I don't understand. I can't see clearly!

SIMONE [*singing*]: We're all perfectly sane here . . .

ALL [*singing*]: We should be free!

[*Laughter. The panels open.*]

MARAT: I hear a chorus of people . . . writhing and screaming!

[*SFX: Sound of a guillotine (made by hitting two food trays against each other). A sharp, metallic sound.*]

   And this machine . . .

[*Shouts and voices in the distance are heard.*]

   [*To* MARQUIS DE SADE] You, sir . . . [*covering his ears*] have brought it here to torment me.

[*The* MARQUIS DE SADE *laughs. He signals to the* CHORUS *to stop making a racket.*]

MARQUIS DE SADE [*before* MARAT]: This is not a plea to reason! [*Ironically*] It's clear you are well-read, Marat, and your speeches are not merely tirades leveled against an angry mob. [*Laughing to the audience*] Journalists always have an agenda! [*To* MARAT] Yours is being

The Friend of the People . . . Oh, but mine . . . Mine is quite the opposite!

[*He rises and walks toward the audience and speaks to them about* MARAT.]

A doctor, a scientist that abandoned his profession to serve his people. Bravo!

[*He applauds. Fanfare: jars, bottles, spoons, voices.*]

MARQUIS DE SADE [*to* MARAT]: For this you get a crown.

[*He walks back to* MARAT *and places a crown upon his head.*]

Laurels to the kings, and to the rich and the powerful.

[INMATES *laugh.*]

. . . But you, my friend, all you get is a crown of thorns.

[*He removes the crown and throws it to the ground. The* CHORUS *runs.* NAPO-LEONCITO *nabs the crown with his sword and places it on his head.*]

MARQUIS DE SADE [*to* MARAT]: Am I right, my friend, wasn't this your choice? [*With rage*] Then, don't question my work . . . ! [*Threatening everyone*] Everyone here gets the role they deserve!

MARAT [*raises his hand*]: People!

[*Sounds, movements. The* INMATES *hide in their cells.*]

MARQUIS DE SADE [*lowering* MARAT'*s hand*]: Don't worry your pretty head. It's of no importance. [*Behind him*] . . . In 1793, after all chaos had stirred the universe, the people were still clamoring for bread. [*Caressing* MARAT'*s head*] Don't you remember?

[*Cries, gestures from the cells.*]

[*To* MARAT] The queues in the bakeries . . .

[*The* INMATES *leave their cells. Pieces of bread are scattered on the ground. They scramble for them. Movement and gesture sequence.*]

The hoarders . . .

[*The* INMATES *rage against the panels and the bars of their cells.*]

[*Indicating the* CHORUS] The smugglers!

JOANNA [*in the cell overhead, shouting*]: Marat, there is no bread!

[*Pieces of bread are thrown. All run and bump into each other to get to the bread.*]

NAPOLEONCITO [*with sword in one hand and bread in the other*]: Respect for property and propriety!

[*The* MARQUIS DE SADE *laughs.*]

SIMONE [*embracing* MARAT]: Marat, the enemies of the people betrayed the Revolution!

MARQUISE: They divided up the palaces!

TOUSSAINT: The land!

ANTOINETTE: The riches!

MARQUISE: And the public offices!

ROUX [*bound*]: Marat, do you want Imperialism to be restored?

[NAPOLEONCITO *poses* (*the very model of a Napoleon statue*). *The* MARQUIS DE SADE *laughs.*]

SIMONE [*to* MARAT]: Get up and go!

JOANNA [*from the ground*]: We're hungry, Marat!

[*Music begins: Street Theme* (*The composition is a variation on* MARAT's *theme*). *As the music plays . . .*]

ANTOINETTE: We want food! We want bread!

TOUSSAINT: The streets are littered with corpses.

ANTOINETTE: Heads are rolling!

JOANNA [*terrified*]: The guillotine never stops . . . never stops . . . never stops!

[*The* MARQUISE *mimics giving* JOANNA *electroshock with the cooking pot in hand. The music grows louder and increases in volume and intensity until a climax is reached.*]

INMATES CHORUS [*singing*]: Marat, it's hard to believe that we don't know where we are headed!

ROUX: With these masters, Marat!

TOUSSAINT [*singing*]: Blood and mud are everywhere . . .

SIMONE [*singing*]: They pile the bodies up at dawn.

ALL: Marat!

NAPOLEONCITO [*singing*]: Haven't you seen the parade of carriages . . . ?

JOANNA [*singing*]: They unload the bodies at dawn!

ANTOINETTE: Marat, it's hard to believe but we don't know where we're to go!

[CHARLOTTE *screams. The metallic sound of the metal pots is heard. All fall to the ground.* TOUSSAINT *picks* CHARLOTTE *up. The music stops.*]

MARQUIS DE SADE [*to the audience, crossing from stage left to right, as if giving a lecture*]: And while all that was happening . . . [*he moves slowly*] . . . Marat was in his bath. Scratching himself . . . cooling himself . . . with beautiful Simone.

[SIMONE *faces the* MARQUIS DE SADE. *The* MARQUIS DE SADE *moves her aside.*]

[*To* MARAT] Don't you think it's right that people should revolt?

[*He looks at the audience.*]

Or was that only possible before . . . and not now?

[MARAT *makes a gesture in rebellion against the* MARQUIS DE SADE. SIMONE *stops him.*]

Typical tyrant!

[*The* MARQUIS DE SADE *gestures in return. The sound of the guillotine is now heard distorted (from afar).*]

[*Above the sound*] And let's not even talk about this infernal machine and its dreadful noise!

[MARAT *hides in the bathtub. From upstage, the image of the cart and the torches is seen. On the cart is* CHARLOTTE'*s decapitated body. Convulsive movements. Dissonant sound. Shouts, cries, whimpers. The* EXECUTIONER, *veiled, turns the cart slowly. In counterpoint to this image, the* MARQUIS DE SADE'*s text is heard. A dense atmosphere envelopes the scene, as if it were* MARAT'*s nightmare or hallucination.*]

[*Very slowly*] I bet you've seen heads rolling . . . [*wheels turn*] while bodies were loaded onto beautiful, beautiful carts . . . [*whimpers, the sound of beating*] that wander through the night.

[*The curtains in the background are drawn. The cart disappears.*]

How are your nights, Marat . . . ? Do you sleep in the bath . . . or snuggled against Simone's gorgeous breasts?

[MARQUIS DE SADE *makes an obscene gesture.*]

We all want those breasts.

MARAT [*rising violently*]: You joined us! You were one of us!

MARQUIS DE SADE [*laughing*]: No . . . no, no, no. Don't misread my essay! Have you forgotten that I'm an aristocrat? A ruined marquis. But a marquis nonetheless! [*Drawing near*] Aren't you suspicious of my kind? As far as I know . . . [*to the audience*] . . . ! Suspicion is one of terror's best weapons . . . ! [*To* MARAT] . . . You suspect me . . . I suspect you . . . [*looking about*] . . . And we all suspect everyone else!

[*Voices, movements.*]

ROUX [*over the voices, to* MARQUIS DE SADE]: You were imprisoned by the old regime!

MARQUIS DE SADE [*laughing*]: Nonsense! People are shocked by four beat-up whores and ten or twelve young studs taking it up the ass . . . !

[*Laughter, mad fanfare.*]

Pure hypocrisy, my friend, because these same people . . . [*To the audience*] . . . including those in powerful positions, have done much worse things . . . [*laughing*] . . . Only they don't publicize them!

[*The* MARQUISE *brings him a tray with food. They all look.*]

MARQUIS DE SADE [*eating*]: In turn, I, like you, sir [*chews bread*], dedicate my art to the people. [*Looking at everyone*] They may not have bread . . . [*chews*], but lots of words to chew on! [*With mouth full*] . . . And as you know: man does not live by bread alone!

[*Mad fanfare: cups and spoons.*]

MARAT [*frantic*]: I don't care about your writings! I'm not a moralist!

MARQUIS DE SADE: You're not . . . [*looking at the curtain in the background*] But they are!

[*A circular, undulating tune: Napoleon's theme. The curtain of rags is drawn and* NAPOLEONCITO *enters, very much the spitting image of Napoleon.*]

MARQUIS DE SADE: He's of both the Old and the New Regime. He's still alive . . .

[NAPOLEONCITO *advances, marches to the tune.*]

. . . Ah, but he can't imagine what comes next! He hasn't the faintest idea what a little soldier, a simple little foot solider can do

[NAPOLEONCITO *is stage center; he executes a military salute.*]

with a head full of schemes and dreams!

[*Music:* NAPOLEONCITO *and the Revolution. Through the curtain, the* INMATES *file in, in full costume of the era. Over the music and movement.*]

NAPOLEONCITO [*in his speech, to the audience*]: Young people of France! From all walks of life!

[CHARLOTTE *approaches.*]

In the spirit of our heroic deeds . . .

[CHARLOTTE, *hand on the sword.* NAPOLEONCITO *does not relinquish.*]

A new world will be born!

[NAPOLEONCITO *raises his and* CHARLOTTE's *hands up.*]

A single, united nation!

[*Silence.*]

MARQUIS DE SADE [*demonstrative, to the audience*]: You see what I mean . . . ? A man who dreams of ruling the world . . . ! And for what?

[*The* INMATES *hide.*]

To impose the Declaration of Human Rights!

[Still image. The MARQUIS DE SADE *goes to* NAPOLEONCITO, *lowers his sword, and they face each other.*]

Human rights . . . ! Disgusting!

[MARAT *stands, in the bath.*]

MARAT: That's not what I wanted!

MARQUIS DE SADE [*against* MARAT]: It wasn't . . . but it is now!

[*The* INMATES *move about. Different poses, actions.*]

MARQUIS DE SADE [*to* MARAT]: You know what? You can never tell where ideas are going to lead! [*Toward the audience, violently*] Think about it . . . The writings of Rousseau and Voltaire . . . led to a revolution. And the Revolution led to . . . Napoleon!

CHORUS [*very softly*]: Napoleon, Napoleon, Napoleon . . . !

MARAT [*surprised*]: Napoleon . . . I don't know him.

MARQUIS DE SADE [*putting on his Joker's Mask*]: He's in your party. A loyal Jacobin! And after . . .

[*The sound of* "La Marseillaise," *quite distant, very distorted.*]

MARAT [*forcefully*]: There is no after.

MARQUIS DE SADE [*to the audience, keeping his joker's spirit alive*]: He just keeps going! He's an egomaniac. [*Mocking, mimicking* MARAT] I am the Revolution! [*Laughing*] And after him . . . nothing.

MARAT: You're a provocateur.

MARQUIS DE SADE [*gesturing with his cape, playing with the audience*]: I'm a pervert . . .

[INMATES *laugh.*]

a madman . . .

[INMATES *hit the bars on their cells.*]

a provocateur . . .

[*Silence.*]

but I'm not a murderer.

[*Shouts, stomps, sounds.*]

ROUX [*shouting*]: Marat, we built the Republic on the blade of a guillotine.

[*Instrumental music. "Cabbage soup" musical theme. All have their cups and spoons in hand. The* MARQUISE *enters with a bowl of soup. It is in the same pot that before was used to mimic giving electroshocks. The* INMATES *form a line in front of the pot as if they were beggars. Beggar-dolls. They all sing while the soup is served.*]

SIMONE [*singing*]: Cabbage soup and bread with beans.

TOUSSAINT [*singing*]: Bloody bones and bloody pits.

SIMONE [*singing*]: The nouveau riche drink their beer.
And eat their breakfast, while we, the poor, go hungry.

[INMATES *gesture with cups and spoons.*]

They have money and luck.

CHORUS OF INMATES AND BEGGARS: While we have dreams . . . full of holes.

ANTOINETTE: I am a hole . . .

TOUSSAINT: I have a hole in pants.

NAPOLEONCITO: I have a hole from my spleen to my kidney.

ALL [*singing*]: Hole, hole . . . we are holes!

SIMONE [*singing*]: In my head there are only . . .

ALL: Holes . . . !

[*Image of the* BEGGARS. *Pose. Freeze. Darkness descends.* MARAT *rises. Tremors through his body. Visions. He can't tell day from night.*]

MARAT: Simone! That Marquis . . . ! And the people . . . laughed!

[SIMONE *embraces him. He leans his head against her. She covers his eyes.*]

SIMONE: You're dreaming, Jean-Paul.

[CHARLOTTE, *stage right, approaches* MARAT. *Sound.*]

MARAT: Is it day or night?

[CHARLOTTE *covers* MARAT *with the black nylon fabric. Bells.*]

SIMONE [*behind* MARAT]: Night.

[*Cries from the* INMATES.]

[SIMONE'*s theme.*]

> [*Singing*] Four years have gone by
> The moment has arrived
> The Revolution has died
> The queen and the hero
> Go down to hell together.
> I hear death howling . . .

[CHARLOTTE *moves.*]

> [*Singing*] And on my lover's breast [*discovers*]
> There is a dagger and a flower

VOICES [*alternating*]: It's time! It's time! It's time!

SIMONE [*singing*]: Time has come
> And all the blood in the world
> Won't save my beloved.

[*Blackout. All enter with candles and flashlights. Strange sounds are heard (nylon bags, garbage, the sounds of the night). Lights flash. Over music and action . . .*]

VOICES ALTERNATING [*very softly*]: Corday! Corday! Corday! Corday!

SCENE 5

Night in Charentón

[CHARLOTTE's *theme is heard. A flashlight shines upon her. Reflections, shafts of light illuminate fragments of her face and body.* CHARLOTTE *is on the stairs, sleeping. Or perhaps she dreams that she is sleeping. Voices awaken her (it's time to play her role). Over the music, with difficulty . . .*]

CHARLOTTE: Poor Marat . . . in his bath.

[MARAT, *stage center, is sleeping. (Is it* MARAT *in* CHARLOTTE's *dream or* CHARLOTTE *in* MARAT's *dream?) The scene should have this air of ambiguity, suspended as it is between reality and dream, between one person's dream and another's. It is a scene suspended in time: It isn't real, but neither is it complete pretense. It is composed of the raw data, the material stuff of dreams exchanged between two delusional beings. Therefore, the scene isn't acted, but rather dreamt up, by one or the other.* CHARLOTTE's *theme is heard during the scene; it is played at a slow tempo, exuding an air of sadness. The sound of "La Marseillaise" is heard slowly, as if from a distance superimposed over* CHARLOTTE's *theme. As the music plays,* NAPOLEONCITO, JOANNA, *and* ANTOINETTE *move the panels toward* CHARLOTTE's *area of the stage. Dim light.* CHARLOTTE *is seen through the panels. Her image superimposes itself over* MARAT's. *Slow movements. As the music plays . . .*]

CHARLOTTE: I, Charlotte Corday, am the first to arrive.

[*The panels turn (sound and light SFX).*]

I come from Caen!

[*Prerecorded sound is heard: hymns, shouts, and the voices of the exiles. A vertiginous effect.*]

Where there's a liberation front!

[*The panels turn. Now only* CHARLOTTE's *theme is heard.*]

[*Facing the audience*] Each one of you . . . saw . . . what Rousseau dreamed of.

[MARAT *stirs in his sleep (sound and light SFX).*]

SIMONE [*singing*]: Once we had the same ideals.

CHARLOTTE [*spoken, from the panels*]: We dreamt the same things.

SIMONE [*singing*]: We dreamt the same things.

INMATES CHORUS [*fragmented images, sung*]: We wanted freedom, liberty!

CHARLOTTE [*to* MARAT]: But for you, liberty . . . [*the panels turn*] was a mountain of corpses!

[*The* CHORUS OF INMATES *are behind the panels.*]

We spoke of Equality . . . but for you, equality meant: the guillotine.

[*The* INMATES' *heads are seen through the bars.*]

SIMONE [*singing with great sadness*]: We wanted freedom!

[INMATES *lower their heads.*]

CHARLOTTE: We dreamt of Fraternity, but all of our brothers are dead.

[*Bells.*]

That is why . . . you must die!

[MARAT *wakes. He is choking. He cannot breathe. Shouts.*]

MARAT: Simone, bring me a glass of cold water! My Proclamation! My Proclamation for the fourteenth of July! They're waiting for me!

[*The* MARQUISE *places her hands in* MARAT's *water.*]

MARQUISE [*terrified*]: The water has turned red!

[MARAT *tries to rise.* SIMONE *holds him back, with rage.*]

MARAT: What does one bathtub full of blood mean, when rivers of blood have been spilled for this country?

[*He walks downstage, toward the audience. He cannot see. He is blind.*]

At first . . . we thought there would only be a few casualties.

[*Shouts, sounds, voices—visions.*]

ROUX [*from offstage*]: Death to the tyrants!

[*The panels move facing* MARAT.]

TOUSSAINT: Death to apathy!

SIMONE: Down with the cowards!

ROUX: Marat, if you don't destroy them, they will put an end to everything.

MARAT [*hallucinating*]: Then there were thousands . . . and it wasn't enough!

[*Sound of military sirens. Panels move. Terror moves in.*]

SHOUTS [*alternating*]: Kill them all, Marat! Kill them all!

MARAT [*in his delirium*]: The dead can no longer be counted . . . ! Because they're everywhere . . . !

ROUX [*indicating*]: Here!

TOUSSAINT: There!

MARAT: On the rooftops!

ROUX: Behind the city walls!

TOUSSAINT: In the basements!

SIMONE [*pointing to* JOANNA, *upstage, above*]: They're hiding.

JOANNA [*wearing red cap and flags*]: No more war, no more war.

MARAT: All those suspected will be arrested! Simone! [SIMONE *embraces him*] We've traitors in our midst, Simone! [*Trembles*] They look the same as us . . . they wear the same clothes . . . the same hats . . . our insignias. But when we take an action, when we take necessary measures . . . they begin to scream.

NAPOLEONCITO [*above, upstage*]: Free the prisoners!

JOANNA: Murderers!

ANTOINETTE: No more dead!

MARAT: What shall we do, Simone . . . ? My skin is burning . . . I can't breathe.

[SIMONE *sets him down to rest and covers his body.*]

[*Trembling, convulsing*] They're screaming at me, Simone. They're screaming inside of me. I am full of screams.

SIMONE [*disturbed by Marat's visions, shakes him*]: There's no one! You're the only one that's screaming!

MARAT [*his body rigid*]: No, Simone . . . I am the Revolution!

[*The stage is illuminated by artificial light. Note the artificiality has to do with the playing of the play within the play.* CHARLOTTE's *theme is heard.* CHARLOTTE *is on one side of the stage. Her hand is extended. She is about to knock on the door. On the opposite side of the stage, the* MARQUIS DE SADE *stands with a bell in hand.* MARAT *and* SIMONE *are stage center.* MARAT *opens his eyes.*]

Is it day or night?

SIMONE: Day. [*Looking at* CHARLOTTE] And she's about to arrive.

[*The* MARQUIS DE SADE *rings the bell.* CHARLOTTE *gestures. She wears white gloves and carries a bouquet of flowers meant for* MARAT. *It is clear from the manner in which they perform that the scene's score (script and musicality) is quite strict.*]

CHARLOTTE: I am here to speak to Citizen Marat.

SIMONE: No visitors allowed.

CHARLOTTE: I'm here to deliver an important message from the city of Caen.

SIMONE [*laughing, with a sheet of paper at the ready*]: Leave us in peace. If you've something to say to Marat [*dangling paper in the air*], you may do so in writing.

[*They execute specific, scored physical movements: slow, coordinated.* SIMONE *with the paper in hand and* CHARLOTTE *with hat in hand.* SIMONE *is in white and red (the* INMATES' *garb and a red sash) and* CHARLOTTE *is in black. They size each other up.* SIMONE *places the sheet of paper on the floor.* CHARLOTTE *steps on it. It is almost as if they were dancing with each other. As* CHARLOTTE *steps on the paper . . .]*

CHARLOTTE: What I have to say to you cannot be written down.

[SIMONE *moves to retrieve the paper.* CHARLOTTE *falls on top of her. Theme: Charlotte at the Fair. The music builds to a climax.]*

I want to see him. I want to see him with my own eyes.

[*They struggle over the paper. It trembles just like* MARAT.]

I want to see him tremble, and watch him sweat. I need to see him.

[*She pulls the dagger out, which up until now has been concealed in the bouquet of flowers.]*

I want to watch him as the tip of my dagger plunges into his skin!

[SIMONE *covers* MARAT. CHARLOTTE *stabs the piece of paper with her knife.]*

Into his flesh. In his blood . . .

[*Blood drips from the flowers onto the piece of paper.]*

. . . with my hands

[*She stains her hands with blood.]*

. . . looking at him . . . looking at him . . . look!

[*She raises the dagger. Standing behind* CHARLOTTE, *the* MARQUISE *grabs her hand, stopping her.]*

MARQUISE: Not yet, Charlotte, not yet!

[*The* MARQUISE *removes the dagger from* CHARLOTTE's *hand. Laughter from* MARQUIS DE SADE *and the* MARQUISE.]

MARQUIS DE SADE: Not yet, Charlotte! You have to come back three times. Go to your door!

[*He turns her so that she faces the audience.* INMATES *laugh. They cross the stage in circles. Street fair music begins. Over the music . . .]*

MARQUIS DE SADE [*tableau with* TOUSSAINT *and* CHARLOTTE]: The Great Fair in . . .

ALL [*entering*]: París!

SCENE 6

Charlotte's Arrival (or the Paris Fair)

[*The mise-en-scène transforms into a street fair. Street* BEGGARS *enter. The* ACTOR-INMATES *dance as if they were dolls in the roles of an old woman, a captain, an executioner, a (female) prostitute, a girl, and the priest. The* ACTOR-INMATES *show the audience their signifying objects: spoons, cups, skeletons, swords, medals, watches, old books, objects from the old regime that have been cast out into the street.* ANTOINETTE *the baker,* JOANNA *the arsonist,* NAPOLEONCITO *the soldier, and* SANSON *the executioner (on stilts).* TOUSSAINT *has been freed from prison, and the* MARQUISE *is in revelry mode. This character display is part of re-presentation of* CHARLOTTE'S *arrival in the city.*]

NAPOLEONCITO [*with his doll, hat, sword, cape, etc., pantomimes being the captain; he is the street fair barker now*]: Charlotte Corday arrived in the city . . .

[*Shouts, voices, simultaneous actions. The cart enters dragged by* SANSON *(after Charles-Henri Sanson), the executioner.* CHARLOTTE *is in the cart.*]

NAPOLEONCITO: . . . and it welcomed her with all its splendor.

[*The cart turns. It is placed center stage.* CHARLOTTE *looks around her. The street vendors call out:*]

NAPOLEONCITO: Acrobats!

JOANNA: Vendors!

ANTOINETTE: Flower-sellers!

NAPOLEONCITO: Charlotte Corday looked in all the shop windows.

NAPOLEONCITO, JOANNA, AND ANTOINETTE [*as a trio*]: . . . because she simply had to find a good knife-maker!

NAPOLEONCITO: See all the great new inventions of our age . . . !

[*He points to* ACTOR-MARAT, *above, who is now acrobat and contortionist. Drumroll. Circus act.*]

. . . The mechanical bird!

[*Laughter, applause.* NAPOLEONCITO *points to* ACTRESS-SIMONE, *who has electric hands and feet.*]

An electric woman . . . !

[*Laughter, voices.*]

NAPOLEONCITO: And to top them all . . .

[*He points to the cart, which is now upside down, as a platform. It's a stage trick: as the cart turns,* CHARLOTTE *is seen tied to the "platform" ready for the knife-throwing magic act with* TOUSSAINT.]

See how a man frees himself from prison and transforms himself, with a little bit of face powder, into . . .

[*Loud percussion: drums.*]

. . . Toussaint the Knife-Maker!

[TOUSSAINT *turns the cart.* CHARLOTTE, *still tied to the cart's back, moves like an animal enraged: kicks, screams, tries to set herself free. Street fair music.*]

TOUSSAINT [*over the sound of the drums, gesturing with his hands*]: In my country there are potions to make a body invisible.

[*He shows his chains.*]

I went through the prison bars . . . [*image of flight*] like a bird. I flew very high and I saw her.

[*He draws close to* CHARLOTTE. *He takes out a knife.*]

[*Aside*] I knew then that what she wanted from me was a knife.

[CHARLOTTE'S *knife trick. Her eyes fixed on him. He turns her head this way and that way.* TOUSSAINT *plays with the knife in* CHARLOTTE'S *mouth. It's*

a circus act. TOUSSAINT *makes the knife appear and disappear.* CHARLOTTE
bites down on the knife.
Another knife appears in TOUSSAINT*'s hand. He nails it between* CHAR-
LOTTE*'s legs.* CHARLOTTE *opens her eyes.*]

[*To the audience*] I gave her the knife . . . and the flower.

[*Laughter, applause from the* BEGGARS *and* INMATES. *A play/game with
chains.* TOUSSAINT *and* CHARLOTTE*'s theme.*]

CHARLOTTE: Who are you?

TOUSSAINT [*transformational poses*]: L'ouverture . . . ! Man . . . Rock . . .
   Animal!

[CHARLOTTE *wraps the chains around her hands. She moves. (Another magic
trick.)*]

CHARLOTTE: Monsieur L'ouverture [*poses with chains*], I thank you for
   the knife . . . and the flower. [*Close to him*] But know this: I am carrying out [*with her hands chained*] . . . a blood oath!

TOUSSAINT [*while caressing her*]: Mademoiselle, I would like very much
   to help you in this endeavor. [*Facing the audience*] Liberating my country was my dream.

CHARLOTTE: I too wish to liberate my people from terrorism.

NAPOLEONCITO [*with the beggar puppet-doll, to the audience*]: She looked
   at the sky and a bird sang!

[JOANNA *makes bird sound.*]

[CHARLOTTE *casts off* TOUSSAINT*'s chains. She runs through the streets
from one side to another. She bumps into the* BEGGARS. JOANNA *places the
blood on the floor.*]

NAPOLEONCITO [*narrating*]: As she crossed through a poor neighborhood . . .

[CHARLOTTE *moves.*]

she stepped into a puddle of blood, which once belonged to a
nobleman.

[CHARLOTTE *falls onto the puddle of blood. Masks of Terror. Over the move-ment . . .*]

She saw the gallows!

[*The music swells.* CHARLOTTE, *from the ground, looks at her hands full of blood.*]

CHARLOTTE: I'm going to kill . . . Marat!

[TOUSSAINT *moves the cart. Bells.* CHARLOTTE *gestures with the knife.* MARQUIS DE SADE *is stage left.*]

MARQUIS DE SADE [*to the audience, narrating*]: And while Charlotte readies herself in the streets, I give you the Tableau of Aristocrats! [*Laughter, declaiming*] The Dead-man's Fair . . . or *Le Petit Trianon*!

[*Music for the Mask Play: trumpet, effects. The Ragged Curtain is drawn by the masked figures/puppets. They are the* INMATE-ACTORS *with the heads of* MARIE ANTOINETTE, *the* KING, *the* NOBLES, *the* GIRL, *and the* CAPTAIN. *They enter with the operatic music, in the order in which they are presented in the following text (pantomime).*]

MARQUIS DE SADE [*singing operatically*]: Queen Slut . . .

[*Laughter and queenly gestures.*]

. . . And the Idiot King . . .

[*The* KING *displays his watch.*]

KING [*singing*]: What perfection, what beauty, not a piece is missing!

[MARQUIS DE SADE *and the queen laugh. Sounds of intrigue.* MADAME *enters.*]

MARQUIS DE SADE [*singing*]: Madame Washed-Out . . . !

[MADAME WASHED-OUT *and the queen pantomime.*]

MADAME WASHED-OUT [*singing*]: The queen has a fever . . . We have to call the doctor!

CHORUS OF NOBLEMEN [*enters, singing*]: Doctor . . . !

[*The* CAPTAIN *enters.* CAPTAIN *and his court enact a mini ballet and pantomime.*]

CAPTAIN [*sword in hand, singing to the queen*]: Here I am, Madame, to heal away . . .

CHORUS OF NOBLEMEN [*singing*]: your royally hot horniness!

[*Erotic pantomime: the queen, the* CAPTAIN, *and* MADAME WASHED-OUT. *Pose. Laughter and gestures from the court (pantomime of gossip, etc.). The* CAPTAIN *penetrates both of them with his sword.*]

CAPTAIN [*gesturing with the sword*]: Do you like my medicine?

[*Laughter. Pleasure Masks. Freeze. Tableaux. The Mask of Death enters dancing with the skeleton of Mrs. Coulmier. Death Minuet. The music becomes more distorted.*]

MARQUIS DE SADE [*to the audience*]: We must call the executioner!

CHORUS OF KINGS AND NOBLEMEN [*in group pose, operatically*]: Sanson . . . !

[SANSON *the executioner enters (on stilts). Applause from all. They sing the Song of the Guillotine.*]

CHORUS [*opera finale*]: *Ce la Gui-llo-tine, Ce la guillo-tii . . . ne . . . !*

SCENE 7

The Beheading Game

[*Light fades. A thick fog envelopes the scene. Shouts and lamentations are heard, and then, the metallic sound of the wheels of the cart as it moves forward slowly, barely visible, toward stage center. Echoes, shadows, sound and distorted figures. The light traverses the fog and creates fragmented images. Above, center,* CHARLOTTE *is seen. What follows is* CHARLOTTE's *subjective vision of the city. Stage right, the* MARQUIS DE SADE *is writing the text of the scene to which the audience is now witness.*]

MARQUIS DE SADE: They're burning the bodies of the dead.

[*The puppet-actors circle the cart. It is hard to distinguish them. The guillotine is heard. Heads roll. Slow movements. The action of the guillotine is veiled. There is a dense atmosphere, akin to Brueghel's* Triumph of Death. *Everything has the quality of a repressed and twisted memory made suddenly, terrifyingly surreal. The headless puppets laugh and contort, in counterpoint to* CHARLOTTE's *text.*]

CHARLOTTE [*veiled by smoke*]: City . . . what city is this . . . where the sun traverses the fog . . . ?

[*Sound of the guillotine. The first heads roll.*]

There's no fog. It is the thick, warm smoke . . . of the slaughterhouses.

[*Voices, screams, sounds; more heads roll.*]

Why do they shout so . . . ? What is it that they carry . . . ?

[*The Mask of Death (on the cart) gathers the heads. Movement.*]

Why do they dance and laugh?

[*Voices, laughter, movement circling the cart.*]

. . . and clap . . . ?

[*Sounds. Actions.*]

The masses strike . . . [*sound of blows*] . . . insult . . . Kill!

[*Distorted sound of "La Marseillaise." Behind the Mask of Death, on the cart,* MARAT *is seen wearing black linen; his head is bandaged as are his hands. Over the image of* CHARLOTTE *and the beheaded ones,* MARAT *speaks in counterpoint to* CHARLOTTE.]

MARAT [*on the cart*]: What happens here cannot be stopped!

[*Simultaneous actions: the Mask of Death continues to gather heads.*]

How much must we put up with before declaring vengeance?

[*Distorted sound of "La Marseillaise." 3-D image.*]

[*Exalted*] Our enemies only see vengeance now!

[*The Mask of Death drags the heads wrapped in cloth. The cart and the puppet-actors freeze.*]

They only see blood now . . . and the measures we've taken!

[*Distorted sound of "La Marseillaise" in crescendo, building to climax.*]

[*Out of control*] We're all suffering from the excesses perpetrated by this gang of thieves and clowns!

[*Movement of the headless bodies.*]

When the people died in war . . . what did they do? They ordered us to fight! [*Convulsing*] But in secret . . . they conspired with the enemy. [*Falling*] Against the people!

CHARLOTTE [*horrified*]: What city is this . . . ?

MARAT [*delirious, shouting*]: Who are our real enemies?

CHARLOTTE [*her whole body trembling*]: . . . where your body shivers in the streets?

MARAT [*in climax*]: Our country is in danger!

[*Sound stops. Light change. (Light accentuates the artifice of one scene shifting to another in the* MARQUIS DE SADE*'s staging.)*]

MARQUIS DE SADE [*interrupting the action, in a soft voice*]: Bravo, Marat! I confess that he moves me. [*To the audience*] Not even the most vile man is immune to the truth!

[MARQUIS DE SADE *approaches* MARAT, *looking at* MARAT*'s bandages.*]

Why does blood excite you?

[MARQUIS DE SADE *moves* MARAT*'s head.*]

Do you really think it's necessary?

[*The cart and the headless ones retreat, very slowly. The* INMATE-ACTORS *begin to take off their puppet clothes and start to change the scene.* MARAT *moves forward, downstage center, foreground, to speak with the* MARQUIS DE SADE*. In the background, the* INMATE-ACTORS *are witness to the scene. Freeze.*]

MARAT [*suffocating, in a whisper*]: I have read in a book of yours, Marquis . . . that the animating force in life . . . [*with effort*] is death.

[*The* MARQUIS DE SADE *laughs. The curtain in the background is drawn. They are alone now.*]

MARQUIS DE SADE [*very slowly*]: That kind of death only exists in the imagination. In mine . . . [*looking at* MARAT] . . . yours . . . [*looking at the audience*] . . . and in those of these poor people who watch us.

[MARQUIS DE SADE *walks toward* MARAT. MARAT'*s breathing is labored.*]

. . . But Nature doesn't recognize this kind of death. Even the cruelest of deaths are met by Nature's absolute indifference!

[MARAT *moves. He is blind. He doesn't know if what he hears is real or something in one of his visions or hallucinations.*]

[*Close to* MARAT] You're right. It's horrifying to see them fall! [*Playing with the metaphor*] These heads, for example, would make excellent fertilizer.

[*He takes* MARAT'*s hand in a bracing grip.*]

And yet . . . [*In his ear, quite loudly*] How sweet and gentle is the guillotine

[*He lowers his hand forcefully, with sadistic delight.*]

compared to other methods of torture.

ROUX [*shouting, hitting the bars of the cell*]: An animal! That man is a feral animal!

[ROUX *cries and resists the straitjacket.*]

How well . . . how well fertilized is this earth with the entrails of our men!

MARQUIS DE SADE [*laughing, to* MARAT]: You see that little monk? He moved a finger . . . and what did he get . . . ? A straitjacket! [*Shouts,* ROUX *moves*].

[MARAT *walks forward. He cannot see what is in front of him but rather sees what he imagines, and that gives him strength.*]

MARAT: The difference between you and me, Marquis, is that I believe in a cause! Your rebellion has neither rhyme nor reason. I want to create a new world . . .

[*He gestures with his hands to the audience.*]

to transform Nature, even if one has to move very carefully . . .

[*He takes the bandages off his hands and casts them to the ground.*]

. . . and to see the world with new eyes!

TOUSSAINT [*in his cell, above, lights match, shouting*]: I am the Liberator of Haiti!

MARQUIS DE SADE [*laughing*]: He's a sad case! [*Mocking him*] The Liberator of Haiti! The Napoleon of America! He'd an army so amazing it was legend!

[*Image of* TOUSSAINT *in his cell with fire.*]

. . . And now . . . [*mocking him, mimicking*] . . . all he does is pursue Charlotte . . . inconsolably.

[*Image of* CHARLOTTE *in her cell; the audience sees just her face and hands.*]

CHARLOTTE [*from offstage, a lament*]: Marat!

MARQUIS DE SADE [*to* CHARLOTTE]: The greatest truth, Marat, is what experience teaches us.

CHARLOTTE [*from offstage, hoarse, out of control*]: Marat!

MARQUIS DE SADE: . . . That the Victim becomes the executioner

[*He turns* MARAT *around.*]

. . . and the noblest of maidens . . .

CHARLOTTE [*from offstage, shouting*]: Marat!

MARQUIS DE SADE [*ending the scene*]: becomes a whore!

[*The* CHORUS OF INMATES *walks out of their cells. They surround* MARAT *and* MARQUIS DE SADE. *They carry costumes.*]

[*Facing forward*] Are we nature's playthings, or are we not, Marat?

[*The* MARQUIS DE SADE'*s musical theme is heard. Lights fade. Near darkness.*]

SCENE 8

The Marquis de Sade's Flagellation

[*Over the music,* SIMONE *and* NAPOLEONCITO *strip the* MARQUIS DE SADE *and* MARAT. *They are left alone, almost nude, wearing only their inmate trousers.* SIMONE *covers his eyes with* MARAT'*s bandage and takes him to his area of the stage (his station). In the foreground, slow movement and sound, delayed and in counterpoint, is seen. This scene is very stark. It should accentuate the loneliness of its characters. They cannot see or hear each other. There is only solitude. Each one is in his own world.*]

CHORUS OF VOICES [*alternating, softly*]: Corday! Corday! Corday! Corday!

[MARAT *is in the bathtub, with the bandage over his eyes.* MARQUIS DE SADE *is in the background. Light and shadow effects.* MARAT *cannot see anything, only shadows. And* MARQUIS DE SADE *has his eyes closed.*]

MARAT [*softly*]: Simone, why is it so dark?

[*First lash of the whip.* NAPOLEONCITO *flagellates the* MARQUIS DE SADE *with his hair.*]

MARQUIS DE SADE [*mask of pain*]: I am in pain!

MARAT [*to* SIMONE]: Where are my papers? I want to dictate the Call to the Nation!

[*Another lash against the* MARQUIS DE SADE'*s body.* MARQUIS DE SADE *experiences pleasure and pain.* CHARLOTTE *enters through the curtain in the background. She is nearly nude. She approaches slowly.*]

MARQUIS DE SADE [*softly*]: I have seen the ambition, the jealousy . . .

[*He receives a lash.*]

and the cruelty of men.

SIMONE [*to* MARAT]: They're here.

[SIMONE *gives him the papers.* CHARLOTTE *is behind* SIMONE. *Her torso is nude.*]

MARQUIS DE SADE [*sighing in relief*]: I'd trade places with Marat a thousand times.

MARAT [*with papers in hand*]: I can't see anything!

[MARQUIS DE SADE *falls upon the chair.*]

MARQUIS DE SADE: But I can't.

[SIMONE *sings.* CHARLOTTE *turns around. She is near* MARAT. *Her skirt is stained with blood.*]

MARAT [*bandaged*]: There's someone at the door.

[SIMONE *and* CHARLOTTE *cross in front of each other.*]

SIMONE [*pulling away*]: It's the young woman from Caen. She has already come twice.

MARAT: What do you want?

CHARLOTTE: To give you a letter.

SIMONE [*dutifully*]: When she visits him again, she will stab him with her knife . . .

[SIMONE *walks toward* MARQUIS DE SADE. CHARLOTTE *embraces* MARAT.]

> And I . . . [*falling to the floor, laughing*] . . . will be left alone . . . crazy . . . [*Looking at* MARAT] I don't even have a son by you [*tearing the pages*]. Only an idea that has vanished . . . [*Tossing the pages*] and that I can no longer touch.

MARAT [*pulling away from the embrace, in his vision*]: Where is Roux?!

[*Faint sound of "The Internationale" is heard. In the background,* ROUX *has red flag in hand. Over the music . . .*]

[MARAT *rises and walks to the audience.*]

Yes, Roux, I now see the men that will come . . . !

[*Laughter, voices, in* MARAT'*s vision.*]

Revolution is upon us!

[*The National Anthem is heard very loudly. Voices. Movements of the* CHORUS *as newspaper vendors (images transform quickly from one thing to another). Quick change of scene.*]

SCENE 9

The National Assembly

[*Over the music, voices and actions of the news vendors are heard. Quick movements. Time passes. The* INMATE-ACTORS *are positioned in different places and levels of the stage. From above, in the background, the red, blue, and white flag of the revolution sways. Placards that are emblazoned with the words Liberty, Equality, Freedom are seen. Calls and shouts from the crowd.*]

NAPOLEONCITO: Wake up, citizens, our country is in danger!

ROUX: A call from the Friend of the People!

TOUSSAINT: They're advancing on Paris!

SIMONE: Those that have left have banded together!

NAPOLEONCITO: Armies from all of Europe!

[MARAT *enters through the ragged curtain. He stands on a raised platform, assuming his position as head of the National Assembly's tribunal.*]

MARAT [*from the platform*]: They want to defeat us by starving us!

[*Panels roll on, demarcating the assembly area. The* INMATE-ACTORS *stand in different poses and in different areas of the stage.*]

NAPOLEONCITO [*to the crowd*]: Let us listen now to Marat in his final address to the National Assembly!

[*Voices, shouts.*]

MARAT: Representative citizens of the National Assembly. [*With a fixed stare at the crowd*] What does it matter if my eyes cannot see . . . ? We must unite against our common enemy!

CHORUS: Marat! Marat!

MARAT: The Minister of Treasury sent wheat for the soldiers!

CHORUS: Kill them, Marat! Kill them all!

MARAT: Most of our generals wait for the day when they can do their jobs!

CHORUS: Off with their heads!

[*Laughter.*]

Kill them, Marat!

MARAT: There's no Money, but the Minister of Finance gives us inflation!

CHORUS: Inflation, inflation, inflation . . . !

MARAT [*indignantly*]: A long time ago I talked about schools, hospitals

[*Voices call out.*]

and homes for the elderly.

CHORUS: Get rid of them, Marat! Throw them out!

MARAT: What will our teachers eat?

VOICE: Grass!

[*Laughter from the* CHORUS.]

MARAT: How will our sick people live?!

[CHORUS *members hide behind the panels. Silence.*]

Have we struggled so much, for so long, only to die of hunger?

[CHORUS *members peer out from behind the panels and shake their heads.*]

We need a leader who is of the people!

[NAPOLEONCITO's *music. The Bosses theme.* NAPOLEONCITO *is seen (wearing his signifying accessories) on* MARAT's *platform. All advance. Drums. Whistles. Different instruments. The March of the* INMATES. *They sing the Bosses song.*]

TOUSSAINT [*singing*]: The bosses we have now are worse than before . . .

SIMONE [*singing*]: They suck our blood the same as before . . .

CHORUS: [*singing*]: And the paper money they give us is only good to wipe our ass . . .

[*Laughter, game.*]

NAPOLEONCITO [*imposing order*]: I'm a soldier of the people! A simple foot soldier, as the Marquis says!

CHORUS [*from the panels*]: Napoleon, Napoleon, Napoleon!

VOICES: Down with Marat! Down with the dictator!

MARAT [*hearing the voices*]: I am not a dictator!

A VOICE: Murderer!

MARAT [*covering his ears*]: We killed to defend ourselves!

ANTOINETTE: Marat, change your tune!

TOUSSAINT: Down with bars on windows and closed doors!

JOANNA: Open the borders, and give us our bread!

[*Cell bars are rattled.*]

NAPOLEONCITO [*on the platform, gesturing with his sword*]: We have orders to search every single corner!

[*Panels move.*]

We will cleanse these streets, basements, and sewers of all of our enemies. Death to the invaders! Long live the nation!

[*The Wheel of History song is heard. Change of scene. Platform is now horizontal.* MARAT *sits on it, as if it were a bed.* SIMONE *sings.*]

SIMONE [*singing*]: The Wheel of History sweeps along
  Its madmen, noblemen, aristocrats, and the poor.
  What's the difference between a madman and one who is not?

[*Laughter, voices.* INMATE-ACTORS *begin placing objects about the space.*]

SIMONE [*singing*]: What does it matter if something's true or false, hidden or exposed . . . What does it matter . . . if we're all mad?

INMATES CHORUS [*singing and dancing*]: . . . It's the Wheel of History!

SIMONE [*singing*]: And in this assembly, Marat, we order you to tell us . . .

CHORUS [*singing*]: What's hiding in the darkness that we cannot see?

[*Light fades.* CHARLOTTE'*s theme is heard* (*the third visit*).]

SCENE 10

Charlotte's Last Portrait

[MARAT *is on the horizontal platform. His eyes are bandaged. The* MARQUIS DE SADE *observes him and gestures.* CHARLOTTE *enters through the curtain in the background. Candles light her way. The entire scene is in black and white.* MARAT *wears thin white linen and white bandages.* CHARLOTTE *is also in white. Their movements are slow. The scene is between light and dark. There are flickers of light. Over music and sound . . .*]

MARQUIS DE SADE: Finally, Marat, I understand. What are all those pamphlets and speeches compared to her . . . she, whose body longs to embrace yours?

[*Flashes of light.* CHARLOTTE *is seen fragmented.* MARQUIS DE SADE *and* MARAT *as well. A trio. Slow movements, precise, ritualized. The final scene of the* MARQUIS DE SADE'*s play.*]

  [*Acting in his play*] A Virgin, Marat . . . a blessed virgin is at your door . . . offering herself to you!

[*A candle lights* SIMONE'*s face. She looks at the* MARQUIS DE SADE *and then to the audience.*]

SIMONE: He loves this scene.

MARQUIS DE SADE [*very slowly*]: Look how she smiles. Marat. There is nothing here. Only her exquisite body . . .

[MARQUIS DE SADE *opens* CHARLOTTE*'s dress.*]

. . . her naked breasts.

[*He caresses her.*]

. . . and under this light fabric, she conceals a dagger [*reveals*] . . . that will give you a most intense . . . [MARQUIS DE SADE *pauses for a moment and then gravely says*] . . . pleasure.

MARAT [*blind, very softly*]: Simone . . . I have seen death. It was a lone woman.

[CHARLOTTE *hugs* MARAT *from behind. Trio.*]

MARQUIS DE SADE [*in his character voice*]: A girl . . . a servant from the country, who's traveled through the heat, and slipped through a window . . .

[CHARLOTTE laughs convulsively.]

Think how these girls wait there (in the country) . . . and dream of men who rule the world.

[*The* MARQUIS DE SADE *and* CHARLOTTE *move. As they do so . . .*]

When I was in prison I learned that this was a world of bodies . . .

[MARQUIS DE SADE *caresses* MARAT *and* CHARLOTTE.]

I dreamt of that body. And it was a dream full of [*gesturing*] strong sensations . . . and violence!

[MARAT *and* CHARLOTTE *are naked. The* MARQUIS DE SADE *has dagger in hand.*]

Marat, the prisons of our bodies are tougher and stronger than those made of stone. And for as long as they remain locked, the entire revolution . . .

[MARQUIS DE SADE *raises the dagger; he offers it to* CHARLOTTE. *Sound.*]

. . . is nothing more than a game of hungry bodies . . . diabolical people.

VOICES [*distorted*]: Corday! Corday! Corday!

[*Slow movement. Delayed action. The* CHORUS *observes.* CHARLOTTE *holds the dagger in her hand, poised over* MARAT.]

CHARLOTTE: Marat, I declare you one of my heroes. I'm not betraying anyone. Because you're dead!

[*Light enters.* NAPOLEONCITO *stops* CHARLOTTE's *hand. Freeze. The action is suspended. Everything begins to spin and blur and deconstruct until only nothingness is left.*]

EPILOGUE

[*An Actors Game: hungry and demonic.*]

NAPOLEONCITO [*holding* CHARLOTTE's *hand*]: Marquis . . . would you like to dance with death?

[*Movement.* CHARLOTTE's *transformational mask in place.*]

She knows that she's about to commit a crime. But you're the one who guides her hand.

[*He takes dagger away from her.*]

Not the enemies of Caen!

[*Everyone observes.* NAPOLEONCITO *places the dagger on the floor. Slow, delayed movement.* CHARLOTTE *laughs. Movement, laughter, voices of the* INMATES.]

MARQUIS DE SADE [*violently*]: Silence!

[*They all stop.* NAPOLEONCITO *and the* MARQUIS DE SADE *are on opposite sides of the stage.*]

[*To* NAPOLEONCITO] In times like these, times of confusion, no one knows what to do. [*Between reality and the world of play*] You thrive on death as much as I did on scandal!

[NAPOLEONCITO advances, sword in hand. They face each other.]

SIMONE [*to the* MARQUIS DE SADE]: Enough!

[SIMONE's *theme is heard, softly, underscoring.*]

[*Over* MARAT's *corpse*] A simple gesture, one hand descends, and Marat's heart stops beating.

[SIMONE *embraces* MARAT's *corpse.*]

[*The* INMATES *draw closer. They surround* SIMONE *and* MARAT. *The women bring red linen to cover them.*]

[*To the* MARQUIS DE SADE] But he couldn't stop this river of people without a history . . .

[*The* CHORUS *opens the red linen fabric, in the background.*]

. . . without a future [*to the audience*] these masses of men and women upon this land.

[SIMONE *caresses* MARAT.]

A land ravaged by hunger . . . sickness . . . death. [*Weeps*] A land that could have been . . .

[*Sound (very softly) of "The Internationale" is heard. The women raise the red linen fabric and cover a section of* MARAT's *body as . . .*]

. . . the Paradise that Marat once dreamt of.

NAPOLEONCITO [*an actor now playing a role*]: He wanted to dignify the soldier and the common man.

MARQUIS DE SADE [*between reality and the world of play*]: You see, in the Revolution the only means to obtain power . . .

NAPOLEONCITO: I abhor blood! [*Grabbing the dagger*] But there was no other way.

MARQUIS DE SADE [*returning to the script*]: is to kill . . . [*looking at* CHAR-
LOTTE] . . . or let her do the killing!

[*An intense, vertiginous sound is heard.* CHARLOTTE *falls upon* MARAT'S
*body, covering him completely with the red linen fabric. Each person places
an offering next to the body:* ROUX *offers his flag,* ANTOINETTE *offers her
bread,* JOANNA *the Mad offers a lit candle.* NAPOLEONCITO *wipes his face
and begins to take off his makeup. He looks at his hands: stained with red and
blue makeup.*]

NAPOLEONCITO [*slowly, stepping out of his role, to the audience*]: It's only
a performance.

MARQUIS DE SADE [*in character, violently*]: Of a play that you're going
to censor!

ACTOR-NAPOLEONCITO: Not me! I just don't like your experiment! I
prefer the street, the smell of blood . . . to this lie!

[*He takes off his hat and tosses it to the ground. He is about to walk away, but
the* INMATES *run to the doors and block his path.*]

MARQUIS DE SADE: Don't you dare exit!

[*They all stop.*]

It's easier to be Napoleon, in the darkness of this basement, where the
mask of play frees him from everything else, than to go out there, into
the street, and face the truth!

[*He points to* MARAT, *stage center.*]

At least he knew how to conduct himself to the very end! Whereas
you . . . You're as changeable as a chameleon.

[*Gales of laughter, mockery, movement from the* CHORUS OF INMATES.
ROUX *shouts, turns around, and bangs the floor. He places* NAPOLEONCITO'S
hat on his head. He mimics him, sword in hand.]

ACTOR-NAPOLEONCITO [*pointing to* MARQUIS DE SADE]: He brought
us here to put on an absurd story about a list of people who were sent
to the guillotine.

ACTRESS-JOANNA [*disconcerted, stepping out of her role*]: We're merely actors . . . a bunch of comedians that you wanted to save . . . in this basement.

MARQUIS DE SADE [*in character, with irony, between reality and the world of play*]: Aren't you working for the King? Aren't you entertaining the court? Don't you cover your face with makeup . . . while the people on the streets suffer hunger, pain, and humiliation?

ACTRESS-SIMONE: Let us out!

ACTRESS-ANTOINETTE: We are not politicians!

ACTRESS-CHARLOTTE: Or heroes!

ROUX [*in character, he cannot get out, shouting*]: Hear! Hear!

[*He runs about the stage. The actors look at him.*]

Marat, a chalice of blood for everyone!

NAPOLEONCITO: Shut up!

MARQUIS DE SADE [*before* MARAT's *body*]: Marat is dead! I wrote his epitaph myself. And you, you covered his body with a . . . cloth.

[ACTOR-NAPOLEONCITO *removes the cloth. He points to* MARAT.]

NAPOLEONCITO: This is nothing more than a crazy, perverted game . . . like all of your work!

MARQUIS DE SADE [*with irony, looking for closure, to the audience*]: A criminal game! Or should I say: the enactment of a crime . . .

[*He points to the* INMATE-ACTORS.]

[*Laughing*] . . . that no one dares to carry out!

[*The* MARQUIS DE SADE *motions to the band to play the last theme. Sound. He lifts* MARAT *up. They look at each other. The* MARQUIS DE SADE's *play is over. Laughter, action from the actors (as if they were madmen, caught in their roles).* ACTOR-NAPOLEON *draws the ragged curtain. They open the gate in the background, which leads to the street outside. We see people passing, cars, and life outside the theater. The* INMATE-ACTORS *run to the door.* NAPO-

LEONCITO *crosses the fence and gets as far as the street. He turns and looks back. He sees the audience, the actors of Charentón, the frayed costumes, the tired makeup, the remains of a performance . . . that will be repeated again and again.*
When he returns, he carries MARAT*'s red linen and repeats the scripted text, as if he were from far off in the distance.*]

ACTOR-NAPOLEONCITO: Young people of France: of all classes and stations, with our actions, with the fervor of our actions, a new world will be born. [*In his own voice*] One world!

[ACTRESS-JOANNA *lights a fire. She burns her mannequin, her work things, etc. Her body is covered in newspapers.*]

ACTRESS-JOANNA: No more war. No more war. [*In her own voice*] No more war.

[*There is a fire glowing, stage center. Lights dim. The actors are positioned in different areas of the stage. Minimal action. There is a repetition by the company of gestures and movements, in and out of character. It is as if the audience is witnessing the play unravel through text and action. The process of shedding character enacted by each actor is different, but for all of them there is a vertiginous return to that first day of work or the first moment when they felt their characters being born.* ACTRESS-ANTOINETTE *undresses. She repeats/recites the text, which is the queen's last letter:*]

ACTRESS-ANTOINETTE: All my shirts are stained with blood . . .

[*She removes her veil.*]

Because of my innate desire to be cleansed . . . when I take my last breath on this long road, I beg you to please leave me alone.

[*She stops. She looks at the audience.*]

[*Out of character, as herself*] Someone will come, two centuries later, to see the sky I never did see.

[ACTRESS-CHARLOTTE *recites her character's text, one she never delivered onstage. She begins as* CHARLOTTE:]

ACTRESS-CHARLOTTE: In my room in Caen, on the table near the window . . . [*as herself*] there is the book of Judith.

ACTRESS-SIMONE [*laughing, in character*]: And I . . . will remain alone, mad . . . I don't even have a child by you . . . [*As herself*] Only an idea that vanishes and that I can no longer touch.

ACTOR-TOUSSAINT [*as himself, on the cart*]: A small island you cannot see.

ACTRESS-JOANNA [*as herself, next to the fire*]: I look out at this city, where all my friends are gone.

ACTRESS-MARQUISE [*as herself, in her corner*]: I can see them in my dreams.

ACTOR-MARAT [*as himself, taking off the bandage*]: Yes, Roux, I see now the men that will come.

[ACTOR-MARAT *and* ROUX *begin to close the panels.*]

ROUX [*in character, between the bars, looking at the audience, laughing*]: Not even a cage can hold me!

MARQUIS DE SADE [*stage center, in character*]: A simple tale of sound of fury signifying nothing!

[*The music the audience heard at the beginning of the piece resumes.* ROUX *and* MARAT *place the panels, as before. Light dims. The actors are now in their dressing rooms/cells. The actors return slowly to their mirrors. Sounds, voices, footsteps are heard.* ACTOR-TOUSSAINT *covers* JOANNA *the Mad's body with a red, white, and blue flag. He returns to his cell. Darkness. Only the music is heard and the sound of the fire.*]

OUR DAD IS IN ATLANTIS

Javier Malpica

Translated from the Spanish by Jorge Ignacio Cortiñas

PRODUCTION HISTORY

In 2006 Javier Malpica earned a grant to go to New York (invited by the Lark Play Development Center) for a translation and a public reading of his play *Our Dad Is in Atlantis*. Also in 2006 he was invited by the Theatre Communications Group (TCG) in Minneapolis for a public reading of his play *Our Dad Is in Atlantis* in a presentation of the Latin American theater and as part of the Global Tapas event. The play was selected for a public reading at the Woolly Mammoth Theatre by the NNPN (National New Play Network) in Washington, D.C. The play also won the Global Age Project Award that was given by the Aurora Theatre Company of Berkeley, California, and was staged in a public reading.

In 2008 *Our Dad Is in Atlantis* was produced by the Working Theatre and Queens Theatre in the Park and opened at the theaters at 45 Bleecker Theater in New York City on April 4 (directed by Debbie Savits). The play also opened in Indianapolis at Phoenix Theatre (directed by Sharin Gamble) on May 8. In 2009 it was staged by the Borderlands Theater in Tucson and several cities in Arizona (directed by Eva Zorrilla). The play was published by *American Theatre* magazine in the July/August 2008 edition. In Mexico *Our Dad Is in Atlantis* was staged in several productions: in Mexico City (directed by Sandra Felix), San Luis Potosí (directed by Jesús Coronado), and Monterrey (directed by Alberto Ontiveros).

In 2010, the playwright was invited by the Goodman Theatre for a public reading of the play as part of the Latino Theatre Festival (directed by Ann Filmer).

Big Brother . . . . Juan Francisco Villa
Little Brother . . . . Remy Ortiz

This translation was commissioned and originally developed at the Lark Play Development Center, New York City, as part of the U.S.–Mexico Playwright Exchange Program. The translation is the sole property of Jorge Ignacio Cortiñas (copyright © 2006). It may not be distributed, copied, or performed, in whole or in part, without permission in writing from ICM, 730 5th Ave., New York, NY 10019 Attn: Val Day. PHOTOGRAPH: Todd Garcia as Big Brother and Remy Ortiz as Little Brother. Photograph by Anthony Aicardi.

CHARACTERS

Big Brother, an eleven-year-old boy
Little Brother, an eight-year-old boy

PLACE: Mexico

TIME: The present

STUFF ABOUT THE COUNTRYSIDE

LITTLE BROTHER: Forty-two, forty-three.

BIG BROTHER: It's so hot!

LITTLE BROTHER: Forty-four cows.

BIG BROTHER: Why are you doing that?

LITTLE BROTHER: What?

BIG BROTHER: Counting cows. Counting cows is stupid. Stop it.

LITTLE BROTHER: I've never seen so many cows in my whole life.

BIG BROTHER: I hate cows. Stop counting cows.

LITTLE BROTHER: All right. I'll count horses.

BIG BROTHER: Don't count horses. Don't count sheep, or goats, or anything. Don't count animals. I hate farm animals.

LITTLE BROTHER: . . .

BIG BROTHER: . . .

LITTLE BROTHER: You think Grandma has horses?

BIG BROTHER: It's so hot here.

LITTLE BROTHER: You told me she has chickens. If she has chickens, maybe she also has a horse.

BIG BROTHER: Are you sure you can't open that window?

LITTLE BROTHER: You saw yourself. It's stuck.

BIG BROTHER: One thing I hate about the country, is the heat. Your clothes stick to your body. And everything smells bad.

LITTLE BROTHER: You think Grandma will let us ride her horses?

BIG BROTHER: Grandma doesn't have horses.

LITTLE BROTHER: How do you know?

BIG BROTHER: The only thing she has is a chicken coop which always stinks like chicken turds.

LITTLE BROTHER: Maybe she does have a horse. Maybe a small one.

BIG BROTHER: You don't even remember Grandma. That's why you're so happy. When you see her again, you'll realize how truly horrible a human being can be.

LITTLE BROTHER: She can't be that bad.

BIG BROTHER: Dad says she used to hit her kids with the Bible whenever they didn't want to go to Mass or when they misbehaved. Later she would make them pray the Our Father. That Bible was as heavy as a rock. He says once she split open Uncle Rodrigo's head and they were pretty sure he started leaking brain juice.

LITTLE BROTHER: I don't think she's going to treat us bad, after all we're her guests.

BIG BROTHER: Guests. What do you think we're doing, taking a vacation?

LITTLE BROTHER: Of course we're taking a vacation.

BIG BROTHER: We're not taking a vacation.

LITTLE BROTHER: Yes we are.

BIG BROTHER: In our entire lives, we've never taken a vacation.

LITTLE BROTHER: There's a first time for everything, right? That's what people say.

BIG BROTHER: Oh yeah? And why now? In the middle of the school year?

LITTLE BROTHER: If Grandma has a little horse, I'm going to ride it every day. I'll feed him alfalfa and we'll be best friends, watch.

BIG BROTHER: I already told you, we're not going on vacation.

LITTLE BROTHER: What difference will that make to the horse?

BIG BROTHER: Enough about farm animals.

LITTLE BROTHER: . . .

BIG BROTHER: . . .

LITTLE BROTHER: If we're not going on vacation, then why are we going to Grandma's house?

BIG BROTHER: You really are dumb.

LITTLE BROTHER: I'm going to tell Dad you're calling me names again.

BIG BROTHER: Go ahead, bother him. See what happens. He meant it when he said he wanted us to sit down and keep our seat belts on.

LITTLE BROTHER: How come you keep saying we aren't going on vacation?

BIG BROTHER: . . .

LITTLE BROTHER: . . .

BIG BROTHER: Dad is going to drop us off there.

LITTLE BROTHER: With Grandma?

BIG BROTHER: I heard him talking with her on the phone. He said stuff like, "It'll just be a month, Mother. I guarantee they won't give you any problems."

LITTLE BROTHER: Where's he going?

BIG BROTHER: I don't know. But he can't take us with him. That's for sure.

LITTLE BROTHER: You're lying. I'm going to ask him and you'll see it's not true.

BIG BROTHER: Why do you think he made us pack all of our clothes?

LITTLE BROTHER: Dad would never do that. He wouldn't leave us behind.

BIG BROTHER: Why do you think we got on this bus when it's so full? Dad is in a hurry to drop us off at Grandma's.

LITTLE BROTHER: Why is he in a hurry?

BIG BROTHER: . . .

LITTLE BROTHER: Is it true Dad is scared of Grandma?

BIG BROTHER: Of course. She used to force them to believe in God by hitting them on the head with a Bible.

LITTLE BROTHER: I don't want Grandma to make me leak brain juices with her Bible.

BIG BROTHER: I shouldn't have told you anything.

LITTLE BROTHER: I thought Dad was going to stay with us.

BIG BROTHER: We'll have to put up with the stink of chicken turds for a whole month.

LITTLE BROTHER: It's just going to be one month then?

BIG BROTHER: Maybe you should go back to counting cows.

STUFF ABOUT TERROR

LITTLE BROTHER: I don't like this house.

BIG BROTHER: You never like anything.

LITTLE BROTHER: It smells old . . . Don't you think it smells old?

BIG BROTHER: What'd you expect? Grandma is old and everything she has in her house is old. Old stuff has to smell old.

LITTLE BROTHER: The furniture has to be a thousand years old. Look at that dresser and that mirror. They have cobwebs they're so old.

BIG BROTHER: You've been complaining since we got here. You haven't done anything but whine.

LITTLE BROTHER: I haven't whined.

BIG BROTHER: If you didn't want to stay, you should have told Dad.

LITTLE BROTHER: This bed is hard. I'm sure nobody's used it. Ever. I want to leave.

BIG BROTHER: You want Grandma to come in here and beat you with her Bible and make you pray? Have you forgotten what I told you about Grandma and her Bible?

BIG BROTHER: . . .

LITTLE BROTHER: . . .

LITTLE BROTHER: I don't like this house.

BIG BROTHER: Just go to sleep already.

LITTLE BROTHER: I can't sleep if you don't turn off the light. You know that.

BIG BROTHER: How do you want me to read with the light turned off? Huh, genius?

LITTLE BROTHER: Grandma said we have to be up at six. Did you hear what I said? . . . If I don't wake up on time, it's going to be your fault. I don't want her to hit me with her Bible so hard that I start leaking brain juice. If you make me oversleep, I'll tell her you're the one she should beat.

BIG BROTHER: I'm right in the middle of the most exciting part.

LITTLE BROTHER: You've already read that book a thousand times.

BIG BROTHER: This is the first time I'm reading it.

LITTLE BROTHER: Don't try to hide it. I can see it through the mirror. It's that same book about vampires. You've read that book more than five thousand times.

BIG BROTHER: So?

LITTLE BROTHER: I'll tell Grandma you're not letting me sleep.

BIG BROTHER: You always whine. That's why me and my friends never took you with us to the train tracks. None of us wanted to hang out with whiny kids.

LITTLE BROTHER: Juan told me all you guys did was throw rocks at the empty train cars . . . I don't want to throw rocks at a bunch of stupid train cars.

BIG BROTHER: Juan is as stupid as you are. He doesn't know anything. We did a lot more than throw rocks . . . You're both stupid.

LITTLE BROTHER: When are you going to turn off the light?

BIG BROTHER: . . .

LITTLE BROTHER: Are you going to turn it off?

BIG BROTHER: I'll turn off the light, but if the devil comes in, I'm not going to defend you.

LITTLE BROTHER: What are you talking about?

BIG BROTHER: The devil, genius. Don't you know he's always around these old houses with all the cobwebs?

LITTLE BROTHER: You're a liar.

BIG BROTHER: He appears inside old mirrors. You didn't know? You yourself said that mirror was as old as Grandma.

LITTLE BROTHER: Mirrors are for looking at yourself and that's all. See? That's just you and me in there and nothing else.

BIG BROTHER: That's when the light is on. Demons are afraid of even the smallest candlelight. Don't you know that fallen angels can't stand the light? But when the lights are turned off that's when they can look and spy on us through the mirrors. Demons get into houses through big mirrors.

LITTLE BROTHER: You're a liar.

BIG BROTHER: In a lot of old houses like this one, people cover up the mirrors at night with black cloth and that way they keep the demons out.

LITTLE BROTHER: You're making that up.

BIG BROTHER: Ask anyone. If we turn off the light, it won't even be ten minutes before a demon comes up through the mirror and the second we fall asleep he'll climb into our beds and steal our memories.

LITTLE BROTHER: You're making it up.

BIG BROTHER: If you want, we can turn off the light so you'll see.

LITTLE BROTHER: I don't believe anything you say.

BIG BROTHER: . . .

LITTLE BROTHER: What are you doing? Don't turn off the light. Don't turn it off.

BIG BROTHER: You'll see. You say you don't believe anything I say? Well you'll see how the devil appears.

LITTLE BROTHER: I'm going to scream for Grandma.

BIG BROTHER: See what a crybaby you are?

LITTLE BROTHER: I'm not a crybaby.

BIG BROTHER: Then I'll turn off the light.

BIG BROTHER: If you turn off the light, I'll scream for Grandma.

BIG BROTHER: If you scream, the devil will come after you. Demons can always hear you. Even when they're hiding in the mirror, they can hear you.

LITTLE BROTHER: I don't believe you.

BIG BROTHER: Lower your voice, he can hear you. He can also see anything that moves.

LITTLE BROTHER: Turn on the light. I don't believe anything you say. The devil doesn't exist.

BIG BROTHER: Then take that blanket off of your head. How do you expect to see that the devil doesn't exist if you cover your head?

LITTLE BROTHER: You're making all of this up.

BIG BROTHER: Hold up. I think I saw something.

LITTLE BROTHER: That's not true.

BIG BROTHER: Take off that blanket.

LITTLE BROTHER: When Dad gets back I'm going to tell him what you're doing.

BIG BROTHER: You'll have to wait a month. Dad isn't coming back for a month.

LITTLE BROTHER: Either way, I'll tell him.

BIG BROTHER: Hold up. Don't move. If you move, the demon is going to come after you.

LITTLE BROTHER: And why not after you?

BIG BROTHER: I already hid behind the bed and he can't see me. Don't you move . . . Be quiet. He's going to hear you. I see it . . . it's like . . . it's like a shadow . . .

LITTLE BROTHER: Are you serious?

BIG BROTHER: Don't move or he'll find you . . . He came out from behind the curtains. I never thought a demon would look like that. He has the face of a really old man. Hold up, his skin isn't red. It's purple, like a dry scab. And his eyes . . .

LITTLE BROTHER: What?

BIG BROTHER: He doesn't have eyes. They're black, like two beetles. His ears are pointy . . . what did I tell you. He's moving his head, looking around the room. Don't you move . . .

LITTLE BROTHER: I want my dad.

BIG BROTHER: Hold up . . . I think he saw you.

LITTLE BROTHER: But I haven't moved.

BIG BROTHER: Your blanket is shaking. It's shaking like a wet dog.

LITTLE BROTHER: Come on, I'm your brother: turn on the light.

BIG BROTHER: I think he's coming in.

LITTLE BROTHER: Turn on the light.

BIG BROTHER: He'll see me.

LITTLE BROTHER: If you don't turn on the light, he's going to steal my memory.

BIG BROTHER: If I turn on the light and make him leave, are you going to let me read?

LITTLE BROTHER: Turn on the light.

BIG BROTHER: Fine. Since you're such a crybaby.

LITTLE BROTHER: . . .

BIG BROTHER: . . .

LITTLE BROTHER: Is he gone? Hello? Can I take off the blanket? Hey? Where are you? Where are you? . . . You better not scare me. Come out already. Demons don't exist . . . Grandma!

BIG BROTHER: . . .

LITTLE BROTHER: The devil kidnapped my brother. Grandma!

BIG BROTHER: Where are you going! Don't bother Grandma.

LITTLE BROTHER: . . .

BIG BROTHER: Can't believe you fell for that. The devil in the mirror . . .

STUFF ABOUT MEN

BIG BROTHER: I've been waiting for you for about a thousand hours. Grandma is going to be mad. She said we had to be home early. Why don't you lift your head? What's wrong?

LITTLE BROTHER: Nothing. Let's go.

BIG BROTHER: Something happen to you?

LITTLE BROTHER: Nothing happened. Let's go.

BIG BROTHER: Why won't you look at me?

LITTLE BROTHER: Grandma said we had to be home early.

BIG BROTHER: Let me see.

LITTLE BROTHER: No. You're going to make fun of me.

BIG BROTHER: Why would I make fun of you?

LITTLE BROTHER: You always make fun of what happens to me.

BIG BROTHER: That's not true. I've never made fun of you.

LITTLE BROTHER: And that time that piñata fell on top of me?

BIG BROTHER: Just that one time.

LITTLE BROTHER: And the time Anna threw me in the pool?

BIG BROTHER: I promise I won't make fun of you this time.

LITTLE BROTHER: Remember what you promised.

BIG BROTHER: Who did this to you?

LITTLE BROTHER: Let's go.

BIG BROTHER: They punched you?

LITTLE BROTHER: I don't like that school anymore.

BIG BROTHER: Did you fight back? Did you punch them back?

LITTLE BROTHER: I want to go back to my old school.

BIG BROTHER: Tell me who it was.

LITTLE BROTHER: I want us to go back to the city.

BIG BROTHER: Answer me, who punched you?

LITTLE BROTHER: . . .

BIG BROTHER: . . .

LITTLE BROTHER: Why did they call me a dirty rat from the capital?

BIG BROTHER: Who called you that?

LITTLE BROTHER: They told me that in this town they didn't like dirty rats from the capital.

BIG BROTHER: . . .

LITTLE BROTHER: What does that mean?

BIG BROTHER: Well it's an insult.

LITTLE BROTHER: They told me that since I was a stinky rat from the capital, I probably had a knife or a gun on me. And probably I was here to mug people and then they said a bunch of other stuff.

BIG BROTHER: This is why I didn't want to come to a town full of cows . . . people here make stuff up that isn't true.

LITTLE BROTHER: I told them I never even owned a gun, so then they wanted to pat me down, but I didn't let them and they told me that if I was so brave, then I had to fight all of them.

BIG BROTHER: How many were there?

LITTLE BROTHER: I don't want to go back to that school.

BIG BROTHER: This is what happens to you for being a crybaby. I've told you before, men don't cry. How do you expect people to respect you if they think you're a girl instead of a man?

LITTLE BROTHER: I'm not a crybaby, and I'm not a girl. I'm sensitive. That's what Grandma says. Besides, the reason they hit me was because they think I'm a dirty rat from the city.

BIG BROTHER: Grandma doesn't know about these things. She's a woman.

LITTLE BROTHER: She might be a woman, but even that guy who sells groceries is afraid of her.

BIG BROTHER: I really don't understand our grandmother, she tells you you're sensitive when you cry but she beats me with her horrible Bible for any little thing I do.

LITTLE BROTHER: Don't tell her they punched me at school.

BIG BROTHER: In that case you're going to have to do what I say and go and punch them back.

LITTLE BROTHER: I'm not a violent person, even if they say I am.

BIG BROTHER: . . .

LITTLE BROTHER: . . .

BIG BROTHER: I'm going to teach you how to box.

LITTLE BROTHER: You don't know how to box.

BIG BROTHER: Of course I do. Thing is you never realized Uncle Rodrigo was giving me lessons. One day I went home with a black eye, just like the one you have, and our uncle gave me private boxing lessons. The next week I found the boy who had punched me, and I challenged him to a boxing match. He didn't even last two rounds. From that day on, everyone respected me.

LITTLE BROTHER: You never came home with a black eye.

BIG BROTHER: My best move was the left hook to the gut.

LITTLE BROTHER: If you had come home with a black eye, Mom would have taken you to the hospital.

BIG BROTHER: Just two or three lessons, and that's all you'll need.

LITTLE BROTHER: I think it'll be better if I tell my teacher what happened.

BIG BROTHER: Are you nuts? If you tell your teacher, all the kids in school are going to be your enemy. You have to honor the code of fistfights. Teachers cannot get involved.

LITTLE BROTHER: . . .

BIG BROTHER: . . .

LITTLE BROTHER: When my teacher asked me what happened, I told her I ran into one of the swings.

BIG BROTHER: That was good. That way they won't ask you any more questions. You weren't a crybaby.

LITTLE BROTHER: But didn't you say I was a crybaby?

BIG BROTHER: Yeah, but it's one thing to be a crybaby at Grandma's house, and another thing to go and be a crybaby to your teacher.

LITTLE BROTHER: So you don't think I need boxing lessons?

BIG BROTHER: You respected the code of fistfights.

LITTLE BROTHER: It was that fat kid.

BIG BROTHER: The one that looks like a pig standing up?

LITTLE BROTHER: Don't say it so loud. He might hear you.

BIG BROTHER: You're right, it's better if you don't fight him. No one could win against that kid, not even Uncle Rodrigo. Or Grandma.

LITTLE BROTHER: . . .

BIG BROTHER: . . .

LITTLE BROTHER: I never saw you with a black eye. Mom would have fainted.

BIG BROTHER: Maybe it's better if I don't give you boxing lessons. I don't think you could have learned the left hook to the gut. It's pretty complicated.

STUFF ABOUT DAD

BIG BROTHER: Don't follow me.

LITTLE BROTHER: Grandma told you to take care of me.

BIG BROTHER: You can't come with me.

LITTLE BROTHER: Where are you going?

BIG BROTHER: Go back to the house.

LITTLE BROTHER: I don't want to.

BIG BROTHER: I'm your older brother and because I'm your older brother, you have to obey me.

LITTLE BROTHER: I don't have to obey you. I only have to obey Dad.

BIG BROTHER: Haven't you ever heard of levels? In a family, whoever's oldest has to be obeyed. When Dad was here, we obeyed him. If we had an older brother, then we would have to obey him too. If you had a little brother or a dog, they would have to obey you. But since it's just you and me, you have to obey me. Therefore I order you to go back to the house.

LITTLE BROTHER: Grandma is the oldest one. She even bosses Dad around.

BIG BROTHER: But she's a woman. If some wild bear attacked us, she wouldn't be able to do anything. Only the oldest man in the house would be able to do something. And that's me. I am the man of the house.

LITTLE BROTHER: Ha ha ha!

BIG BROTHER: Why are you laughing? I order you to stop laughing.

LITTLE BROTHER: You can't be the man of the house.

BIG BROTHER: Why not? What's wrong with you?

LITTLE BROTHER: You're afraid of Grandma.

BIG BROTHER: And you're afraid of mirrors.

LITTLE BROTHER: Besides there are no bears here.

BIG BROTHER: You want me to punch you?

LITTLE BROTHER: Do it and I'll tell your friends you're afraid of Grandma.

BIG BROTHER: I order you to go back to the house.

LITTLE BROTHER: Who are you going with? Are you going with Miguel?

BIG BROTHER: That's not important.

LITTLE BROTHER: Where are you going? To throw rocks at the trains?

BIG BROTHER: I told you to beat it.

LITTLE BROTHER: I don't think there are any trains that go through here.

BIG BROTHER: If you don't beat it, you're the one I'm going to throw rocks at.

LITTLE BROTHER: I don't like Miguel and you told me you thought he was a jerk.

BIG BROTHER: Are you going or not? I'm tired of you following me. You follow me everywhere. You're like my shadow. Worse than my shadow, because at least my shadow leaves me in peace when there isn't any sunlight.

LITTLE BROTHER: . . .

BIG BROTHER: I'm not going to throw rocks. I'm not going to see Miguel either. I just want to be alone and think awhile.

LITTLE BROTHER: That's a lie. Nobody likes to be alone. Why would you want to be alone?

BIG BROTHER: Think whatever you want.

LITTLE BROTHER: . . .

LITTLE BROTHER: Fine, I'll go. But just tell me one thing.

BIG BROTHER: Why do you insist on bugging me?

LITTLE BROTHER: Do you know where Dad is?

BIG BROTHER: What are you talking about?

LITTLE BROTHER: I asked you if you know where Dad is?

BIG BROTHER: Of course I don't know. Nobody knows.

LITTLE BROTHER: Well I know. And I'm not going to tell you unless you take me with you.

BIG BROTHER: You're crazy. How could you possibly know where Dad is? Even Grandma doesn't know.

LITTLE BROTHER: I've been investigating and he's someplace really fantastic. It's someplace everyone thinks sank, but that isn't true. This place is fantastic. And he's going to take us there.

BIG BROTHER: You're crazy. You should go back to the house before the sun completely melts your brain.

LITTLE BROTHER: Our dad is in Atlantis.

BIG BROTHER: Where did you say he is?

LITTLE BROTHER: In Atlantis. I'm sure you don't know what that is. I asked my teacher and she told me it was a fantastic place where everyone was happy.

BIG BROTHER: Atlantis never existed. Everyone knows that.

LITTLE BROTHER: Of course it exists. They made up the part about it sinking so it wouldn't become too crowded with too many people.

BIG BROTHER: Atlantis is like Neverland. It's a fantasy. You better go back to Grandma's house with your fantasies.

LITTLE BROTHER: Of course Atlantis exists.

BIG BROTHER: You want me to punch you like the fat kid from your class did?

LITTLE BROTHER: My teacher told me that was a huge island where a lot of Greek people lived and they all had a lot of books. She says a wise man named Plato used to talk a lot about how well people lived there. She also told me the island sank but I'm sure it didn't sink and that it's still there.

BIG BROTHER: That place never existed.

LITTLE BROTHER: Atlantis even has a post office.

BIG BROTHER: Disneyland also has a post office.

LITTLE BROTHER: Then how come Dad wrote to us from there if it doesn't exist?

BIG BROTHER: Dad didn't write us and you know it.

LITTLE BROTHER: I'll go but I won't show you what I took from Grandma.

BIG BROTHER: What do you have there?

LITTLE BROTHER: You can't be the man of the house because you're afraid of Grandma and you wouldn't have dared to do what I did. But I was brave enough to go into her bedroom.

BIG BROTHER: What did you take?

LITTLE BROTHER: . . .

BIG BROTHER: A letter from Dad?

LITTLE BROTHER: Didn't you want to go hang out with your new friends?

BIG BROTHER: Let me see it.

LITTLE BROTHER: I think I'll go back to the house.

BIG BROTHER: Let me see it.

LITTLE BROTHER: . . .

BIG BROTHER: . . .

LITTLE BROTHER: You see? It comes from Atlantis. The envelope says so.

BIG BROTHER: It doesn't say Atlantis, jackass. It says Atlanta.

LITTLE BROTHER: Seriously? I thought it said Atlantis.

BIG BROTHER: Why doesn't it say anything about when he's coming back?

LITTLE BROTHER: Where's Atlanta?

BIG BROTHER: He just says hello, but he doesn't say when he's coming back for us.

LITTLE BROTHER: Is Atlanta far?

BIG BROTHER: There's no return address.

STUFF ABOUT MOM

LITTLE BROTHER: It's seven–four, bottom of the ninth. The best hitter in the entire league is about to take a swing. Bases are loaded. Remember, my friends, this Mexican hitter has more than fifty home runs this season. He's broken all the league's records and those of the universe and he's going for one more. Two balls and no strikes. Here comes the pitch and it's a . . . strike. This can't be! The hitter swung with such force, you could have sworn that ball was going to fly out of the park. He's knocked that ball over the back fence four times this afternoon and he's looking to do it a fifth time. Here comes the pitch and it's a . . . it's a ball! The greatest hitter of all time stays alive my friends. The pitcher winds up, checks the bases and . . . another strike! No, it's not possible, ladies and gentlemen. Looks like the Atlanta Braves could lose this game. Here comes the payoff pitch. This is his last chance, the runners are ready. It's a . . .

BIG BROTHER: What are you doing?

LITTLE BROTHER: This can't be. Because of you the Atlanta Braves lost the World Series.

BIG BROTHER: You didn't even like baseball before and now you watch it every day.

LITTLE BROTHER: When we get to Atlanta, I'm going to play baseball and one day I'll play for the Atlanta Braves.

BIG BROTHER: It's ridiculous that you're playing baseball using a sponge as a ball and a broom as a bat.

LITTLE BROTHER: I asked Grandma for money for a bat but instead she gave me this broomstick.

BIG BROTHER: You're lucky she didn't beat you with it.

LITTLE BROTHER: What about you? What are you going to do when we get to Atlanta?

BIG BROTHER: They say people in that country don't like foreigners.

LITTLE BROTHER: Of course they do. Their biggest baseball stars are all from other countries.

BIG BROTHER: Maybe that's the case in baseball, but the people in that country don't want foreigners working at any other jobs. Why do you think all the foreigners over there end up cleaning bathrooms or picking fruit?

LITTLE BROTHER: I don't think Dad is going to end up cleaning bathrooms.

BIG BROTHER: Pass me the ball. I'll toss it to you.

LITTLE BROTHER: Top of the game, ladies and gentleman. The Atlanta Braves return to the World Series.

BIG BROTHER: If Mom was here, Dad would never have gone to another country to clean bathrooms.

LITTLE BROTHER: Throw it more to the center.

BIG BROTHER: Mom would never have allowed the family to separate.

LITTLE BROTHER: When she died I cried for a week.

BIG BROTHER: If Mom hadn't died, Dad could have kept working as a teacher.

LITTLE BROTHER: I can't even imagine Dad as a teacher.

BIG BROTHER: This one is going down the middle.

LITTLE BROTHER: And what a hit. The ball is flying, it's flying and it's a home run, ladies and gentlemen, a home run from the best hitter in the entire history of the Atlanta Braves.

BIG BROTHER: . . .

LITTLE BROTHER: . . .

BIG BROTHER: Sometimes I think you can't remember anything. Like the time Dad sold our apartment so he could get out of debt.

LITTLE BROTHER: Maybe now he's teaching in Atlanta.

BIG BROTHER: All we ate was beans and noodles. Beans and noodles.

LITTLE BROTHER: Of course I remember the beans and noodles.

BIG BROTHER: Mom and Dad were a great team.

LITTLE BROTHER: I always liked the noodles.

BIG BROTHER: Just like a baseball team.

LITTLE BROTHER: . . .

BIG BROTHER: . . .

LITTLE BROTHER: I miss Mom.

BIG BROTHER: Every time they had an anniversary, Dad would buy her a stuffed animal.

LITTLE BROTHER: I miss the lime pie she used to make.

BIG BROTHER: I never understood why he did that, then later they told me how they had met at the zoo. They loved telling that story.

LITTLE BROTHER: I once helped her bake a cake.

BIG BROTHER: They always celebrated their anniversaries with cake.

LITTLE BROTHER: Maybe, if I ask her, Grandma will bake me a cake just like the ones Mom used to bake.

BIG BROTHER: I hope Dad doesn't forget about us.

LITTLE BROTHER: Let's keep playing. Throw me the ball.

STUFF ABOUT PASSING AWAY

BIG BROTHER: Stop banging the chair.

LITTLE BROTHER: What time is our uncle coming to get us?

BIG BROTHER: I don't know. Stop banging the chair.

LITTLE BROTHER: He's late. Should we go back to the wake?

BIG BROTHER: No. He told us to wait here.

LITTLE BROTHER: But he gave you money to pay the bill, right?

BIG BROTHER: Yeah, but he said we should wait here.

LITTLE BROTHER: . . .

BIG BROTHER: . . .

LITTLE BROTHER: Hey . . . did you . . . love her?

BIG BROTHER: Grandma?

LITTLE BROTHER: Yeah.

BIG BROTHER: Did you love her?

LITTLE BROTHER: I don't know. I think I did. She was our only grand-mother, right?

BIG BROTHER: I never understood why she beat me more than she did you.

LITTLE BROTHER: . . .

BIG BROTHER: Stop beating that chair up. You're going to piss off the waitress.

LITTLE BROTHER: I don't think you loved her. You didn't cry when they told us about the hospital. Or when you saw her in her coffin.

BIG BROTHER: Just because you always cry doesn't mean I have to act the same way.

LITTLE BROTHER: Well it made me sad. She didn't even say good-bye.

BIG BROTHER: How was she supposed to say good-bye, if her pain came all of a sudden. She barely had time to hail a taxi.

LITTLE BROTHER: We should have gone with her.

BIG BROTHER: And what about school, stupid? Besides, even if we had gone with her, that wouldn't have changed anything.

LITTLE BROTHER: No, but she could have said good-bye. I don't know. She might have given us advice.

BIG BROTHER: . . .

LITTLE BROTHER: We should go back to the wake.

BIG BROTHER: You said you were hungry. Besides, they're probably still praying the rosary.

LITTLE BROTHER: Luis Medina told me that the wake lasts all night and then the next day they bury her. What's the point of a wake any-way? Do we have to stay up all night praying?

BIG BROTHER: I don't know. It was different with Mom.

LITTLE BROTHER: Yeah. With Mom it was different.

BIG BROTHER: . . .

LITTLE BROTHER: You think Dad is going to be sad when he finds out?

BIG BROTHER: She was his mother, wasn't she?

LITTLE BROTHER: When Mom died you cried. I remember that.

BIG BROTHER: Either way, he's never called here.

LITTLE BROTHER: Who?

BIG BROTHER: Maybe I should order a soda.

LITTLE BROTHER: But he's going to call, right? He has to call someday, doesn't he?

BIG BROTHER: He must be busy. In the United States, you have to constantly be working or they kick you out. Stop banging the chair with your fat feet.

LITTLE BROTHER: Dad's a hard worker, isn't he?

BIG BROTHER: Of course he's a hard worker. If he wasn't, he wouldn't have lasted over there. And obviously, he's been there a long time. If he wasn't a hard worker, they would have sent him back. That's why he hasn't called. That's the reason. You hear me? That's why.

LITTLE BROTHER: I know.

BIG BROTHER: We don't have enough money for another soda.

LITTLE BROTHER: Hey . . . what if it's true? That they're going to take us to Hermosillo?

BIG BROTHER: Where did you hear that?

LITTLE BROTHER: Felipe told me. He told me we're going to go live with them.

BIG BROTHER: It's not true.

LITTLE BROTHER: Yes, it is. And I heard our aunt ask Mrs. Meche to help her pack our stuff.

BIG BROTHER: It's not true. You're making this up.

LITTLE BROTHER: I swear.

BIG BROTHER: Well maybe you're going to go live with them because I'm not going anywhere.

LITTLE BROTHER: That's not true. We're both going.

BIG BROTHER: I just told you, you're the only one leaving. I'm going to stay in Grandma's house.

LITTLE BROTHER: But they're not going to let you stay there by yourself.

BIG BROTHER: Don't worry about it.

LITTLE BROTHER: That's what you say, but they're not going to let you.

BIG BROTHER: We'll see.

LITTLE BROTHER: . . .

BIG BROTHER: . . .

LITTLE BROTHER: Let me stay with you.

BIG BROTHER: No. It's better if you go with them. That way you won't bug me.

LITTLE BROTHER: Please. Let me stay with you. I promise I won't bother you.

BIG BROTHER: No. Besides, you get along with Felipe and with Hector.

LITTLE BROTHER: That's not true. I hate those two.

BIG BROTHER: Did I or did I not see you playing with Felipe and his toy soldiers?

LITTLE BROTHER: Yeah, but I still don't like him. I hate him, I swear. This morning he stole one of my stamps and he twisted my arm like this.

BIG BROTHER: Well you can't stay. You don't know how to take care of yourself.

LITTLE BROTHER: Neither do you. You're too young. You try and act like a grown-up but you're still too young. Uncle isn't going to let you.

BIG BROTHER: . . .

LITTLE BROTHER: Grandma looked really bad. All dried out, right? You think Mom looked that way?

BIG BROTHER: Of course not, stupid. Mom was young and Grandma was old. Don't be stupid.

LITTLE BROTHER: Death is pretty ugly, huh? Even though she looked dried out and pale, I thought she was going to open her eyes when I leaned over her.

BIG BROTHER: . . .

LITTLE BROTHER: Maybe I didn't love her either.

BIG BROTHER: I didn't say I didn't love her.

LITTLE BROTHER: . . .

BIG BROTHER: Why don't you go find our uncle and ask him for some money for a soda?

LITTLE BROTHER: Go yourself. I'm not thirsty.

STUFF ABOUT GOD AND HEAVEN

LITTLE BROTHER: I believe you.

BIG BROTHER: What good was a sack of sugar going to do me?

LITTLE BROTHER: It's true. There's no way you could have sold it.

BIG BROTHER: I bet it was Hector. It's always something with him.

LITTLE BROTHER: But I think it's better this way.

BIG BROTHER: What's better?

LITTLE BROTHER: At least they punished us by not letting us go to Mass. It's better.

BIG BROTHER: You didn't even get punished. You could have gone.

LITTLE BROTHER: Yeah, but I didn't want to go. You know what Mom wanted to name me?

BIG BROTHER: Of course I know.

LITTLE BROTHER: Nils. Nils Holgerson.

BIG BROTHER: She would read us that story every night.

LITTLE BROTHER: Every time I wanted to skip Mass she would scare us with that. I was always afraid some elf was going to come and put me on top of a goose and fly me over some gloomy country. Weren't you afraid of that?

BIG BROTHER: I bet you it was Hector.

LITTLE BROTHER: Did you know the Braves made it to the play-offs?

BIG BROTHER: You know I don't like sports.

LITTLE BROTHER: At least on Sunday there aren't any customers. So we can watch television or read comic books.

BIG BROTHER: You could have gone with them.

LITTLE BROTHER: Thing is, that priest makes me nervous. He's always asking me things about catechism that I don't know.

BIG BROTHER: Because you never did your first Communion. Besides, I don't think that priest likes you. He never quizzes me.

LITTLE BROTHER: He asked Felipe one time. And he knew the answer.

BIG BROTHER: It's a good thing that priest doesn't ask me any questions, because he'd be in for a big surprise.

LITTLE BROTHER: Yeah, because you don't believe in heaven, do you?

BIG BROTHER: If heaven existed, then Mom would have tried to get in touch with us, you can be sure of that.

LITTLE BROTHER: Grandma too, right?

BIG BROTHER: No. Not Grandma, because I'm sure she doesn't miss us. But Mom for sure.

LITTLE BROTHER: Yeah. Definitely Mom.

BIG BROTHER: . . .

LITTLE BROTHER: What are you doing? You're drawing hearts.

BIG BROTHER: You see? Now you're going to start bugging me. That's why I said you should have gone to Mass with your uncle.

LITTLE BROTHER: I know why you're drawing hearts. For Graciela.

BIG BROTHER: Go shelve the soda bottles, why don't you.

LITTLE BROTHER: She's pretty, isn't she?

BIG BROTHER: I said go shelve the soda bottles. Don't piss me off. Uncle asked you if you were going to help me and you told him yes. So now you have to help me.

LITTLE BROTHER: I'll help you at the counter. If a customer comes in, I'll take care of them.

BIG BROTHER: I said no. Now go or I'll send you home.

LITTLE BROTHER: Why can't me and Felipe help at the counter? I know how to add things up.

BIG BROTHER: If you're not going to help with the soda, then don't do anything but don't give me any lip either.

LITTLE BROTHER: . . .

BIG BROTHER: . . .

LITTLE BROTHER: Heaven is suppose to be the most beautiful thing there is, right?

BIG BROTHER: I'm going to tell Uncle that the only reason you didn't go to Mass is because you're lazy and you wanted to bug me. Don't think he's not going to hit you.

LITTLE BROTHER: Can I tell you something? In heaven they have swimming pools everywhere. And games, like in the park.

BIG BROTHER: . . .

LITTLE BROTHER: And all they feed you is pastries and chocolate malt shakes.

BIG BROTHER: I bet you can't eat more than ten pastries without throwing up.

LITTLE BROTHER: I could eat up to a thousand pastries.

BIG BROTHER: You're so full of it. You'd throw up.

LITTLE BROTHER: In heaven I bet they show movies all day and all night.

BIG BROTHER: Monster movies too?

LITTLE BROTHER: No. They don't show monster movies.

BIG BROTHER: See? You're always saying stupid things.

LITTLE BROTHER: You're just saying that because you don't believe in heaven. But I believe. And one day, you'll see I'm right.

BIG BROTHER: What will I see? You think when you die you're going to heaven and I'm not? I swear, you are so incredibly full of it. How am I even suppose to see that? Don't be retarded.

LITTLE BROTHER: What if Graciela ended up in heaven?

BIG BROTHER: There you go again with Graciela. Shut up already. Why don't you turn on the television. Since you won't shut up, at least turn on the television.

LITTLE BROTHER: You see? You're turning red.

BIG BROTHER: Shut up. I'm going to hit you I swear. Shut your mouth already.

LITTLE BROTHER: . . .

BIG BROTHER: . . .

LITTLE BROTHER: I wish I could go to school. I'm tired of always having to go everywhere with our aunt and then helping out in the store.

BIG BROTHER: And what about me? You think I like always having to be here, like a slave?

LITTLE BROTHER: You know who I can't stand anymore? Hector. If I could smash his face in, I would.

BIG BROTHER: Don't be a big mouth. Why don't you break Felipe's face? Him you could handle.

LITTLE BROTHER: Because he doesn't call me a freeloader and Hector does. But the thing is Hector is really fat and really tall. He'd knock out one of my teeth or break my nose.

BIG BROTHER: I'm telling you if I find out it was Hector who took that bag of sugar, I'm the one who's going to knock out his teeth or break his nose.

LITTLE BROTHER: You could use the left hook to the gut that Uncle Rodrigo taught you.

BIG BROTHER: . . .

LITTLE BROTHER: . . .

BIG BROTHER: Give me that!

LITTLE BROTHER: See? I told you. They are hearts.

BIG BROTHER: You're so nosy. You better watch out tonight. I'm going to put a scorpion in your bed.

LITTLE BROTHER: Don't, I'm sorry.

BIG BROTHER: I'm going to put a scorpion in your bed like the one we saw the other day. While you're sleeping. And you'll never wake up.

LITTLE BROTHER: Don't, I'm sorry. I'll help you with the soda bottles.

BIG BROTHER: You're nosy. Watch out tonight. I know a place full of scorpions. All I need is one so I can put it in your bed.

LITTLE BROTHER: Don't, I'm sorry! I'm sorry!

BIG BROTHER: Don't start crying. You deserve it.

LITTLE BROTHER: . . .

BIG BROTHER: Shut up already.

LITTLE BROTHER: . . .

BIG BROTHER: All right already. I won't do it. But shut up. I don't know why you're so nosy and such a crybaby.

LITTLE BROTHER: . . .

BIG BROTHER: Go on, turn on the television. See if there are any cartoons on.

LITTLE BROTHER: . . .

BIG BROTHER: . . .

LITTLE BROTHER: She's pretty, isn't she?

BIG BROTHER: Who? Graciela? Kind of.

LITTLE BROTHER: Maybe she'll come on Wednesday.

BIG BROTHER: Uncle said she would. He said he invited her whole family. She has to come.

LITTLE BROTHER: You think they're going to throw me a party on my birthday like they're doing for Felipe?

BIG BROTHER: Of course not.

LITTLE BROTHER: How do you know? Maybe they will throw me a party. It's coming up in less than two months. Maybe if I behave.

BIG BROTHER: Yeah, sure. Maybe they'll even buy you a thousand pastries. Ha ha.

LITTLE BROTHER: No, stupid. But they can still get me one big one.

BIG BROTHER: Dry your eyes. They're going to see that you cried and they're going to blame me.

LITTLE BROTHER: You know what else they have in heaven? A baseball stadium.

STUFF ABOUT FAMILY

LITTLE BROTHER: See how he's stopped screaming? They've given him some medicine or put something on it.

BIG BROTHER: Good. I couldn't stand his screaming anymore.

LITTLE BROTHER: It's not even that big a deal, right?

BIG BROTHER: That's because you've never had a toothache, but you'd be just like him, shrieking.

LITTLE BROTHER: I don't complain as much as Felipe.

BIG BROTHER: No. You're worse.

LITTLE BROTHER: . . .

BIG BROTHER: I hope he stays in there forever. I don't know why they made us come with him, it's not like anything is going to happen to him.

LITTLE BROTHER: It's just a little while, that's what our aunt said. Just until the man from the gas company comes.

BIG BROTHER: She made that up so she wouldn't have to come.

LITTLE BROTHER: That's not true, if they don't fill up our tank today we have to wait till Tuesday till the truck comes by again. And if we run out of gas we'll have to take cold showers.

BIG BROTHER: It's not that big a deal. It's been hot lately anyway.

LITTLE BROTHER: But at five in the morning it's cold. And that's when we have to go with uncle to buy the fruit, right?

BIG BROTHER: Probably they're going to pull out his tooth. And then he'll start screaming again.

LITTLE BROTHER: Are you still sore from yesterday?

BIG BROTHER: Sore from what?

LITTLE BROTHER: When Hector and his friends grabbed you.

BIG BROTHER: No. Not anymore.

LITTLE BROTHER: I didn't think you would ever come out. They were on top of you for like ten minutes, weren't they?

BIG BROTHER: It was longer. I was suffocating. It was longer.

LITTLE BROTHER: I yelled for our aunt to come but she didn't listen to me.

BIG BROTHER: Of course she didn't listen to you.

LITTLE BROTHER: ...

BIG BROTHER: What did you tell her?

LITTLE BROTHER: That they had all ganged up on you, that they were piled on top and that you were stuck down there and probably they had broken all your bones.

BIG BROTHER: And what did she say?

LITTLE BROTHER: That they were just playing, and that I shouldn't worry.

BIG BROTHER: Of course.

LITTLE BROTHER: She would have done something if it had been Hector, right? Or Felipe. Like just now. She went pale. Then later she sent us over here. She even paid for a taxi. It's not even that big a deal.

BIG BROTHER: All for the screams of your cousin . . .

LITTLE BROTHER: He's your cousin too.

BIG BROTHER: He's more your cousin than mine. You play with him sometimes.

LITTLE BROTHER: Which one of them bugs you the most?

BIG BROTHER: I don't know. I'm sick of it.

LITTLE BROTHER: Of what?

BIG BROTHER: Nothing. Pass me that magazine, the one about cars.

LITTLE BROTHER: It's cool.

BIG BROTHER: Give it to me. I asked you for it so I could look at it, not you.

LITTLE BROTHER: Lend it to me for a second.

BIG BROTHER: I said no, if you wanted to see it why didn't you grab it before.

LITTLE BROTHER: Is that a Lamborghini?

BIG BROTHER: No. It's a Porsche.

LITTLE BROTHER: It's cool. When I grow up, I'm going to invent my own car.

BIG BROTHER: Oh yeah? I'd like to see that.

LITTLE BROTHER: I'm going to use really big rims and it's going to be super-fast. It's going to have black windows and flames on the doors.

BIG BROTHER: When you get older you're not going to do any better than run a grocery store and that's if you're lucky. To invent a car first you have to go to school.

LITTLE BROTHER: Uncle said that next year he'd enroll us in a school. Not this year because he doesn't have enough money, but next year he's going to enroll us.

BIG BROTHER: And you're so stupid, you believed him.

LITTLE BROTHER: That's what he said.

BIG BROTHER: He also said he was going to take us on vacation. And only the four of them went. You and me had to stay at the neighbor's. And he also said he's spoken with Dad a bunch of times.

LITTLE BROTHER: It's not true?

BIG BROTHER: What do you think?

LITTLE BROTHER: He told me he can't stay on the phone too long because the gringo police can trace the call and that's why he's never passed us the phone. But he says Dad says hello and that he's happy.

BIG BROTHER: And you're so stupid you believed him.

LITTLE BROTHER: Why are you saying it isn't true?

BIG BROTHER: Because it's not. Ask him what state Atlanta is in and you'll see he doesn't know. Ask him what school he plans to enroll us in.

LITTLE BROTHER: I want to go to the school around the corner, the one with the fountain.

BIG BROTHER: Get used to the idea that you're going to end up working in a store.

LITTLE BROTHER: . . .

BIG BROTHER: I told you they were going to pull out his tooth. He started screaming again.

LITTLE BROTHER: I want to go to the school with the fountain. I've already started keeping the pencils and erasers that Felipe doesn't want. And I have two notebooks that are practically new.

BIG BROTHER: If I had a car like this one, no one could hold me back. I'd leave everyone behind, until I crashed into the sea.

LITTLE BROTHER: . . .

BIG BROTHER: I'm sure our aunt didn't want to come. That's why she sent us to take care of your cousin.

LITTLE BROTHER: Yesterday I was looking at a map of Mexico that was on the wall of the stationery store. Did you know that Hermosillo is the capital of Sonora and that Sonora is right next to the United States?

BIG BROTHER: . . .

LITTLE BROTHER: . . .

BIG BROTHER: That one was pretty gruesome. People probably think he's being murdered.

LITTLE BROTHER: . . .

BIG BROTHER: What did you just ask me?

LITTLE BROTHER: Nothing. Hey . . . what was that blond kid's name, the one with the motorcycle?

BIG BROTHER: Who?

LITTLE BROTHER: The one who came by the store the other day, the one who's dating Graciela.

BIG BROTHER: I don't know. What do I care?

LITTLE BROTHER: Is he a gringo?

BIG BROTHER: How can he be a gringo? Of course not. Don't be so stupid.

LITTLE BROTHER: Does he know English?

BIG BROTHER: I don't know. What do I care?

LITTLE BROTHER: It's that he was carrying a magazine like this one, but it was about motorcycles. And it was all in English. Is it hard to learn English?

BIG BROTHER: I don't know. I don't think so. If that idiot knows how to speak English, then it must not be very hard. Actually, it's probably the easiest thing in the world. As easy as riding a motorcycle which any idiot can do.

LITTLE BROTHER: What do you want to be when you grow up?

BIG BROTHER: If I had a car like this one . . . you'd be eating my dust.

LITTLE BROTHER: Maybe it's like knowing how to swim. As long as you're not afraid. I remember Dad became really happy when I learned how to swim. Or how to ride a bicycle. Or how to work with fractions. The other day, I looked in one of Felipe's notebooks and realized that I still knew how to add fractions. Maybe one day I can invent my own car if I still know how to add fractions, which is pretty hard.

BIG BROTHER: That one sounded just like a girl! If he's screaming like that, they must be pulling out all his teeth one by one. What were you saying?

LITTLE BROTHER: Nothing. So what do you want to be when you grow up?

BIG BROTHER: I don't know. I haven't thought about it. Maybe a dentist.

LITTLE BROTHER: You think our aunt is ever going to show up?

STUFF ABOUT THE GRINGOS

LITTLE BROTHER: Are we there yet?

BIG BROTHER: If you ask me that one more time, I'm going to ask the driver to pull over and leave you on the side of the road.

LITTLE BROTHER: It's just that . . .

BIG BROTHER: It's that what?

LITTLE BROTHER: I have to pee.

BIG BROTHER: So go to the bathroom. It's in the back.

LITTLE BROTHER: Come with me.

BIG BROTHER: Why do you want me to go with you? Nothing's going to happen to you.

LITTLE BROTHER: Come with me.

BIG BROTHER: No, because two people can't even fit in that bathroom.

LITTLE BROTHER: Wait for me outside, please.

BIG BROTHER: I said no. Stop bugging me. If you want to go to the bathroom, go. If not, don't.

LITTLE BROTHER: It's that there's a man there who every time I turn around, he stares at me in a really evil way.

BIG BROTHER: Which one?

LITTLE BROTHER: The one with the mustache and the jacket.

BIG BROTHER: Oh yeah, I see him.

LITTLE BROTHER: Come with me.

BIG BROTHER: He's not going to do anything. Besides, it's logical, dummy. Just now when I leaned over, he looked at me too. It's logical. If you lean out, he sees you, but that's because he's staring ahead, not because he wants to look at you.

LITTLE BROTHER: I better wait. We're almost there.

BIG BROTHER: You're a scaredy cat. I'm sure that man thinks that you're the one who doesn't stop looking at him. He's probably thinking that if you turn around one more time, he's going to go ask the driver to kick you off the bus.

LITTLE BROTHER: That's not true.

BIG BROTHER: That's what I would do.

LITTLE BROTHER: I'm not going to look anymore. Besides, we're almost there. Look. I drew a map. Here's Hermosillo. Here's Nogales. The way I figure, we're right about here, which means we're almost there.

BIG BROTHER: You're stupid. We're over here.

LITTLE BROTHER: That's not true.

BIG BROTHER: Oh yeah? We're right about here. You'll see. You should go to the bathroom and get it over with, later you can take a nap because otherwise you won't be able to hold it.

LITTLE BROTHER: I can hold it.

BIG BROTHER: Whatever.

LITTLE BROTHER: . . .

BIG BROTHER: . . .

LITTLE BROTHER: Can I have one of the sandwiches?

BIG BROTHER: No. Don't even think about it. It's too soon.

LITTLE BROTHER: Can I just take a little bite?

BIG BROTHER: Far as I'm concerned, you can eat all four of yours if that's what you want. But don't go complaining later that you're hungry, because I'm not going to give you any of mine.

LITTLE BROTHER: You should have bought me a little pastry. Or some potato chips.

BIG BROTHER: We don't have much money. Hardly enough to get there. And we still have to figure out how we're going to cross. And on the other side we're going to need money also. And all you can think about are potato chips and pastries.

LITTLE BROTHER: Well I'm hungry.

BIG BROTHER: You are not hungry. You just feel like bugging me. I know you. Just a minute ago you wanted to go to the bathroom and now you're hungry. Just go to sleep.

LITTLE BROTHER: Did you make sure that this was the bus that said Nogales?

BIG BROTHER: Stop bugging me. Just go to sleep.

LITTLE BROTHER: . . .

BIG BROTHER: . . .

LITTLE BROTHER: What words do you know in English? I know the word for bathroom.

BIG BROTHER: What good is that going to do you if you can't even take a piss by yourself?

LITTLE BROTHER: Also I know the words for "money," and for "home run" and the word for "strike" and . . . "double play." Also the word for "baby." And I know how to say, "Stop, Motherfucker!" I know how to say that in English.

BIG BROTHER: Where did you learn that?

LITTLE BROTHER: In this cop movie. This Italian guy came out. And he yelled in English, "Stop, Motherfucker!" when he took out his gun. And he also yelled, "Freeze, Police!"

BIG BROTHER: What good is that going to do you over there?

LITTLE BROTHER: I don't know. What if someone wants to mug me or something.

BIG BROTHER: Now you've started saying stupid things again. If somebody wants to mug you, you better play dead, because over there people are seven feet tall or more. You know how tall that is? Like double your height. Any one of those gringos can squash you like an insect if you're not careful.

LITTLE BROTHER: . . .

BIG BROTHER: . . .

LITTLE BROTHER: Whoa. I thought Hector lost that at school?

BIG BROTHER: That's what he thought. But I took it from his backpack the day he stuck that nail in my shoulder.

LITTLE BROTHER: It's so cool. Does it have batteries?

BIG BROTHER: No. But that doesn't matter. We'll buy them later.

LITTLE BROTHER: So cool. Too bad you didn't buy any in the bus terminal. We could have played the whole trip.

BIG BROTHER: Yeah but it doesn't matter. We'll buy them later.

LITTLE BROTHER: It really made me mad that he made you bleed with that nail.

BIG BROTHER: Give it back already. You're going to break it.

LITTLE BROTHER: Let me hold it for a little while.

BIG BROTHER: No. Besides what's the point if you can't see anything on the screen.

LITTLE BROTHER: But let me press the little buttons at least.

BIG BROTHER: Enough. You already pressed them. Relax. Give it to me. Give it.

LITTLE BROTHER: This must be the English word for "Stop." Here it says "Stop." And over here it says "Start."

BIG BROTHER: No. It says "On" and "Off."

LITTLE BROTHER: Really? So in English, when you say "Stop, Mother-fucker," is that the same as saying "Off"? So basically, when you turn "off" a TV or something like that, should I say, "Stop, Motherfucker TV"? "Please"?

BIG BROTHER: They're the same words you use when you say, "Shut your mouth. Give me the game. You're going to break it."

LITTLE BROTHER: I was listening to Uncle's rock records to see if I could make out what they were saying, but I couldn't. The only thing I could understand was when they said, "Baby." Why do they say "Baby" so much in rock music? Are they like lullabies for babies or something?

BIG BROTHER: Don't be retarded, how can they possibly be lullabies for babies?

LITTLE BROTHER: Then why do they keep singing, "Baby Baby"?

BIG BROTHER: Well it's their custom. Customs that the gringos have. Every country has its own way of doing things.

LITTLE BROTHER: There they play baseball and we play soccer. They're blond and we're brown. There they sing rock 'n' roll to their babies and we sing lullabies.

BIG BROTHER: —

LITTLE BROTHER: You'll see how happy Dad is going to be when he sees us. First thing I'm going to ask him for is to take me to the movies.

BIG BROTHER: A monster movie.

LITTLE BROTHER: Stop bugging me. Of course not. We'll see a movie about ships. Or about dinosaurs.

BIG BROTHER: . . .

LITTLE BROTHER: Did you give Graciela that letter?

BIG BROTHER: The letter? Yeah sure.

LITTLE BROTHER: What did she tell you?

BIG BROTHER: Nothing.

LITTLE BROTHER: Why nothing?

BIG BROTHER: She wasn't there. I left it in her mailbox.

LITTLE BROTHER: That was dumb. You should have waited till she got back.

BIG BROTHER: That's what you would have done, right, genius? Because you, you've had what, like a million girlfriends?

LITTLE BROTHER: Did you kiss her?

BIG BROTHER: How could I have kissed her? Didn't you hear she wasn't there?

LITTLE BROTHER: No. I mean, did you ever kiss her?

BIG BROTHER: What do you care?

LITTLE BROTHER: You never even kissed her?

BIG BROTHER: What do you know?

LITTLE BROTHER: You should have waited till she got back.

BIG BROTHER: You're right. I should have waited for her to come back. And I should have sent you to Nogales by yourself. Since you can't even take a piss on your own.

LITTLE BROTHER: . . .

BIG BROTHER: . . .

LITTLE BROTHER: Too bad she didn't even notice you because she sure was pretty.

BIG BROTHER: . . .

LITTLE BROTHER: You think our aunt and uncle are going to miss us? Even just a little? I mean, when they realize we're not coming back, you think they're going to worry about us? You think they'll miss us just a little bit? Sometimes when I went with our aunt to run her errands, she and I would make each other laugh. And you helped Uncle in the store a lot.

BIG BROTHER: . . .

LITTLE BROTHER: I just remembered that the bus did say Nogales. I just remembered.

STUFF ABOUT THE DESERT

LITTLE BROTHER: It's really dark.

BIG BROTHER: . . .

LITTLE BROTHER: I don't want to go anymore.

BIG BROTHER: Shut up and keep walking! . . . What's wrong with you? Why are you stopping?

LITTLE BROTHER: I'm really thirsty. And it's too dark.

BIG BROTHER: What did you expect? It's nighttime and it's cloudy.

LITTLE BROTHER: What if we went back?

BIG BROTHER: When we were in Hermosillo sometimes we would walk down streets when it was dark and there wasn't a moon and you didn't complain then.

LITTLE BROTHER: You can't even see the ground. I could fall. We have to wait till the moon comes out.

BIG BROTHER: It's better this way. This way no one can see us.

LITTLE BROTHER: We should go back.

BIG BROTHER: You were the one who wanted to go see Dad. You cried at least once a week. And now you say you want to go back?

LITTLE BROTHER: I don't cry anymore.

BIG BROTHER: Yeah, you cry. I heard you cry yesterday.

LITTLE BROTHER: It's too dark.

BIG BROTHER: Are you going to shut up?

LITTLE BROTHER: Wait a minute. I'm tired. And we haven't eaten since we finished those sandwiches and those cookies we bought.

BIG BROTHER: If we wait, it's going to get worse.

LITTLE BROTHER: They say people who cross the desert get mistaken for wolves or coyotes and then they get shot.

BIG BROTHER: Those are just stories people make up. They're trying to scare people so they don't try and cross. You can't believe everything you hear.

LITTLE BROTHER: We should go back. They could kill us like we're coyotes that's how much they don't want us to cross. We should go back.

BIG BROTHER: Keep walking.

LITTLE BROTHER: It's still a long way off. You even said Atlanta was so far away that it didn't even fit on my map.

BIG BROTHER: I told you that so you wouldn't get your hopes up. And so that you wouldn't finish the food so fast. But it's not that far, really.

LITTLE BROTHER: I'm thirsty.

BIG BROTHER: Just think about the look on Dad's face when he sees us.

LITTLE BROTHER: Yeah. He's going to be really happy, right?

BIG BROTHER: He won't even believe it.

LITTLE BROTHER: . . .

BIG BROTHER: . . .

LITTLE BROTHER: What was that?

BIG BROTHER: I don't know. It was nothing.

LITTLE BROTHER: Are there snakes around here? Could it have been a snake?

BIG BROTHER: I don't know but it wasn't a snake. Just a twig that snapped.

LITTLE BROTHER: It's starting to get cold. Is it true that in the desert it gets so cold at night that you can freeze?

BIG BROTHER: Of course not. It's the desert. Deserts are hot. And at night, well . . . it's less hot. But not cold.

LITTLE BROTHER: Well I'm cold. And really thirsty.

BIG BROTHER: Don't think about that anymore. Think about something else.

LITTLE BROTHER: Maybe Atlanta is like Atlantis and it has all the water you can possibly imagine.

BIG BROTHER: And if we lose our way? I should have brought a compass, I'm so dumb.

LITTLE BROTHER: What did you say?

BIG BROTHER: Nothing. Keep talking.

LITTLE BROTHER: And well I bet you there's a bunch of swimming pools everywhere you go. And more water than you can believe. And you can drink all you want. In Atlanta you can never be thirsty, not ever ever.

BIG BROTHER: What if we took a wrong turn?

LITTLE BROTHER: What did you say? What if what?

BIG BROTHER: Nothing. Keep walking. Talk to me.

LITTLE BROTHER: I don't want to talk anymore. I want to go back. I'm thirsty. I'm tired.

BIG BROTHER: Don't start crying. I'm serious. Don't start crying.

LITTLE BROTHER: I'm not crying, but I'm tired.

BIG BROTHER: Tell me about the car you're going to invent when you grow up, go on.

LITTLE BROTHER: I don't want to. I want to go back.

BIG BROTHER: Don't stop. Please. Don't stop.

LITTLE BROTHER: Here. Just a little while. Look, right here in this soft sand. I'm so sleepy.

BIG BROTHER: Don't go to sleep.

LITTLE BROTHER: Why not?

BIG BROTHER: I don't know. I heard it's bad. Don't sleep. Please. Talk to me.

LITTLE BROTHER: Here. Sit by me. Look.

BIG BROTHER: . . .

LITTLE BROTHER: Here in this soft sand.

BIG BROTHER: All right. We'll rest for a little bit.

LITTLE BROTHER: Yeah. Lean against me. That way we'll be less cold. We should have bought batteries.

BIG BROTHER: We should have bought batteries and we could have played . . .

LITTLE BROTHER: . . .

BIG BROTHER: . . .

LITTLE BROTHER: Aren't you sleepy?

BIG BROTHER: Kind of.

LITTLE BROTHER: Are you sure there aren't snakes around here?

BIG BROTHER: Of course not. And it doesn't get cold either. How can it be cold in the desert. Those are just stories people make up.

LITTLE BROTHER: It's true. You're right.

BIG BROTHER: . . .

LITTLE BROTHER: You know what else is in Atlanta besides tons of swimming pools?

BIG BROTHER: Tell me.

LITTLE BROTHER: There's games, just like in the park. And there's always pastries to eat. And chocolate malt shakes.

BIG BROTHER: That's cool.

LITTLE BROTHER: And all day and all night they show movies.

BIG BROTHER: . . .

LITTLE BROTHER: Right now I could eat a thousand pastries and drink a thousand chocolate malt shakes . . .

BIG BROTHER: Me too.

LITTLE BROTHER: . . .

BIG BROTHER: . . .

LITTLE BROTHER: . . .

BIG BROTHER: Think about the look on Dad's face when he sees us.

LITTLE BROTHER: . . .

BIG BROTHER: . . .

LITTLE BROTHER: . . .

BIG BROTHER: Did you fall asleep? Huh?

LITTLE BROTHER: . . .

BIG BROTHER: . . .

LITTLE BROTHER: . . .

BIG BROTHER: Did you fall asleep?

APPENDIX: PROGRAMMING IN THE GOODMAN LATINO THEATRE FESTIVAL

2003

Teatro de Ciertos Habitantes (Mexico) *El Automóvil Gris*

Compañia Marta Carrasco (Barcelona, Spain) *Mira'm* (*se Dicen Tantas Cosas*)

Goodman Theatre *Electricidad* by Luis Alfaro

Goodman Theatre *Psst . . . I Have Something to Tell You, Mi Amor* by Ana Castillo

Aguijón Theater Company (Chicago) *La Casa de Bernarda Alba* by Federico García Lorca

Teatro Luna (Chicago) *The Maria Chronicles*

Teatro Vista (Chicago) *The Messenger* adapted by Cecilie Keenan from the novel by Mayra Montero

2004

Culture Clash (Los Angeles) *Culture Clash in AmeriCCa*

La Fábrica de Teatro Imaginario (Bilbao, Spain) *Yuri Sam*

Luis Alfaro (Los Angeles) *No Holds Barrio*

Teatro Vista (Chicago) *Let the Eagle Fly* book by John Reeger, music by Julie Shannon

Aguijón Theater Company (Chicago) *Bodas de Sangre/Blood Wedding* by Federico García Lorca

2006

Comediants (Barcelona, Spain) *Las Mil y Una Noches*

Pia Fraus (Brazil) *Bichos do Brasil*

Compañia Marta Carrasco (Barcelona, Spain) *Ga-Gá* and *Aiguardent*

Universes (New York City) *Blue Sweat*

Aguijón Theater Company (Chicago) *Yerma* by Federico García Lorca

Staged Reading Series

The Book of Titus and Other Latino Bible Stories by Luis Alfaro
Dark Play, or Stories for Boys by Carlos Murillo
El Grito del Bronx by Migdalia Cruz
Quita Mitos by Tanya Saracho
The Crossing/El Viaje de los Cantores by Hugo Salcedo

2008

Compañia Marta Carrasco (Barcelona, Spain) *J'arrive*

Emmanuel Márquez Company (Mexico) *De la Oreja al Corazón* by Mercedes Gómez Benet

Adriana Sevan (Los Angeles) *Taking Flight*

Culture Clash (Los Angeles) *Chavez Ravine/Culture Clash in AmeriCCa*

Albany Park Theater Project (Chicago) *Aquí Estoy*

Chicago Children's Theatre *Esperanza Rising,* based on the book by Pam Muñoz Ryan, adapted by Lynne Alvarez

Laura Crotte (Chicago) *Al Son Que Me Toques, Lorca*

Luna Negra Dance Theater (Chicago) *Antojito*

Teatro Vista (Chicago) *Little Certainties* by Bárbara Colio

Teatro Luna (Chicago) *Jarred* by Tanya Saracho

Aguijón Theater Company *Hasta los Gorriones Dejan su Nido* by Raul Dorantes

2010

Teatro Buendía (Cuba) *La Visita de la Vieja Dama; Charentón* by Raquel Carrió and Flora Lauten

Goodman Theatre *The Sins of Sor Juana* by Karen Zacarías

Teatro de Calle Sarruga (Barcelona, Spain) *Insectos* performed at Millennium Park

Albany Park Theatre Project (Chicago) *Feast*

Aguijón Theater Company (Chicago) *Las Soldaderas*

Teatro Vista (Chicago) *El Nogalar* by Tanya Saracho, staged reading

Sandra Delgado (Chicago) *Para Carmen*

Gustavo Leone (Chicago) *The Leader*

Elbio Rodríguez Barilari (Chicago) *On "Sor Juana,"* a new opera

Memory of Fire based on the books by Eduardo Galeano adapted by Jessica Mills, Henry Godinez, and the 2010 Latina/o Theatre "Staging Revolution" class at Northwestern University. Performed with the Grant Park Music Festival conducted by Miguel Harth-Bedoya.

Lark Play Development Center Staged Readings

Our Dad Is in Atlantis by Javier Malpica translated from the Spanish by Jorge Cortiñas

A Lover's Dismantling: Fragments of a Scenic Discourse by Elena Guiochins, translated from the Spanish by Andy Bragen

Deserts by Hugo Alfredo Hinojosa Diaz translated from the Spanish by Caridad Svich

Of Princes, Princesses, and Other Creatures by Paola Izquierdo translated from the Spanish by Susana Cook

Yamaha 300 by Cutberto López Reyes translated from the Spanish by Mando Alvarado

ABOUT THE AUTHORS

ALBANY PARK THEATER PROJECT, founded in 1997, is a multiethnic youth theater ensemble based in the Albany Park neighborhood of northwestern Chicago that inspires people to envision a more just and beautiful world. The ensemble creates original theater based on the life experiences of people whose stories might otherwise go untold: urban teens, immigrants, and working-class Americans. The members are invested in creating a space where teenagers engage critically and creatively with the world as artists, thereby embarking on a purposeful life as adventurous dreamers and accomplished achievers. The project was founded by David Feiner and Laura Wiley and is housed at the Laura Wiley Theater in the Eugene Field Park, a facility of the City of Chicago Park Service.

LUIS ALFARO is a writer and performer known for his work in theater, performance art, poetry, short fiction, and journalism. A Chicano born and raised in the Pico-Union district of Los Angeles, he is also a producer and director who spent ten years at Center Theatre Group's Mark Taper Forum as director of new play development and codirector of the Latino Theatre Initiative. His plays and performances have been seen throughout the United States, Mexico, and England. They include *Electricidad, Down Town, No Holds Barrio, Body of Faith, Straight as a Line, Bitter Homes and Gardens, Ladybird, Black Butterfly,* and *Breakfast, Lunch & Dinner.* Alfaro is the recipient of a MacArthur Foundation Fellowship, a National Endowment for the Arts/Theater Communications Group (NEA/TCG) Theatre Residency Program for Playwrights grant, and the Pen Center Literary Award in Drama. A member of New Dramatists, he is also the recipient of Kennedy Center Fund for New American Plays awards, Rockefeller Foundation Multi-Arts Production (MAP) grants, a University of California Regents Fellowship, L.A. Weekly's Queen of the Angels Award, and the 2005 James A. Doolittle Ovation Award for his body of work. A highly anthologized writer, he is featured in the collections *Resurrecting Grace: Remembering Catholic Childhoods* edited by Marilyn Sewell (Boston: Beacon Press, 2001), *Cootie Shots* edited by Norma Bowles with Mark E. Rosenthal (New York: TCG Books, 2000), *Another City* edited by David L. Ulin (San Francisco: City Lights Books, 2001), *Extreme Exposure* edited by Jo Bonney (New York: TCG Books, 1999), *Plays from South Coast Repertory* (New York: Broadway Play Publishing, 2000), *Out of the Fringe* edited by Caridad Svich and Maria Teresa Marrero (New York: TCG Books, 2000), *O Solo Homo* edited by Holly Hughes and David Roman (New York: Grove Press, 1998), and *Corpus Delecti* edited by Coco Fusco (New York: Routledge, 1999). His short film *Chicanismo* was created at KCET/PBS, and his solo spoken-word CD, *Down Town,* was recorded on the label New Alliance/SST. Alfaro is an associate artist with Playwrights' Arena and Cornerstone Theater Company in Los Angeles. He currently teaches at the University of Southern California and California Institute of the Arts. Alfaro took classes as a teenager at the Inner City Cultural Center and is grateful for the many playwriting workshops; most notable and life-changing were the experiences he had with María Irene Fornés, Paula Vogel, Eduardo Machado, Mac Wellman, and the performance workshops of Scott Kelman.

RAQUEL CARRIÓ was born in Havana, Cuba. She is a professor, playwright, and essayist. She is the founder of the Institute of Scenic Arts at the University of Arts of Havana and of the International School of Theatre of Latin America and the Caribbean (EITALC). She is a professor of drama and theater research. She has received numerous awards for her essays and critical studies. She is dramaturge and playwright for Teatro Buendía.

JORGE IGNACIO CORTIÑAS has received many awards including fellowships from the National Endowment for the Arts and the New York Foundation for the Arts; as well as the Helen Merrill Playwriting Award; playwright of the year in *El Nuevo Herald*'s 1999 year-end list; a Writers Community Residency from the YMCA National Writer's Voice; and the Robert Chesley Award for Lesbian and Gay Playwriting, among others. His first play, *Maleta Mulata,* was produced by Campo Santo + Intersection for the Arts in San Francisco. His second play, *Sleepwalkers,* was produced by the Arena Stage in 1999, where it was awarded a Carbonell Award for Best New Work given by the South Florida Critics Circle. *Sleepwalkers* was further developed and remounted by the Alliance Theatre in 2002. *Tight Embrace* was produced by INTAR Theatre in New York, and his play *Blind Mouth Singing* recently completed a run at Chicago's Teatro Vista, a production the *Chicago Tribune* praised as having "visionary wit." *Blind Mouth Singing* will be remounted by the National Asian American Theatre Company in New York this spring. His most recent play, *Bird in the Hand,* was developed at this year's Eugene O'Neill National Playwrights Conference. He has been commissioned by the Mark Taper Forum, South Coast Repertory, and Hartford Stage. He is a Usual Suspect at New York Theatre Workshop and a member of New Dramatists and the Playwrights' Coalition at MCC Theater.

HENRY GODINEZ is the resident artistic associate at Goodman Theatre and the curator of the Latino Theatre Festival. He directed Karen Zacarías's *The Sins of Sor Juana* at the Goodman as part of the fifth Latino Theatre Festival in 2010. He also directed José Rivera's *Boleros for the Disenchanted* at the Goodman, as well as its world premiere at Yale Repertory Theatre. His other world premieres at Goodman include Karen Zacarías's *Mariela in the Desert,* Regina Taylor's *Millennium Mambo,* and Luis Alfaro's *Straight as a Line.* Godinez also directed *The Cook* by Eduardo Machado, *Electricidad* by Luis Alfaro, *Zoot Suit* by Luis Valdez, and *Red Cross* by Sam Shepard (in Regina Taylor's *Transformations*) at the Goodman; the Goodman/Teatro Vista coproduction of José Rivera's *Cloud Tectonics;* and the 1996–2001 productions of *A Christmas Carol.* Mr. Godinez's other Chicago credits include *A Year with Frog and Toad* and *Esperanza Rising* for Chicago Children's Theatre, Nilo Cruz's *Two Sisters and a Piano* (Apple Tree Theatre/Teatro Vista co-production), and *Anna in the Tropics* for Victory Gardens Theater. Mr. Godinez is the cofounder and former artistic director of Teatro Vista, where he directed *Broken Eggs, El Paso Blue, Journey of the Sparrows, Santos & Santos,* and *The Crossing.* His other directing credits include work at Portland Center Stage, Signature Theatre Company in New York City, Kansas City Repertory Theatre,

Oak Park Festival Theatre, Colorado Shakespeare Festival, and several seasons of *Stories on Stage* for WBEZ Chicago Public Radio. As an actor, Mr. Godinez appeared most recently in the Goodman/Teatro Vista world premiere of José Rivera's *Massacre* (*Sing to Your Children*) and on TV in *The Beast,* in *Chicago Code,* and in a recurring role on *Boss.* Born in Havana, Cuba, Mr. Godinez is an associate professor in the Department of Theatre at Northwestern University and has served as a site evaluator and panelist for the National Endowment for the Arts, the Illinois Arts Council, and the Evanston Arts Council. He serves on the Board of Directors of the Illinois Arts Council and Albany Park Theater Project. Mr. Godinez is the recipient of the 1999 Theatre Communications Group (TCG) Alan Schneider Director Award and the Distinguished Service Award from the Lawyers for the Creative Arts, and he was honored as the 2008 Latino Professional of the Year by the Chicago Latino Network.

JAVIER MALPICA was born in Mexico City in 1965. After receiving his bachelor's degree in physics, he completed the Diploma in Literary Creation at the Writers' School of SOGEM (The General Society of Mexican Writers). He has written more than ten plays (many of them cowritten with his brother Antonio), most of which have been produced. He has received various prizes and honors for his work, including the Victor Hugo Rascón Banda Prize for *Our Dad Is in Atlantis.* His other plays include *Letters in the Matter* (winner, National Institute of Fine Arts of Mexico [INBA] National Prize for Theater), *Seventh Round, Maria Frankenstein, Canon* (winner, Theater Prize for Young Creators), *Return to Midnight* (finalist, New Theater), *The Last Journey* (second place, Tomás Urtusástegui Prize for Theater for Young Audiences), *All the Voices* (Honorable Mention, Manuel Herrera Prize), *The End of History* (winner, New Theater), *Essay of a Coma* (Program of Collaborations), *Mujer on the Border,* and *Five Shots in the City of Palaces.* He has given courses and lectures in Mexico and abroad. He has also published and received prizes for his works of fiction for children.

RAMÓN H. RIVERA-SERVERA is associate professor and director of graduate studies in the Department of Performance Studies at Northwestern University. He is the author of *Performing Queer Latinidad: Dance,*

Sexuality, Politics (Ann Arbor: University of Michigan Press, 2012), coeditor with Harvey Young of *Performance in the Borderlands* (Basingstoke, U.K.: Palgrave, 2011), and coeditor with E. Patrick Johnson of *solo/black/woman: scripts, essays, and interviews* (Evanston, Ill.: Northwestern University Press, 2013). His articles and reviews on Latino performance have appeared in *Modern Drama, Text and Performance Quarterly, Theatre Journal, TDR, Trans, emisférica,* and *Ollantay Theater Magazine.* He is currently working on a book manuscript, *Exhibiting Performance: Race, Museum Cultures, and the Live Event,* which argues that performance has played a central role in shaping the ways in which museums of history and anthropology across the Americas collect and exhibit race at the beginning of the twenty-first century. Rivera-Servera serves on the board of the Society of Dance History Scholars, the advisory committee for LGBT history at the Chicago History Museum, and the editorial board for *Theatre Topics.*

MILDRED RUIZ-SAPP is a founding member of Universes. She is a playwright, actress, and singer who received her B.A. from Bard College. She has been awarded the 2008 Theatre Communications Group (TCG) Peter Zeisler Award; the 2006 Career Advancement Fellowship from the Ford Foundation through Pregones Theater; the 2002–2004 and 1999–2001 TCG National Theater Artist Residency Program Award; and a BRIO (Bronx Recognizes Its Own) Award. She was a cofounder of The Point, a community arts organization in the Hunts Point neighborhood of the Bronx, and a former board member of the National Performance Network and the Network of Ensemble Theaters.

STEVEN SAPP is a founding member of Universes. His credits include playwright/actor for *Ameriville* (directed by Chay Yew) from Curious Theater's Denver Project (directed by Dee Covington); *One Shot in Lotus Position* from Curious Theater's *The War Anthology* (directed by Bonnie Metzger); *Blue Suite* (directed by Chay Yew); *Rhythmicity* (Humana Festival); and *Slanguage* (New York Theater Workshop, directed by Jo Bonney). He was playwright, actor, and director for *The Ride;* assistant director for *The Architecture of Loss;* director of Will Powers's *The Seven* at the University of Iowa; and director of Alfred Jarry's *Ubu Enchained* at Teatr Polski in Warsaw, Poland. His awards and affiliations include

2008 Jazz at Lincoln Center Rhythm Road Tour; the 2008 Theatre Communications Group (TCG) Peter Zeisler Award; the 2002 TCG National Directors Award; 2002–2004 and 1999–2001 TCG National Theater Artist Residency Program Award; 1998 and 2002 BRIO (Bronx Recognizes Its Own) Awards; a Van Lier Playwriting Fellowship at New Dramatists; cofounder of The Point; and a Usual Suspect at New York Theatre Workshop. He has a bachelor's degree from Bard College. His publications include *Universes: The Big Bang* (New York: TCG Books, 2009) and "Slanguage" in *The Fire This Time* (New York: TCG Books, 2002).

ADRIANA SEVAHN NICHOLS is an award-winning actress and playwright. Her critically acclaimed solo show, *Taking Flight*, garnered her a San Diego Theatre Critics Circle Award and a Los Angeles Women's Theatre Festival Award, and the CD was a finalist for a 2008 Audie Award. Her plays have been published by Samuel French and Smith and Kraus. She has developed and performed her work at the Sundance Institute Theatre Lab, South Coast Repertory, Mark Taper Forum, Goodman Theatre, L.A. Theatre Works, Stages Theatre, The Fountain, INTAR Theatre, and the Lark Play Development Center. In 2008, she received the Middle East America Distinguished Playwright Award, which gifted her with a commission to write a play inspired by her Armenian grandparents' survival of the Genocide of 1915. The play, *Night over Erzinga*, was developed by the Lark and director Daniella Topol through several workshops, culminating with a BareBones production in New York, followed by a rolling world premiere, beginning in San Francisco, with Golden Thread Productions, and continuing in 2012, at Silk Road Rising, in Chicago. As an actress, Adriana has appeared in multiple guest-starring roles on television including roles in *Law & Order, The Unit, Sex and the City*, and *Law & Order: Criminal Intent*. Highlights of her theater credits include SCR, the Public Theatre, Boston Court, the Goodman, Kirk Douglas Theatre, ACT, and Yale Repertory Theatre. One of Adriana's biggest passions is bringing theater and young people together to give them the opportunity to unleash and express their full creative potential. She has taught theater workshops nationally and internationally, at the ORRAN Center for at-risk youth in Yerevan, Armenia; Goodman Theatre; CalArts; and the University of California, Santa Barbara; and she has run a mentoring program for adolescent girls living in group homes in Los Angeles. She is currently working on her new play, *Running on Roller Skates*. Adriana is honored to be included in this anthology. She wishes to express her deepest gratitude to directors Giovanna Sardelli and Tony Plana for all they contributed in helping her bring *Taking Flight* to life.

CARIDAD SVICH is a U.S. Latina playwright, translator, lyricist, and editor whose works have been presented across the United States and abroad at diverse venues, including the Denver Center, Mixed Blood Theatre, Cincinnati Playhouse in the Park, Repertorio Espanol, 59East59, McCarren Park Pool, 7 Stages, Salvage Vanguard Theatre, Teatro Mori (Santiago, Chile), ARTheater (Cologne, Germany), and Edinburgh Fringe Festival in the United Kingdom. She received the 2011 American Theatre Critics Association Primus Prize for her play *The House of the Spirits*, based on the novel by Isabel Allende, and has been short-listed for the PEN Award in Drama three times, including in 2010 for *Instructions for Breathing*. Her key works include *12 Ophelias, Alchemy of Desire/Dead Man's Blues, Iphigenia . . . A Rave Fable, Love in the Time of Cholera* (based on Gabriel Garcia Marquez's novel), *The Way of Water*, and the multimedia collaboration *The Booth Variations*. An alumna of New Dramatists, she holds an M.F.A. in theater-playwriting from the University of California, San Diego, and has taught creative writing and playwriting at Bard College, Barnard College, Rutgers University–New Brunswick, and Yale School of Drama.

TEATRO BUENDÍA is the most celebrated independent theater company in Cuba. It is renowned for its poignant adaptations of classic texts whose themes reflect the struggles and challenges of contemporary Cuban society. Teatro Buendía was founded in 1986 by actress, teacher, and artistic director Flora Lauten, with graduates from the Instituto Superior de Arte. Lauten and playwright Raquel Carrió contextualize western and European classics in a uniquely Cuban setting, with an ensemble of actors who have trained rigorously under Lauten's tutelage.

UNIVERSES is an ensemble of multidisciplinary writers and performers who fuse poetry, theater, jazz, hip-hop, politics, down-home blues, flamenco, and Spanish boleros to create moving, challenging, and entertaining theatrical works. The group breaks the bounds of traditional theater to create its own brand of performance, inviting old and new generations of theater-makers as well as theatergoers and newcomers to reshape the face of American dramas.